Assiniboine Park

Designing and Developing a People's Playground

DAVID SPECTOR

GREAT PLAINS
PUBLICATIONS

Copyright © 2019 David Spector

Great Plains Publications
1173 Wolseley Avenue
Winnipeg, MB R3G 1H1
www.greatplains.mb.ca

All rights reserved. No part of this publication may be reproduced or
transmitted in any form or in any means, or stored in a database and
retrieval system, without the prior written permission of Great Plains
Publications, or, in the case of photocopying or other reprographic copying,
a license from Access Copyright (Canadian Copyright Licensing Agency),
1 Yonge Street, Suite 1900, Toronto, Ontario, Canada, M5E 1E5.

Great Plains Publications gratefully acknowledges the financial support
provided for its publishing program by the Government of Canada through
the Canada Book Fund; the Canada Council for the Arts; the Province of
Manitoba through the Book Publishing Tax Credit and the Book Publisher
Marketing Assistance Program; and the Manitoba Arts Council.

Design & Typography by Relish New Brand Experience
Printed in Canada by Friesens

LIBRARY AND ARCHIVES CANADA CATALOGUING IN PUBLICATION

Title: Assiniboine Park : designing and developing a people's playground /
    David Spector.
Names: Spector, David, 1951- author.
Identifiers: Canadiana 20190068256 | ISBN 9781773370125 (softcover)
Subjects: LCSH: Parks—Manitoba—Winnipeg—History. | LCSH: Zoos—
    Manitoba—Winnipeg—History.
Classification: LCC FC3396.65 S64 2019 | DDC 971.27/43—dc23

Canada

FSC
www.fsc.org
MIX
Paper from
responsible sources
FSC® C016245

ENVIRONMENTAL BENEFITS STATEMENT

Great Plains Publications saved the following
resources by printing the pages of this book on
chlorine free paper made with 10% post-consumer
waste.

TREES	WATER	ENERGY	SOLID WASTE	GREENHOUSE GASES
2	400	1	8	900
FULLY GROWN	GALLONS	MILLION BTUs	POUNDS	POUNDS

Environmental impact estimates were made using the Environmental Paper Network
Paper Calculator 4.0. For more information visit www.papercalculator.org.

Contents

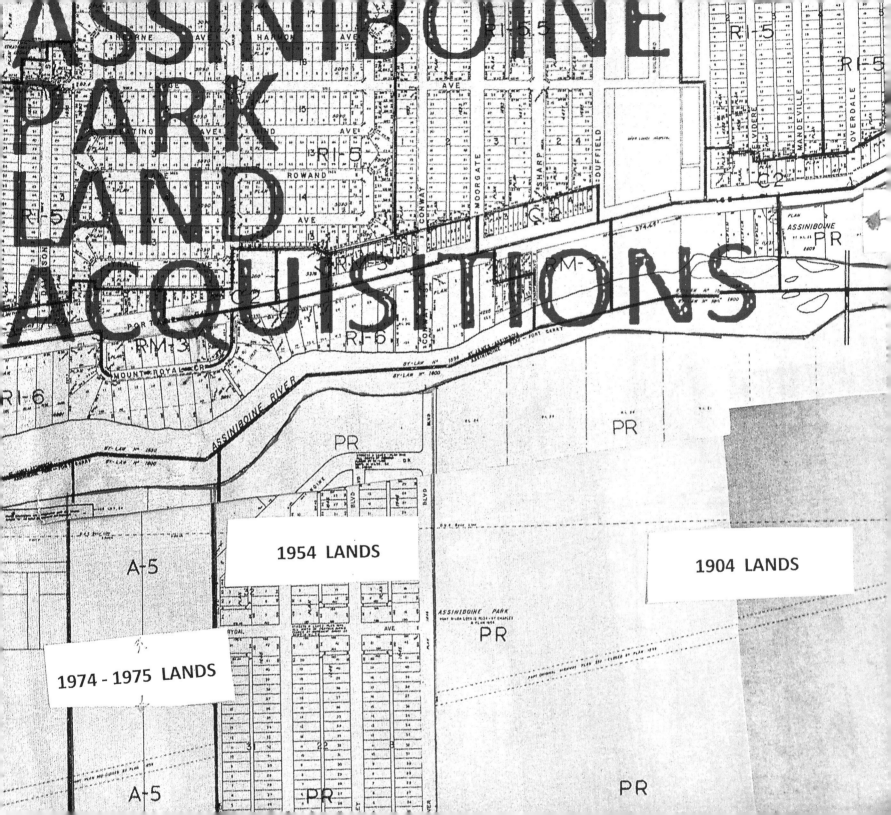

ASSINIBOINE PARK LAND ACQUISITIONS

1954 LANDS

1904 LANDS

1974 - 1975 LANDS

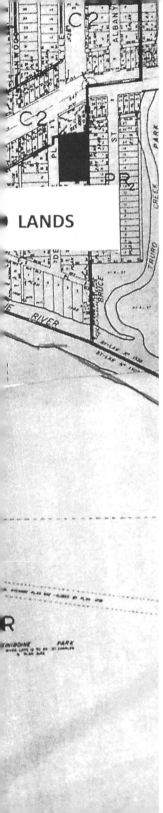

LANDS

Acknowledgments

In the mid-1950s, my parents introduced me to the attractions and delights of Assiniboine Park. They guided me through the luscious subtropical foliage in the first Conservatory and the floral displays in the English Garden. And of course, my favourite place was the zoo, where the black, grizzly and polar bears, the lions, tigers and monkeys provided endless amusement. My parents inculcated me with a sense of Winnipeg's and Canada's history. As a teenager, I became curious about Assiniboine Park's past – an interest that has continued throughout my adult life. This book is dedicated to their memory.

After a long career with Parks Canada in Ottawa, I returned to Winnipeg and decided to pursue my interest in Assiniboine Park. When I found no one had written an in-depth history of the park, I decided to tackle it myself. However, this story of the park could not have become

OPPOSITE
Land Acquisition
Reference Plan

possible without the assistance of various individuals and institutions: My long-time friend, Randy R. Rostecki, reviewed the manuscript in its final stages. His comments, suggestions and insights into Winnipeg's history have improved this work immeasurably. From his vast private database, Randy pointed me to newspapers, articles and publications which would otherwise have been missed. Another long-time friend, Henry Trachtenberg, provided me with useful articles and references. My friend Miriam Greene happily tolerated my never-ending monologues on the history of Assiniboine Park. Thank you, friends.

The holdings of the City of Winnipeg Archives comprise one of the main sources of information for this book. Archivists Sarah Ramsden and Martin Comeau provided much-needed assistance in identifying pertinent collections. Last but not least, the staff of the City Archives granted me the use of their private lunch room so I could sustain myself during long days of research!

Librarians with the Manitoba Legislative Library, Monica Ball,

Stuart Hay and Jason Woloski, provided valuable reference services including the identification of historic publications on Winnipeg containing articles and photos of Assiniboine Park.

Many of the photos in this book have been sourced from the photo collection of the Provincial Archives of Manitoba. Archivist Chris Kotecki assisted me in navigating the computerized databases in order to locate pertinent illustrations. Several *Winnipeg Tribune* photos from The Tribune Collection at the University of Manitoba Archives have also been used. Archivist James Kominowski provided valuable assistance to me in copying photos from this collection and authorizing their use in this publication.

Great Plains Publications deserves credit for publishing this history of Assiniboine Park. The fine editing of Ingeborg Boyens has made this a much better book.

Introduction

Tuesday, July 7, 1908 was a warm summer day with a temperature of 27 degrees Celsius. At 3:30 PM, members of city council, the Board of Control, the Public Parks Board and a press contingent assembled in front of the picturesque, gingerbread-style city hall for an inspection trip to what Parks Board Secretary James H. Blackwood called "Winnipeg's new suburban playground." Awaiting to transport the dignitaries was a convoy of open-air automobiles – a manifestation of the progress in Winnipeg's booming economy.

The route taken to Assiniboine Park was a showcase of the city's new affluent southwestern suburbs. Travelling down Main Street, the cars likely turned right on Portage Avenue, passed the massive Eaton's department store, and continued west to Maryland Street. Veering south, the convoy crossed the Maryland Bridge and entered Crescentwood with its grand residences of the city's commercial elite. Continuing west, the cars travelled down Academy Road, skirted the newly-emerging, middle class residential development of River Heights and eventually arrived at the southeastern gate of the park. Here the inspection began in earnest.

The park which Mayor J.H. Ashdown; seven aldermen; Public Parks Board members F.W. Drewry, R.D. Waugh, E.W. Sharpe, H.C. Stovel, F.W. Handel; and Controllers Latimer, Baker and Harvey entered

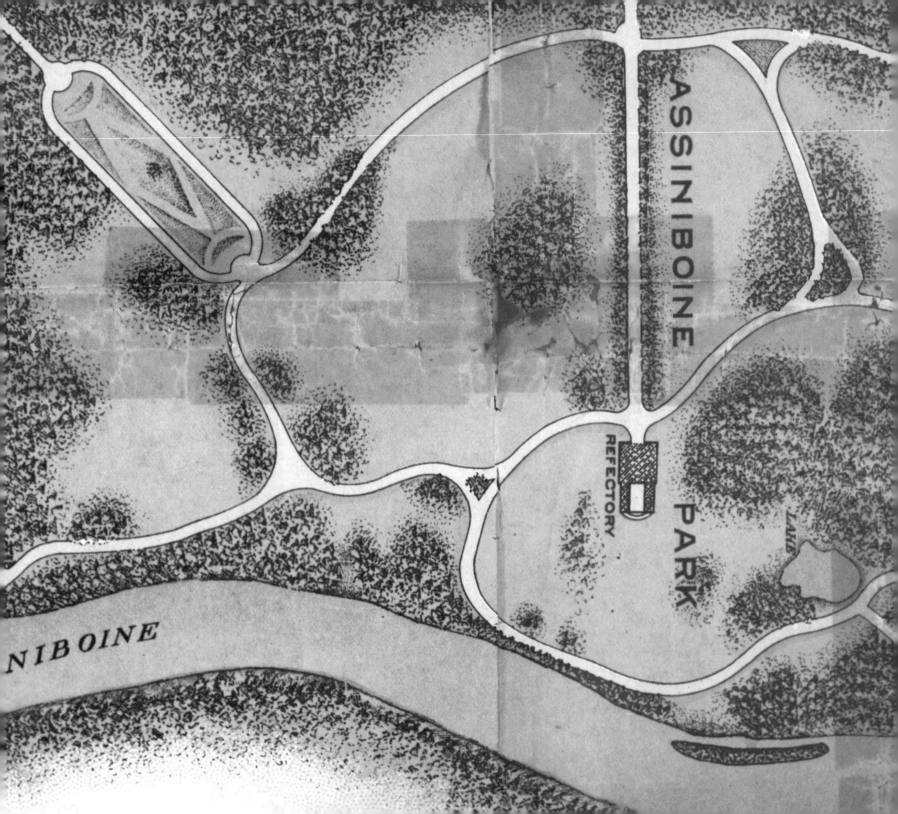

ASSINIBOINE PARK

REFECTORY

ASSINIBOINE

NIBOINE

LAKE

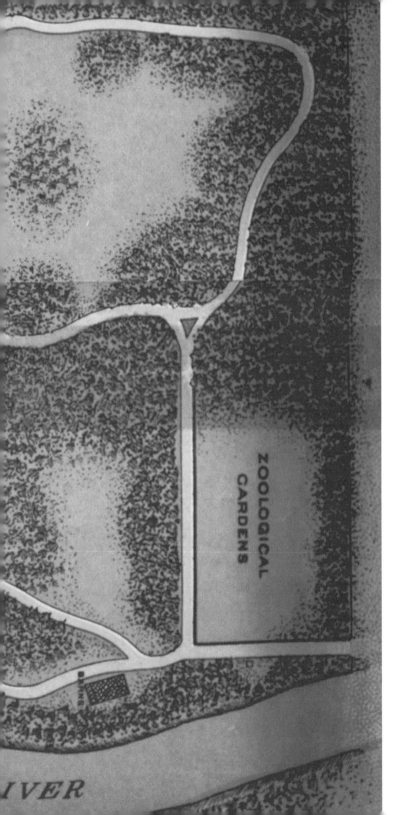

ZOOLOGICAL GARDENS

...IVER

had been transformed in four years from a cow pasture to an idyllic, urban and Arcadian breathing space. Rapidly nearing completion in 1908, its design echoed those of parks in other cities – Point Pleasant Park in Halifax, Mount Royal Park in Montreal, High Park in Toronto, Stanley Park in Vancouver, Central Park in New York City and above all, Como Park in St. Paul, Minnesota. The visiting party expressed its delight with the newly-completed winding gravel driveways, the flower beds in full bloom, the three-acre plant nursery with its hundreds of flowering plants, trees and shrubs destined for transplanting, the duck pond under excavation, and the immense pavilion to which workers were adding the finishing touches. The party singled out the zoo for special attention. At this time, it was confined to native Western Canadian animals, housing three bears, five red deer, three buffalo, one elk and two eagles. The visitors concluded that the zoo should be expanded, and more animals should be acquired.

Mayor Ashdown struck one discordant note that day. He expressed

Plan of Assiniboine Park, 1912. *THE DOMINION, VOLUME 3, NUMBER 4, APRIL, 1912*

Mayor James Ashdown,
ca. 1915. MANITOBA
ARCHIVES PHOTO

concern about public access to the park and demanded adequate and frequent streetcar service. However, until a permanent footbridge was erected over the Assiniboine River in 1931 to connect with the Portage Avenue streetcar routes, the issue would remain unresolved.

Assiniboine Park never celebrated an official grand opening. No brass bands played, and no municipal politicians delivered self-congratulatory speeches. Instead, the city extended an invitation to the public to visit the park throughout the park's developmental phase from 1904–08. The zoo constituted the first part of the park to be completed. On November 3, 1906, the *Winnipeg Free Press* reported that the zoo was "thronged with visitors" who had come despite a several-mile-long hike from the streetcar terminus at the old Agricultural College (now the Jewish Community Campus). On Victoria Day, 1909, most of the visitor facilities were operational. The *Free Press* noted:

> Assiniboine Park …was like the scene of a country picnic, and the first thing noted was that there was no harsh rattle of amusement devices, no discord of hawkers. Except for the park-like aspect lent by the pavilion, the picnicker might have imagined himself cut quite loose from the city's toil and law… For parties who wished to chat over ice cream or sandwiches, there was the pavilion with its refreshment counter, its roomy verandahs, its tea rooms. For the couple who felt that two were company but a trio a multitude, there were the woody paths where roughness provided an excellent excuse for mutual support. Perhaps the place of greatest activity was the refreshment counter on the ground floor of the pavilion where thirsty picnickers clamored for lemonade and other drinks.

For almost 110 years, Assiniboine Park has provided an idyllic escape from the hustle and bustle of city life. While much of the park has been altered, the overall concept remained unchanged until recently. The following pages tell the story of Assiniboine Park from its inception to the present day. Surprisingly little has been written on the history of Assiniboine Park beyond works commissioned by the city itself – namely a 1972 essay and in 1993, a history book to commemorate the 100th anniversary of Winnipeg's park system. A general history dealing exclusively with Assiniboine Park's unique issues was clearly needed. For instance, what role did Assiniboine Park play in the social history of Winnipeg? Who used the park and in what activities did these people engage? How did Assiniboine Park compete for visitors with its rivals, including the commercial River and Elm Parks, Winnipeg and Grand Beach, and more recently Birds Hill Provincial Park and The Forks? How did the zoo evolve from a basic caged menagerie of Western Canadian animals for children's entertainment to a centre for the preservation and breeding of endangered species? It is these questions that this book addresses.

Throughout its life, Assiniboine Park has reflected the evolution of Winnipeg and its societal values. This book explains how Assiniboine Park metamorphosed from a pleasure playground oriented to relaxation, contemplation and family recreation to a 21st-century theme park at the forefront of popular botanical and zoological education and Indigenous teachings. It reports the controversies in assembling the park's real estate and documents the development of the park in terms of landscaping and gardens, physical structures, playing fields and the zoo.

This book shows how Assiniboine Park evolved from an Anglo-Saxon weekend sanctuary for liturgical music where swings were disconnected from their moorings and the merry-go-round tethered on Sundays, to a seven-day multi-cultural playground offering music and activities to people of all backgrounds. During its development, the park bore witness to all the great events of the 20th century – the First and Second World Wars, the Winnipeg General Strike, the royal visits and the 1960s counter-culture movement. All these events are covered. With its $200-million state-of-the-art zoo, conservatory, duck pond and playground redevelopment, Assiniboine Park will attract new generations of Winnipeggers from all walks of life and play an important role in the city's future.

For almost 110 years, Assiniboine Park has provided an idyllic escape from the hustle and bustle of city life.

Chapter One: Beginnings

In the 1870s, Winnipeg was stretching from its gangly village youth into a burgeoning frontier prairie town. By 1876, a few substantial brick buildings had risen along Main Street to complement the majority of inexpensive false-fronted wooden structures. To achieve an aura of respectability, residents constructed churches and formed drama and musical societies. Yet Winnipeg's future remained clouded. Unless the new transcontinental railway selected Winnipeg as its divisional point, the city would fade into an obscure backwater.

Laying out the Formal Garden
(now site of Diversity Gardens), 1909
CITY ARCHIVES, PUBLIC PARKS BOARD
ANNUAL REPORT, 1909

Winnipeg's decision to finance a railway bridge over the Red River enticed the Canadian Pacific Railway to route its line through the city and ensured its rise as a regional centre. A period of dramatic growth ensued. Eighteen months in 1881 to 1882 saw a massive real estate boom with wild bidding, daily land auctions, houses thrown up in twenty-four hours and hundreds of would-be speculators camped out in tents on the streets. Although a recession hit in 1883, a prosperous future for Winnipeg was ensured. The election of 1884 replaced a gang of speculators, crooks and possibly whorehouse owners with a business-dominated city council and reform-minded Mayor Charles E. Hamilton, confirming that Winnipeg had emerged as a responsibly-administered, growing urban centre.

Experienced and talented business people migrated to Winnipeg and transformed the city into a major grain marketing centre. Entrepreneurs also entered the wholesale business; between 1896 and 1901, Winnipeg realized its potential as a centre of the Western Canadian wholesale trade. According to Ruben Bellan in *Winnipeg, First Century – An Economic History*, by 1901, Winnipeg's 103 factories employed 3,155 people and produced $8,616,000 worth of goods – a figure which would quadruple within a decade. Building permits reflected Winnipeg's growth most accurately. In 1900, $1.4 million in building permits were issued. A year later, the number increased to $2.4 million and skyrocketed to $9.7 million in 1904. All these economic activities were labour intensive, and newcomers arrived daily from the East to take up jobs.

As the clock chimed in the New Year of 1902, Winnipeg had reached a crossroads in its development. It stood on the threshold of emerging from a small regional centre to the metropolis of Western Canada. In 1901, Winnipeg had logged a population of 42,340, up from 25,639 a decade earlier; Winnipeg would double its numbers to over 90,000 by 1906. The rapid expansion of the prairie wheat economy in the late 19th century was funneling new settlers and merchandise westward through the city. And grain and cattle were moving along the rail system to eastern Canada and world markets. The Canadian Pacific Railway planned to expand its shops and yards to deal with the increasing rail traffic. In 1908, it would employ a workforce of 4,000 people in Winnipeg.

According to early 20th century thought, extensive green space was needed to maintain a contented, crime free, healthy urban population and workforce. Yet in 1902, Winnipeg had only a few small parks. It desperately needed a large suburban park to meet rising citizens' expectations for recreational lands.

Rapid urban growth had outpaced the expansion of the city's park system, which had remained fixed for almost a decade. While still affordable, municipal politicians, the press and business operators expected land prices to rise suddenly. It was felt that it was now or never for Winnipeg to establish a large suburban park and join other North American cities which had created large urban breathing spaces decades earlier.

The early Parks System in Winnipeg

At the height of the frenzied economic activity, there were thoughts about parks – an idea that had not surfaced earlier. Thanks to a land donation, Winnipeg developed its first, but short-lived, large, suburban park. Captain Hugh S. Donaldson gave the city eighty acres (thirty-two and a half hectares) opposite Brookside Cemetery on Notre Dame

Avenue, land that was predicted to be central to the city's core in future years. Prepared and executed by city council on February 13, 1882, an agreement between the two parties

was signed but not registered in the Land Titles Office. In 1882 and 1883, the city landscaped Donaldson Park with tree plantings. However, the park attracted few visitors because of its considerable distance from

Pavillion, River Park, 1900.
MANITOBA ARCHIVES PHOTO

downtown. According to historian R.R. Rostecki in *Brookside Cemetery: A Celebration of Life* "the locale remained so isolated that the caretaker of the Cemetery was given to grazing his cow in the park." In 1885, the city abandoned Donaldson Park and the lands probably reverted to their donor. It would take two decades before a second, more successful suburban park, Assiniboine, would be developed.

During much of the 1880s, Winnipeg functioned as an urban centre without parks, but with many undeveloped open spaces. City councils of the period concentrated their efforts in constructing the basic infrastructure of roads, sewers, police and fire protection as well as a picturesque city hall and a jail. In an unpublished essay, "The Pre-Parks System of Winnipeg, 1880 – 1893," Rostecki points out that Winnipeg had many open spaces, and within "a few-minute walk away from any building the problems of a big city appeared far away."

People did appreciate recreational spots for exercise, picnicking and courting. In part, private groves

Pontoon Bridge – River Park, 1911.
MANITOBA ARCHIVES PHOTO

In sharp contrast to the relatively idyllic Elm Park, River Park across the river functioned as a commercial amusement park.

Street Car at
River Park,
Early 1900s.
MANITOBA
ARCHIVES PHOTO

fulfilled that function. On July 8, 1885, the *Winnipeg Daily Times* described two popular pleasure spots. Located off Main Street north of St. John's Cathedral, both were accessible by a short walk from the streetcar terminus and offered lovely forested river views. Owned by banker Duncan McArthur and situated at the east end of McAdam Avenue, the northernmost of the groves provided scenery similar to "the primeval forest of an Ontario back township instead of on the treeless prairie" and extended "for nearly half a mile back from the river and down the river for miles." The owner permitted "picnic parties and pleasure seekers" to use the space for free. These unofficial picnic spots sufficed until 1890 when the Winnipeg Electric Railway Company opened River and Elm Parks to the public.

In 1890, A.W. Austin and his Winnipeg Electric Railway Company laid out the city's first large privately-owned urban park. Comprising nearly 100 acres (forty and a half hectares) on both sides of the Red River at today's Kingston Row, the east side was named Elm Park and the west side, River Park. An old-growth forest of stately elms and oaks stretched along the riverbanks. During summer of 1890, workers cleared the underbrush, fenced the properties, and installed park benches under the trees. At Elm Park a footpath was laid along the Red River and a large pavilion-dance hall with refreshment stands was erected.

The Winnipeg Electric Railway Company planned Elm Park for picnicking, hiking and dancing. In sharp contrast to the relatively idyllic Elm Park, River Park across the river functioned as a commercial amusement park. Swings, a merry-go-round, a firing range, and children's rides were laid out. Later, company officials added a small zoo. To attract paying customers, in 1890 the company constructed a streetcar line through wooded and undeveloped Fort Rouge to River Park. At that time, a ferry, and two years later, a floating bridge carried park goers between the two parks.

Throughout its existence, the River Park-Elm Park development brought multitudes of Winnipeggers through its turnstiles. On its grand opening in August 1890, 3,000 people picnicked within its confines. On Dominion Day 1895, 5,000 visitors paid the ten-cent streetcar fare which included park admission. Labour Day also proved popular with visitors; on that holiday in 1895, Elm Park witnessed thirty public picnics.

In a class-conscious city that was often divided by racism, the two parks welcomed all classes and ethnic groups. On Saturdays, workingmen and their families crowded into the parks while church and synagogue groups held picnics on weekdays at Elm Park. At times vandalism became an issue. On Dominion Day 1892, the *Free Press* reported that young men destroyed incandescent light bulbs on the illuminated trails with their walking sticks. The Winnipeg Electric Railway Company hired a private detective to oversee the crowds and deter future culprits.

Overall, in the 1890s, River and Elm Parks functioned as a focal point for Winnipeg's recreational activities. Yet the parks remained a purely commercial venture of A.W. Austin.

David D. England, Winnipeg's
First Chief Gardener, 1903.
MANITOBA FREE PRESS, AUGUST 29,
1903, P. 19

Once within its boundaries, park patrons were encouraged to spend money on amusements and at food outlets. For the longer term, the company envisaged greater revenue opportunities. It was hoped the street railway would foster residential development in Fort Rouge and thus greater ridership on the line. The lands comprising River and Elm Parks would increase in value. The eventual sub-division and sale of the two parks into residential building lots would enrich the Winnipeg Electric Railway Company far more than the operation of an amusement park. In short, River and Elm Parks were developed as investment opportunities and never places for people to relax and regenerate their bodies and souls in idealized natural surroundings.

By the late 1880s, slow and steady growth in Winnipeg had filled open spaces in the city's core and near suburbs with buildings. Children and adolescents could not find places to play and to engage in organized and unorganized sports. The press and city council called for improvements.

In September 1889, the *Manitoba Sun* wrote that the city "should have a few breathing spaces." Three months later, the *Sun* advocated that "a good number of small parks or playgrounds would be of infinitely more value than two or three large parks." On September 16, 1889, city council appointed a special committee to consider the question of parks and to report in two weeks time. However, city council did not act and recommended that the matter be re-considered in 1891. Procrastination continued for two years. Not until 1893 did city council establish a system of small urban parks.

The provincial Public Parks Act of April 20, 1892 established the legislative framework for the creation and administration of municipal parks in Manitoba's cities and towns. Drafters of the Act largely modelled it on similar provincial legislation in Ontario of nine years earlier. Parks could be created in cities upon a petition of 300 electors if assented to in a regular municipal election. A Public Parks Board made up of the mayor, the chairpersons of the finance and works committees of council and

At the turn of the century, it had become apparent to all that a large, scenic suburban park was needed to fulfil the requirements for recreation and relaxation of Winnipeg's rapidly expanding population.

six other city residents appointed by council, would operate the park. The Act authorized the Board to acquire land by donation or purchase for public parks not exceeding 600 acres (242.8 hectares) in total for cities with more than 25,000 inhabitants. Under the terms of this Act, the City of Winnipeg created the Public Parks Board in 1893, purchased lands and laid out a number of small municipal parks for the purposes of community breathing spaces. According to the *Free Press* of August 23, 1894, "women and children and the toilers of the shops and factories might spend a pleasant hour amidst the leafy trees or green swards under the broad expanse of heaven."

Distributed in every residential district, the parks created were compact. St. John's Park boasted the largest area at ten and a half acres (four and a quarter hectares) followed by St. James Park at six acres (nearly two and a half hectares). Notre Dame Park at almost four acres (one and a half hectares), Central Park at three and a half acres (nearly one and a half hectares), Selkirk and Dufferin Parks at two acres apiece (almost one hectare) and Victoria Park at nearly one acre (a third of a hectares) completed the list. In March 1894, the Public Parks Board asked local architects to prepare and submit plans for the parks. On March 27, 1894, elected and appointed officials comprising Parks Board Chairman E.L. Drewry, the Parks Board members, the mayor, and two aldermen selected the winning entries in the competition. The city accepted architect S. Frank Peters' plans for Central Park and Selkirk Park while St. John's Park, the original Assiniboine Park (now Fort Rouge Park) and Victoria Park would be laid out pursuant to H.S. Griffith's designs. The one engineer, Walter J. Holyoake, achieved success. His plans for Notre Dame Park and St. James Park would also be executed. In early April 1894, the city hired a thirty-year-old landscape gardener from the United Kingdom, David D. England, to implement the architects' design and operate Winnipeg's new park system. England would be employed as chief city gardener until 1906 when a conflict of interest forced his resignation.

Premier Rodmond
Palen Roblin,
Architect of City of
Winnipeg Charter
of 1902. MANITOBA
ARCHIVES PHOTO

As the clock chimed in the New Year of 1902, Winnipeg had reached a crossroads in its development.

At the turn of the century, it had become apparent to all that a large, scenic suburban park was needed to fulfil the requirements for recreation and relaxation of Winnipeg's rapidly expanding population. In his 1900 Annual Report to the Parks Board, the city's chief gardener recommended "that Winnipeg should have an outside park where citizens can go and spend the day and play cricket, lawn tennis and other games; at the present time…no park is suitable for this purpose." Moreover, the existing "small parks are heavily visited…because we have no large park." The daily press concurred. In their editorials they gave particular voice to these sentiments. On October 24, 1901, the *Winnipeg Tribune* wrote that within a short period of time Elm Park and River Park would be too small for the city, and with increasing land values there was no guarantee that they would remain open to the public. The *Tribune* recommended that city purchase land for a large recreational ground while real estate prices remained moderate. The *Winnipeg Telegram* offered its opinion: It too feared that the Winnipeg Electric Railway Company would subdivide Elm and River Parks into building lots. Then Winnipeg would be bereft of sizeable recreation grounds. On August 27, 1903, the *Telegram* called for a park comprised not of "bare prairie or even a piece of prairie with monotonous poplar. It is desirable if possible to find some picturesqueness in the landscape and some variety in the timber together with a river front and a good beach." These arguments, among others, influenced city council and the Public Parks Board to consider the idea of a large suburban park.

In 1902, the City of Winnipeg took the first tentative steps in creating a suburban recreation ground. The City of Winnipeg Charter authorized the city to purchase lands outside Winnipeg for this purpose. In existence since 1893, a Public Parks Board stood ready to construct and administer the new park. One hurdle remained before a large suburban park could be created outside city boundaries – enabling legislation. The Public Parks Act of 1892 stood silent on this issue. The provincial Conservative government of Rodmond Roblin acted. In 1902, Manitoba passed a Charter for the City of Winnipeg that stipulated the terms by which Winnipeg would be governed. The legislation repealed all previous acts and parts of legislation in conflict with its terms. The charter also addressed the requirement for a suburban park. Section 691 authorized city council to pass bylaws for the acquisition by purchase or expropriation of land for cemeteries, parks, agricultural or exhibition grounds within or outside city limits. Moreover, the council could erect buildings thereon and issue regulations for their operation. As with all capital expenditures, any bylaw setting aside funds or raising capital by debentures for public works would need approval of the electors.

The City of Winnipeg Charter of 1902 restricted who could vote on bylaw plebiscites. Only those with land assessed at $400 or more could vote on bylaws requiring municipal borrowing. To pass a money bylaw,

two-thirds approval was needed. The result became valid only if at least three-tenths of all registered electors voted. The City of Winnipeg Charter incorporated women's right to vote on money bylaws. In 1903, women as well as men would approve or reject a bylaw authorizing the expenditure of funds for the creation of a large suburban park.

The Concept of the Large Suburban Park

The concept of the large suburban park originated in England. In the English-speaking world, Birkenhead Park was the first example. Located on the Mersey River across from Liverpool, it opened to the public in 1847. Designed by Sir Joseph Paxton, who later achieved fame for the Crystal Palace in London, the park encompassed 125 acres (over fifty hectares) and according to Charles E. Beveridge's and Carolyn F. Hoffman's introduction to *The Papers of Frederick Law Olmsted*, featured winding paths with an undulating surface surrounded on all sides with "every variety of shrubs and flowers all set in borders of green turf." In

1850, the pioneer of American landscape architecture, Frederick Law Olmsted, visited the park and later imported the concepts to the United States and Canada. He launched his career by partnering with British émigré architect Calvert Vaux and winning a design competition for Central Park in New York.

Olmsted developed a comprehensive philosophy of park design, the purpose of which he believed lay in providing scenery "that would counteract the psychological stress of urban life." Towards that goal, his designs incorporated elements of border planting, open postcard landscapes and passages through "picturesque sylvan scenery." No attempt was made to preserve nature. According to William H. Wilson in *The City Beautiful*,

> Olmsted's parks were massive public works designed to reshape the land in basic ways. He did not respect existing natural features unless they could be subordinated to his plans. Olmsted's parks were built in the romantic or postcard modes. They were inventions – not natural but products of naturalistic construction.

In his park designs, Olmsted aimed to fill a void in working class lives and counteract the effects of the saloon. Children benefitted from playing, exercise and natural scenery. Parks strengthened family ties in cities by bringing families together.

New York City's Central Park, North America's first large urban park, inspired city councils across the United States and Canada to create similar green spaces. First proposed by New York City Mayor Ambrose Kingsland on May 5, 1851, the park became a reality after marginal rocky and swampy land useless for commercial activity was expropriated from impoverished Irish, German and black families. In October 1857, New York City held an architectural competition for development of the original 778-acre (314.8 hectare) expanse. Olmsted and Vaux beat out thirty-one other competitors for the $1.5-million park, which included a parade ground, three playgrounds, sites for an exhibition or concert hall, flower garden, skating rinks, fountain and lookout tower. Central Park opened to the public between 1858 and 1860 and was expanded in 1863. According to Roy Rosenzweig and Elizabeth Blackmar in *The Park and The People: A History of Central Park*, Olmsted believed that the park offered "an artistically designed landscape [which] would provide a refreshing antidote to the city's competitive pressures and dreary buildings."

Soon other urban centres emulated New York City's example. Olmsted, Vaux & Company received contracts for the design of large urban parks in Buffalo, Chicago and Albany. Philadelphia, Baltimore, Boston, Hartford and Detroit joined the bandwagon and took steps to create their own large parks. In Canada, Montreal developed its most distinctive geographical feature – Mount Royal. In 1869, the Quebec legislature amended the city's charter by authorizing it to borrow $350,000 for a park on that site. In 1874, Frederick Olmsted was contracted to design the park. It opened on Victoria Day, 1876, with a parade, speeches and cannon fire.

Toronto, Halifax and Vancouver followed next, developing large urban parks at minimal cost to taxpayers. High Park in Toronto originated as a land donation from John Howard in 1873 and by 1890 became accessible to the public by streetcar and by the increasing popularity of bicycling. In Halifax, in 1866, the Imperial Government leased Point Pleasant peninsula for park purposes to the directors of Point Pleasant Park for a term of 999 years at a rental charge of one shilling per annum. The preamble of the agreement extolled the "salubrity and beauty of its position, by its proximity to the city and by the opportunities it would afford to all classes of the community for healthful recreation and exercise." When it opened to the public on June 23, 1873, it featured newly-constructed roads and pathways; extensive tree and shrub plantings and a road to the southern tip of the peninsula became a reality over the next six years. Stanley Park in Vancouver was created in 1887 from a largely unused military reserve. As the 1880s came to a close, large urban parks had been laid out in most major urban centres in the United States and Canada.

More than the large green spaces in Eastern Canada and the American Seaboard, Como Park in St. Paul, Minnesota influenced Assiniboine Park's creation and development. Historian Andrew J. Schmidt has written about Como Park's past. According to Schmidt, in 1873, a special commission of the City of St. Paul purchased 257 acres (104 hectares) for park purposes on the north and west sides of Lake Como within St. Paul's boundaries, "the lands [being] an oak savannah ecosystem with a naturally rolling surface covered with prairie grass and groves, primarily of oak trees…punctuated with bare gravelly ridges and low marshy areas."

For fourteen years, the lands lay undeveloped. In 1887, the St. Paul Board of Park Commissioners was established and provided the impetus for park development. Additional lands were purchased, and landscape architect Horace Cleveland began work. Cleveland's design echoed those of Frederick Olmsted for Central Park and Mount Royal Park. His plan called for a natural-istic park preserving the rolling hills alongside Como Lake and with a variety of trees, shrubs and vines planted along the drives. Como Park would provide for passive recreation – horseback riding, unstructured play, walking and picnicking and "a naturalistic escape from city life." In the 1890s, newly-appointed St. Paul Parks Superintendent Frederick Nussbaumer modified Cleveland's plan. He added floral gardens, a conservatory, aquarium, zoo and playing fields to the mix. It was this hybrid concept which Winnipeg would adopt for Assiniboine Park.

More than the large green spaces in Eastern Canada and the American Seaboard, Como Park in St. Paul, Minnesota influenced Assiniboine Park's creation and development.

Chapter Two:
A Parade Of Land Speculators, 1903

The years 1903 and 1904 can be described as momentous in the history of Winnipeg's public parks system. After years of debate, the Public Parks Board and city council finally approved the creation of a large suburban park. In these years, the necessary money bylaw was approved by ratepayers, the land purchased, and after considerable discussion, the park named.

J. Smith Property – One of the Land
Parcels acquired for Assiniboine Park,
c. 1903 MANITOBA ARCHIVES PHOTO

The Public Parks Board in 1903 and 1904

The Public Parks Board was instrumental in creating Assiniboine Park. Effectively an adjunct to city council and subject to its funding, the Public Parks Board was comprised partly of the publicly elected mayor and finance and public works committee chairmen. To create Assiniboine Park, the Parks Board benefitted from the leadership of two mayors, John Arbuthnot (1901–03) and Thomas Sharpe (1904–06). Before his election in 1901, Arbuthnot, an Ontario-born railway contractor in Port Arthur (now Thunder Bay) and lumber company owner in Winnipeg, served as both an alderman and Parks Board chairman. His successor, Thomas Sharpe, boasted similar qualifications. Irish-born and with experience as a bank clerk in Ireland and paving contractor in Toronto and Winnipeg, he served as alderman for four years, three of those as public works chairman. Both politicians brought considerable business and administrative experience to the Parks Board.

John Arbuthnot, Mayor of Winnipeg in 1903 *REPRESENTATIVE MEN OF MANITOBA – HISTORY IN PORTRAITURE,* THE TRIBUNE PUBLISHING COMPANY, WINNIPEG, 1902

In addition to three politicians, six citizens were appointed to the Parks Board. Selected by city council, the appointees served three-year terms in rotation, with two members retiring each year. In 1903 and 1904, Winnipeg city aldermen looked to capable, politically reliable and civic-minded friends and business colleagues to fill the unpaid Parks Board positions. The civilian appointees were made up of a number of Winnipeg's leading business operators, long-time Winnipeggers, and several individuals who had enriched themselves through land speculation. These officials fulfilled their duties under the revised Public Parks Act of 1902 which reiterated and confirmed terms of the 1892 statute.

Among the most prominent civilian members of the Public Parks Board was Henry Sandison. Appointed chairman of the Parks Board in 1903 and re-appointed a year later, Sandison was born

Thomas Sharpe, Mayor of Winnipeg, 1904
MANITOBA ARCHIVES PHOTO

in Scotland and apprenticed as a tailor at age twelve. At nineteen, he emigrated to Canada and settled in Winnipeg where he opened a tailor shop. Most notably, Sandison made a fortune in land speculation after Winnipeg's 1881–82 real estate boom turned to bust. According to the *Free Press*, "when the despair of depressed times seized so many and brought progress to a standstill Mr. Sandison was one of the sanguine citizens who took advantage of depressed times to invest in city property."

At the young age of forty-one, Sandison retired and took an active interest in public life. He devoted himself to the Public Parks Board

where he became instrumental in the creation of Assiniboine Park.

The board members included Donald Andrew Ross, a realtor whose attitudes complemented those of Sandison. He established a real estate company at the age of twenty and was well-regarded in the business community. In the view of F.H. Schofield in *The Story of Manitoba,* "his opinions are yet received as expert authority upon matters relating to real estate in this city and the importance of the realty transfers which he negotiated placed him prominently among the foremost representatives of this line

Henry Sandison – Father of Assiniboine Park

Henry Sandison took early retirement after making a fortune in land speculation when others were scared off. Still a young man, he dedicated himself to public service, particularly the establishment and development of public parks. Sandison served on the Public Parks Board for fourteen years, including three as chairman. He spearheaded the effort to establish Assiniboine Park as a multi-use playground free to all citizens, complete with vast open spaces, a pavilion, zoo, conservatory and greenhouses. For his accomplishments, the voters in Ward 2 elected him to city council in 1905 and again in 1906. As an alderman, Sandison continued to play a prominent role in developing Assiniboine Park and securing its boundaries. Appointed to city council's Buffalo Committee he also became involved in relocating the city's herd of bison from Silver Heights to the newly created Assiniboine Park Zoo.

Sandison died in 1942 at the age of eighty-five. In his obituary, the *Winnipeg Tribune* wrote that "he was instrumental in obtaining Assiniboine Park for the city."

Henry Sandison, Public Parks Board Member and Chairman, 1903
CITY OF WINNIPEG ARCHIVES, INTRODUCTION TO PUBLIC PARKS
BOARD ANNUAL REPORTS, 1893–1910

of business in the city." The knowledge and experience of Ross and Sandison would prove invaluable in assessing the lands offered for the suburban park by Winnipeg's land speculators.

Charles Napier Bell provided the Public Parks Board with general business expertise which complemented the realty knowledge of Sandison and Ross. He served in a number of influential posts, including secretary of the Winnipeg Board of Trade, secretary of the Winnipeg Grain Exchange, and secretary of the Royal Commission on Shipment and Transportation of Grain. His knowledge of Winnipeg's history, economy and growth potential enabled Bell to make a valuable contribution to selecting the site for Winnipeg's suburban park.

Frederick William Drewry brought the only sportsman's perspective to the Parks Board table. With his brother Edward Lancaster Drewry, he had opened Redwood Breweries. He also was an avid sportsman, serving as director of the Winnipeg Lacrosse Club, president of the St. John's College Cricket

Club and president of the Manitoba Rugby Association.

On June 3, 1903, the members of the Public Parks Board assembled for their regular meeting at Winnipeg's picturesque city hall. They appointed a committee consisting of Chairman Sandison, and Members Ross, Bell and Drewry to enquire and report into the matter of acquiring what they called an "outside park." On June 15, 1903, the committee recommended the creation of a suburban park like those in other major cities. To begin the process, the Parks Board ordered a money bylaw be prepared and voted on by ratepayers – a requirement for all capital projects at the time. Given the fickleness of Winnipeg property owners, its outcome was uncertain.

The 1903 Money Bylaw and Plebiscite

In late July 1903, the City of Winnipeg held the referendum to allow the city to raise $50,000 through taxes to purchase and develop a suburban park site. Parks Board Chairman Sandison led the campaign for a park. In an open

FREDERICK WILLIAM D Manufacturer, Winnipeg.

Frederick William Drewry, Public Parks Board Member, 1903
REPRESENTATIVE MEN OF MANITOBA – HISTORY IN PORTRAITURE, THE TRIBUNE PUBLISHING COMPANY, WINNIPEG, 1902

Sandison envisaged a multi-use park, with something for everyone. He proposed it would be used "for the purpose of promoting the study of natural history."

letter that appeared in the *Free Press* on July 28, 1903, Sandison argued that the city needed a park that was "owned and controlled by the citizens of Winnipeg." He explained that the city's rapid growth necessitated the acquisition of land. And that action was needed while property was affordable. He pointed out that it was better to have a park under public control instead of private ownership – a park with "ample facilities for all our athletic associations to exercise themselves free from exorbitant charges and restrictions … under private ownership."

Sandison envisaged a multi-use park, with something for everyone. He proposed it would be used "for the purpose of promoting the study of natural history. The establishment of zoological and botanical gardens will be the means of exhibiting to strangers visiting the city the fauna and flora of our new and progressive country. Our buffalo herd can secure in such a park a congenial home and these can be supplemented by other wild animals. Our horticultural products too can be given an impetus under such conditions as will be afforded in a suburban park." Sandison proposed the construction of a conservatory and greenhouses and the development of a nursery to supply plants, trees, flowers and shrubs for all of Winnipeg's parks.

To benefit the public, he proposed to "put up a large and commodious pavilion for the amusement and recreation of citizens." The park would be located on either the Red or Assiniboine River to offer the public facilities for boating, canoeing, aquatic sports and bathing. Sandison's vision was indeed grand and comprehensive.

Henry Sandison's imaginings for Winnipeg's suburban park may have been inspired by Como Park in St. Paul. Sandison probably visited Como Park as railways provided frequent passenger service between Winnipeg and Minneapolis-St. Paul. He likely corresponded with St. Paul Parks Superintendent Frederick Nussbaumer as park officials throughout the United States and Canada regularly exchanged ideas and information. There is no explicit record of communication, but Sandison's vision for Winnipeg's suburban park was strikingly similar to the Nussbaumer concept of the park as a naturalistic getaway but one which provided recreational facilities and attractive horticultural and zoological exhibits.

The phrasing and timing of the plebiscite question demonstrated an intense desire by the Public Parks Board and city council to expedite passage of the parks bylaw. The question placed before Winnipeg ratepayers on July 29, 1903 circumvented the usual requirement for two-thirds approval for raising municipal debentures. Instead, voters were requested to authorize a $50,000 expenditure for a suitable park site owned and controlled by Winnipeg's citizens. Moreover, the vote was held at the height of a hot prairie summer. Prior to the advent of central air conditioning, affluent Winnipeg ratepayers sweltered in the heat along with the less fortunate. The cool escape of a large park must have seemed quite appealing. The *Free Press* wrote in an editorial "the parks bylaw should need no recommendation to the citizens particularly these

hot days when everyone is longing for a place where he or she may go and enjoy a respite from the heat and dust."

Ratepayers approved the bylaw overwhelmingly by a vote of 685 for versus 346 against. The *Free Press* concluded that "the want of an outside park was badly felt for some time and those instrumental in getting the park bylaw submitted were jubilant last evening on account of its success."

However, the work to secure suitable property was just beginning. The *Free Press* predicted the Public Parks Board would "have a long and harassing squabble before the site is decided on and purchased. There are many options in the hands of the Board." The *Winnipeg Tribune* echoed these sentiments. It declared that "the only difficulty remaining is to decide on the site… and the present was thought to be the most opportune time to purchase, as land values in the vicinity of the city are rapidly advancing."

The Land Selection Process

The location of the new suburban park became the subject of intense debate. Two visions for a site emerged – the first supported by the press, the public and the Parks Board, and the second supported by land speculators. Only one vision could prevail. There were more than six months of false starts, accusations and negotiations before the Parks Board finalized purchase of its selected property.

The Parks Board formulated a rudimentary vision of suitable lands for its suburban park. According to the *Free Press* of June 26, 1903, "the board has in view a large tract of land of very pretty park-like property with a fine stretch of river front." Schemes of the speculators differed greatly from the Parks Board. On September 12, 1903, the *Free Press* explained that some of the sites eyed by the Parks Board were held by speculators and possessed "a very real estate speculator aspect upon them. They would sell to the city at a low figure but reserve the choicest fronts and locations to be enhanced in value by the work of the Parks Board on the adjoining but less advantageously situated parts." In essence, with its limited budget the city would be forced to select lands with limited river frontage, scrub bush and swamp bisected by roads and railway tracks. Speculators would benefit from large public expenditures to improve the marginal park land. They would sell at exorbitant and outlandish prices the adjacent well-treed, drained and scenic residential lots. The Parks Board would require all the expertise of its members to outwit those sharks.

Initially the Parks Board did not develop a selection process to identify suitable lands for a suburban park. Instead, it invited land owners and real estate companies to submit proposals. They did not evaluate proposals against fixed criteria. Board members were experienced businessmen who had made decisions throughout their long careers according to their business instincts and their intuition. That is how they had achieved success in Winnipeg's rough and tumble business community.

They flew by the seats of their pants. And that's what they intended to do here.

Until summer's end of 1903, the Public Parks Board received no proposals from citizens, real estate companies or speculators. But as summer turned to autumn, a parade of land speculators came forth in an effort to persuade the Parks Board to purchase their marginal lands. The Board instructed Chief Gardener D.D. England to report on the suitability of various sites.

The *Free Press* objected to the unstructured selection process. In an October 7, 1903 editorial, it concluded that given multiple offers, the site selection question was difficult to solve. It recommended securing "the opinion of some landscape architect or experienced park superintendent familiar with the park system and park experience of North American cities, who could advise as to the adaptability of the various

propositions for park purposes and also as to the way the public of other cities regard distance and accessibility."

Exactly one month after England had presented his report, the *Free Press* reiterated its call for an outside expert. It noted England's lack of expertise: "The Parks Board erred we think, not taking the opinion of a competent outsider, instead of exposing one of its own officials to unfair public criticism. The Park Superintendent's Report is that of a gardener. He determines the suitability of land for a park based on the actual count of the trees and actual acreage of different classes of land on each particular site. If it is bog land he says so very candidly and if it is suitable for a park he says so with equal candor."

The *Free Press* continued to push, arguing only an outside park expert could make a selection based upon park accessibility, the future direction of Winnipeg's growth and the experience of other communities. However, The Public Parks Board did not follow the *Free Press* recommendation. The allocation of $50,000 for park acquisition and development left little financial wiggle room.

Land Offers – the Options

The Public Parks Board entertained many offers from real estate companies and land speculators but gave serious consideration to only four offers: the O'Meara Option, now near Crescent Park, Nugent's Point, now Wildwood Park, the Archibald Wright lands on the south side of the Assiniboine River west of the current St. James Bridge, and the Munroe Pure Milk Company lands among others.

The O'Meara Option was the first site seriously considered. It was located five and a half miles (8.5 km) south of city hall and about three miles (4.8 km) south of the terminus of the Elm Park streetcar line on the west side of the Red River. It possessed a river frontage of forty-four chains (885 metres). John O'Meara offered the lands to the city at $50 per acre.

Since it fell within the city's budget, on September 17, 1903 the Parks Board recommended purchase of the lands, subject to a site inspection by both its members and city council.

The site visit on Saturday, September 19, 1903 left Parks Board members and city aldermen unimpressed. According to the *Free Press*, "the site is void of large trees and is covered with willow and poplar while the western portion is now used for hay." The land was low lying and the Canadian Northern Railway line bisected the property. One alderman labelled it as hay swamp trimmed with willow. Mayor John Arbuthnot remarked that he "does not consider the site a good one." Two weeks after the inspection, the *Free Press* commented that the site "was not selected because of the superiority over other sites … but because it came within the limits of the price set by vote." Embarrassed by the criticism of its political masters, the Parks Board quietly rescinded its purchase offer.

The rejection of his proposition did not deter land promoter John O'Meara. In early November 1903, he purchased full page advertisements in Winnipeg's daily newspapers. The ads extolled his property's virtues including a deliberately misleading three-quarters of a mile (1.2 kilometres) of river frontage. To facilitate a sale, he reduced his asking price by $10 to $40 per acre. There were no takers at the Public Parks Board or city council.

A second offer arrived at the Parks Board office in late September 1903 – the William Pearson & Company's Nugent Point site. The property was located south of the Elm Park streetcar line in what is now Wildwood Park. The lands, totalling 1,340 acres (546 hectares), comprised Lots 1 to 9, Parish of St. Boniface from the Red River to the Pembina Highway and Lots 35 to 57, Parish of St. Vital. According to William Pearson "we did not limit the board to any given proposition whatever, as we thought they could select an area of land… which would suit their purpose." Pearson set various prices for the lots – higher for river frontage and lower for rear portions. A slick salesman and later a town planning advocate, Pearson promoted the virtues of his lands vigorously. Being one of the most beautiful places in the vicinity of the city, he claimed that Nugent's Point had been a favourite destination of campers for many years. Treed with large elms, oaks and maples, it supposedly featured high riverbanks and the most beautiful of river views. Water accessibility constituted a strength. The property could be reached by the largest river steamers – "an advantage which cannot be got on the Assiniboine." Judging by his sales pitch, Pearson's Nugent's Point should have been irresistible to the Parks Board.

The Public Parks Board entertained many offers from real estate companies and land speculators but gave serious consideration to only four offers.

However, the site elicited mixed press commentary. The weekly entertainment broadsheet *Town Topics* supported Pearson's proposal vigorously. In a laudatory editorial of October 10, 1903 – which could have been penned by Pearson himself – it wrote that:

Nugent's Point is well known to canoeists and summer campers as one of the most picturesque spots on the Red River. The distance from Winnipeg is just right for a river trip, about an hour by canoe. The whole property is heavily treed; in fact, the bush is if anything too thick in places. If this property can be acquired at anything like a reasonable figure the city fathers should certainly not pass it over without the gravest consideration.

The *Free Press* was more ambivalent in its evaluation. In an editorial dated October 7, 1903, it simply noted that Nugent's Point came "within the amount stipulated." It pointed out that proponents of the site claimed that it "offers more natural and park features."

The Public Parks Board took no steps to acquire Nugent's Point. While Park Superintendent D.D. England praised Nugent's Point for its rolling ridges with large groves of trees and good river frontage, the Parks Board remained unimpressed.

On November 28, 1903, William Pearson issued an ultimatum. He said the Nugent's Point property was on the brink of being sold to private investors. If the Parks Board did not purchase park lands almost immediately, his offer to the city would be withdrawn. The Parks Board searched elsewhere for a park site.

The Archibald Wright property constituted the third site considered by the Parks Board and city council. Located on the south side of the Assiniboine River, it extended westward from today's St. James bridge. The owner, Archibald Wright, proposed selling 500 (202 hectares) or 1,000 acres (404 hectares) below market value to the city in order to boost the value of his surrounding lots. Wright appears to have promoted his lands with a planted letter to the editor of the *Free Press*. Signed "Parks" a week before his offer, the writer described driving around Winnipeg on his horse and buggy. The driver noted a site on the south side of the river next to the Canadian Pacific and Canadian Northern Railway tracks which would make "one of the prettiest pieces of land imaginable for a park." In the letter, he suggested that the city purchase 200 acres (81 hectares) of the front facing the Assiniboine River for a park and 100 acres (40.4 hectares) to the south for exhibition grounds. The letter voiced objections to a park along the Red River.

> I notice Red river below Elm park suggested. Has it appealed itself to anyone what this location would mean? We have already two parks in this direction, one which is now used for a show ground for cheap attractions very necessary in their way but to my mind altogether undesirable along the city suburban park line as these parks draw a class of people that detract from the quiet protection and safety that residents would feel if they knew their children are passing through on their way to a park situated beyond.

In mid-October 1903, a city alderman inspected the Wright property. The Parks Board requested Wright to submit a proposal for the riverfront portion of his lands. However, by November 1903, the Parks Board interest in the Wright property had waned. In his report on the possible site, D.D. England noted the river frontage was a straight line with a mud bank, and securing a water supply would be problematic. The search for a suitable park site would continue.

After two months of reviewing proposals by land companies and speculators, it had become evident to the Parks Board and city council that none of the offers presented were satisfactory. The lands contained only limited river frontage, scrub bush and swamp. It was time to identify a scenic acreage, preferably along the Assiniboine River, and request that the land owners of the desired parcels come forth with offers.

Negotiations with the Monroe Pure Milk Company and Others

In October 1903, public pressure had mounted to locate the suburban park on the south side of the Assiniboine River. In an editorial on October 7, the *Free Press* wrote that momentum was gathering for a park on the south of the stream opposite St. James Church or Sturgeon Creek at its juncture with the Assiniboine. The *Winnipeg Telegram* commented that the scenery along the Assiniboine River was much prettier than along the Red. The appetite for a park along the river was strong, but there was the understanding that the $50,000 approved under the bylaw might not be enough to buy and develop the land needed. The Parks Board hoped that landowners along the Assiniboine would come forward with reasonable offers.

On October 23, 1903, the Munroe Pure Milk Company responded to the Parks Board call for Assiniboine River frontage. The *Telegram* noted that the Munroe lands bordered the Archibald Wright frontage to the east. The Munroe offer differed greatly from previous propositions. While land companies and speculators had presented river frontages of half a mile (.8 kilometre) or less and depths of two miles (3.2 kilometres), the Munroe lands extended for a mile along the Assiniboine River and totalled one-mile square. If the City needed less depth, Munroe would comply. On November 12, 1903, the Munroe Pure Milk Company broadened its

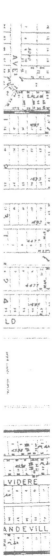

proposal. It presented seven distinct offers covering areas of different sizes and shapes. The *Free Press* commented that "these run from the whole tract which is 75 chains [1509 meters] by two miles [1.6 km] down to one of 42 chains [845 meters] by one half mile [.8 km]. This last offer covers the whole river frontage of his property and includes the best of the park lands. It has all the finest trees and groves and riverbank." Munroe hoped that the Public Parks Board would express an interest in one of the options.

From the outset, Mayor John Arbuthnot viewed favourably the possibility of acquiring the Munroe lands. He argued that if Assiniboine River's water power were harnessed, fifty acres (20.2 hectares) of the land would be submerged. "This would be a tremendous advantage to the park, as the expansion of the river at this point would give the city a little lake without the expenditure of a single dollar by the Parks Board. There is a knoll in the low lands which would make a pretty island and a jutting point would give an added touch to the scenic effort." Arbuthnot's idea of

channelling the Assiniboine River's power never happened as the province focused its efforts on Winnipeg River hydro developments.

The Munroe lands could be made accessible, Arbuthnot further argued, by public transit. With the proposed extension of the Portage Avenue streetcar line to Silver Heights, a bridge over the Assiniboine River could convey passengers to the park.

The Munro lands were not contiguous. Several small land owners held lots between the Munro parcels and were unwilling to sell. Consequently, for most of November and December in 1903, the Parks Board delayed the selection of a park site. As his term drew to a close, Arbuthnot exercised his authority under the City of Winnipeg Charter and refused to sign the park bylaw passed by ratepayers the previous July. Arbuthnot also demanded public consultations. In an interview with the *Free Press* on December 22, 1903, Arbuthnot asserted "I will not sign the parks bylaw until I know where the park is going to be. After selection, the parks board should give the public an opportunity of

saying whether they approve of the site or not…The selection of the park is a matter on which the public are keenly interested." If his term expired without his signature, the bylaw would die. Without re-submission to ratepayers the following year, the project to establish a suburban park would be abandoned.

On December 28, 1903, the Parks Board tabled a report on the park site. It recommended the city buy Lots 12 to 15 and 18 to 24 inclusive from the Assiniboine River to a point a half-mile back containing 320 acres (129.5 hectares) from the Munroe Pure Milk Company and that the portion of Lots 16 to 17 and 18 to 19 not owned by Munroe be expropriated. Two days later, a special meeting of city council was held. Open to the public, anyone could address the aldermen on the park site. Following council approval and public assent, the mayor would sign the park bylaw. At the meeting, Nugent's Point sales representative James Scott vented his anger at the Parks Board for not selecting his site. He criticized the Munroe lands as being grub-infested swamp and during certain seasons a morass while the two enclaves between them possessed rich, deep and valuable soil which would cost "a mint of money to acquire. Setting forth loud and continuous laughter by the assembled aldermen, the council members nevertheless referred the proposed purchase back to the Parks Board." On December 31, 1903, the Public Parks Board and city council held a special meeting to discuss an amended offer from Munroe. The City secured an option with a sizeable frontage on acceptable terms.

Negotiations to purchase the south Assiniboine properties continued throughout winter and subsequent spring. In February, Sandison reported that "the suburban park question is still at a standstill and is apparently no nearer a settlement than ever." To acquire the recommended properties comprising Lots 18 to 24, Municipality of St. Charles required negotiating with five parties: Archibald Wright, Munroe Pure Milk, J. Chiswell, P. Smith and John Smith. According to Sandison "the first three were very reasonable and

the propositions submitted by them very fair indeed. The other two were the very opposite and I think the only course for the board to take is to make them an offer for the land." The two Smiths asked for $400 to $500 per acre for their land [Lots 18 & 19] "when we can buy land on either side of them for $100 per acre." Sandison believed that the Smiths' asking price constituted a stalling tactic. The Parks Board had proposed expropriation, but city council possessed no inclination to utilize the process. The Smiths capitalized on city council's reluctance to deploy forceful measures.

On May 5, 1904, after months of negotiations, a deal for the acquisition of the Munroe Pure Milk Company properties and the other lands was struck "without recourse to expropriation." The *Free Press* noted Chairman Sandison "had a satisfied smile" as he explained the advantages

From the outset, Mayor John Arbuthnot viewed favourably the possibility of acquiring the Munroe lands.

of purchasing the Munroe property to the assembled Parks Board. His views were shared by the members and after a short discussion they unanimously recommended to city council the purchase of the lands for a total of $37,000. Eleven days later, city council unanimously adopted the Parks Board resolution. The Parks Board was authorized to complete the transaction. The suburban park would become a reality.

The press enthusiastically welcomed the decision. On May 18, 1904, the *Free Press* penned the following editorial:

> The final purchase of the suburban park will be hailed with satisfaction by the citizens generally. After the exercise of a good deal of patience the chairman of the parks board, Mr. H. Sandison was able to secure the selected land without recourse to harsh measures. Naturally the owners who had resided on the land for quite a number of years and had come to regard it as their permanent home, were reluctant to see it pass out of their hands. The public are thoroughly in sympathy with such a sentiment and for this reason will be glad to learn their land has been secured by the tactful negotiations of the parks board committee and not by expropriation measures.

The *Telegram* would not be outdone in its support. In an editorial on the same day, it praised Sandison and his colleagues for the work accomplished and city council for approving the Parks Board recommendation. It celebrated the site as being centrally located "with a mile of waterfront and a sunny and picturesque stretch of the Assiniboine affording many delightful vistas." The site, it continued, possessed "a varied and undulating landscape much of it already a natural park." The support of Winnipeg's daily newspapers boded well for the park's development.

The Public Parks Board moved quickly to finalize the land transactions. On June 1, 1904, the board examined the revised park plan and forwarded it to the city solicitor for review and completion of the land deals. Five days later, the Parks Board authorized the issuance of cheques. The *Free Press* noted the breakdown: John Smith, 42.72 acres (17.3 hectares) at $250 each; Patrick Smith, one acre (1.4 hectares) at $300; Grace Smith, 22.68 acres (9.2 hectares) at $300 each; R.W.J. Chiswell, 12.63 acres (5 hectares) at $125 each; and the Munroe Pure Milk Company, 203.27 acres (82.31 hectares) at $100 each. With interest the cheques totalled $39,903.

A review of the payments yielded several interesting conclusions. Although listed as a vendor, Archibald Wright received nothing. The sums disbursed to the Munroe Pure Milk Company and R.W.J. Chiswell appear paltry given the location of their lands. John Smith, Patrick Smith and Grace Smith received three times the value of the Munroe and Chiswell properties. However, dwellings and outbuildings on these lands may have affected prices. The Smiths had won by holding out for more cash. However, the city had assembled the land parcels required for a picturesque suburban playground. There were no losers.

Naming the Park

The deal was done, but the park needed a name. Public Parks Board members, city councillors, the press and the public proposed their favourite names. Until the end of 1904, the issue would remain unresolved.

The entertainment weekly *Town Topics* first addressed the matter. On September 3, 1904, it commented on Parks Board member Charles Napier Bell's suggestion that La Verendrye should be the name. It wrote:

Should not the memory of the fathers of the West be perpetuated in our western place names? La Verendrye was the father of them al [sic]. He was the first white man to come west of Lake Superior. Long before the first representative of the Hudson's Bay Company came down from York Factory to the Red River country, La Verendrye established at the junction of the Red and Assiniboine in 1731, a little stockaded trading post which he named Fort Rouge, then he went on to ascend the Assiniboine and was the first white man to cross the continent to the Rockies.

He was the first white man to discern the advantages as a centre of trade possessed by the site upon which Winnipeg has grown to be the commercial metropolis of Western Canada and yet there is

Charles Napier Bell, Public Parks Board Member, 1903
REPRESENTATIVE MEN OF MANITOBA – HISTORY IN PORTRAITURE, THE TRIBUNE PUBLISHING COMPANY, WINNIPEG, 1902

CHAS. N. BELL, F.R.G.S., Secretary Grain a Secretary Board of Trade ; Secretary Grain a Produce Exchange, Winnipeg.

Almost three months elapsed until the Parks Board met on December 29, 1904 to select a park name. A count was taken and "Assiniboine" garnered three votes. Norquay, St. Charles, King Edward, Alexandra and La Verendrye received only one vote apiece.

nothing in Winnipeg to commemorate his name.

What could be more fitting than that it should be commemorated in the title of the park on the Assiniboine and that at some time in the future his statue should stand in that park looking upon the river which his name deserves to be for all time associated.

Town Topics clearly endorsed Bell's recommendation.

At its meeting on September 7, 1904, the Public Parks Board debated the issue of the park's name. Board member Bell reiterated his argument for the name La Verendrye. One alderman suggested Assiniboine. Mayor Thomas Sharpe and board member Stewart Mulvey agreed. Other names suggested included King Edward, Alexandra and Norquay. The Parks Board deferred its decision to a later date.

On September 10, 1904, *Town Topics* approached the park name issue again. In response to its conclusion that no "musical" Indigenous names existed, letter-to-the-editor writer "W.A." disagreed. He suggested three possibilities. Aywaypewin (rest) and Nepowin (sleep), he wrote "are the most musical." Muskootay (prairie) "is not so bad, only there might be more truth than poetry in the suggestiveness of mosquito." Suffice to say, no members of the Parks Board or daily press followed up on W.A.'s suggestions.

Almost three months elapsed until the Parks Board met on December 29, 1904 to select a park name. A count was taken and "Assiniboine" garnered three votes. Norquay, St. Charles, King Edward, Alexandra and La Verendrye received only one vote apiece. On a second vote, Parks Board members acclaimed the park "Assiniboine." (They re-named the existing small riverfront Assiniboine Park as Fort Rouge.) So it came to pass that Assiniboine became the official name of the new suburban park. However, throughout its history many people continued to call it by its unofficial name – City Park.

As the year 1904 drew to a close, Winnipeg Public Parks Board members could feel justifiably proud of their achievement in establishing a large suburban park. But their work was only beginning. New challenges would arise in developing Assiniboine Park with the limited funds at their disposal without starving the other parks within Winnipeg's system of cash.

Chapter Three:
The Formative Years, 1904–1913

In spring 1904, Winnipeg had laid the foundation for a new suburban park. The city owned the land – two hundred and eighty acres (over one hundred and thirteen hectares), featuring a one-mile (more than one and a half kilometres) run of prime Assiniboine River frontage. On April 28, 1904, the *Winnipeg Telegram* described the property as having "one of the most picturesque stretches of the Assiniboine. The banks of the stream at this place run down to the water in gravel beaches or almost to the water in turf and slopes. The soil is excellent and well drained. Good drinking water is abundant and there are many fine trees."

People on Assiniboine Park River Trails, ca. 1910–1913 MANITOBA ARCHIVES PHOTO

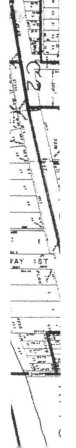

In a follow up editorial of May 18, 1904, the *Telegram* praised the park as having "rich, well drained soil and undulating landscape, much of it already a natural park." Various species of trees ascended skyward from the riverine forest floor. The editorial praised the unusual landform in the centre of the park – a natural depression that extended for more than 600 yards (549 metres) and could be used to form a "beautiful lagoon."

Despite the ample praise, the park space was far from pristine. It had been farmed for a generation and had been cultivated with pasture and crops. Houses and outbuildings stood on the former Munroe Pure Milk Company and John Smith properties. How would the lands be transformed into a suburban park attractive to Winnipeggers?

Securing the Park Boundaries

The first order of business was to secure the park's boundaries. The process entailed adding the lands to the city, closing the existing east-west highway and re-routing it to the south. In the course of these steps, the Parks Board came into conflict with the Municipality of Assiniboia. The municipality lay immediately to the west of the city boundaries. Indeed, much of the land lay with the RM's jurisdiction. Anticipating a significant loss to its tax base, Assiniboia deployed all means at its disposal to delay the opening of Assiniboine Park.

The Public Parks Board and City of Winnipeg had acted unilaterally in acquiring Assiniboine Park. No consultation with the Municipality of Assiniboia took place. And there was no offer of compensation for lost property tax revenue. But Assiniboia needed the funds. Since its creation in 1880, parts of the RM had grown from a rural municipality to a virtual residential suburb of Winnipeg. To service an infrastructure of roads west of today's Polo Park, substantial capital infusions were required.

An amendment to the province's City of Winnipeg Charter assented to on January 31, 1905 deleted lands from the Municipality of Assiniboia comprising Assiniboine Park and added them to Winnipeg. Assiniboia retained the road bisecting the park. Ownership of that road would be the municipality's trump card in stalling Assiniboine Park's completion.

At first, the Municipality of Assiniboia attempted to tax the new suburban park. In early 1905, it issued a Notice of Assessment to the City of Winnipeg for the park lots. The city contested the tax notice. In a letter, city clerk C.J. Brown reminded his Assiniboia counterpart that Assiniboine Park had officially became part of Winnipeg by the amendment to the city charter.

To justify its position, Assiniboia secured a legal opinion. Its solicitor wrote that "the Municipal Boundaries Act has not been amended in any way affecting the Municipality of Assiniboia and [its lands] … The land is therefore liable for taxation." However. the city argued that Assiniboia's solicitor had misinterpreted the Municipal Boundaries Act. That Act only defined outer boundaries of municipalities – not enclaves like the one that made up Assiniboine Park. It was not amended in 1905 because Assiniboia's outer boundaries had not changed. Only a small enclave had been withdrawn.

On June 10, 1905, Winnipeg's appeal against the assessment was heard. The city succeeded in its appeal. Henceforth, Assiniboia could only make its displeasure known by stalling the park's development through other avenues.

At the October 15, 1904 Assiniboia Council meeting, a delegation from Winnipeg proposed closing the east-west road that ran through the park. In replacement, a new thorough-fare south of the new recreational grounds would be constructed at the city's cost.

Assiniboia deferred the matter until November, so it had time to interview property owners affected by the proposed changes. By February 1905, no progress had been made. The *Tribune* reported that the road closure issue required discussions by repre-sentatives of the city and Assiniboia. Another three months elapsed as

Despite the ample praise, the park space was far from pristine. It had been farmed for a generation and had been cultivated with pasture and crops.

Parks Board Chairman T.W. Taylor, Aldermen Latimer and Henry Fry, City Engineer H.N. Ruttan and D.D. England waited for Assiniboia Council. To break the impasse, the city reiterated its willingness to pay for the road diversion. But Assiniboia council remained intransigent. It requested that the offer be submit-ted in writing with plans attached. On June 1, 1905, Assiniboia council only hesitatingly and conditionally authorized the preparation of a bylaw setting terms for its consent. It said that at a future date the reeve would approve the terms of the road closure.

Frustration set in amongst Public Parks Board members and Winnipeg aldermen. Would Assiniboia ever agree to the road closure and re-routing? According to the *Telegram* of June 19, 1905, some Winnipeg aldermen were saying that if the road could not be closed, the city should sell Assiniboine Park and purchase land elsewhere.

Despite growing misgivings, the city continued negotiating. On July 5, 1905, Alderman Henry Sandison, City Solicitor Isaac Campbell and Chief Gardener England met with Assiniboia Council regarding the road closure. Assiniboia's solicitors prepared a draft bylaw closing the east-west road through the park and a portion of McCreary (now Shaftesbury) Road between Lots 17 and 18 and opening a new road in substitution. The bylaw contained a surprise – extending and maintaining the existing ferry road to form a connection with the new highway (now Corydon Avenue). On September 22, 1905, the *Telegram* reported that "the road difficulty is

now practically settled." As time would tell, it was mistaken.

Construction commenced in earnest in 1906. In July, Parks Board Secretary James H. Blackwood urged his Winnipeg Board of Works counterpart to "open and grade the new road running along the south boundary of Assiniboine Park at your earliest convenience. Until this work is done, it is impossible to make progress in carrying out the proposed improvements."

One year later, the road work was finally complete. The old road would be closed, and Blackwood notified the Municipality of Assiniboia accordingly. But Assiniboia resumed its stalling tactics. On July 30, 1907, its council passed a motion prohibiting the road closure until a committee of council was "satisfied that the new road is in sufficient good repair to allow the public to make use of same for general traffic." Three months later, Assiniboia approved another motion "that the Council cannot agree to the closing of the road through the park until Councillors Bourke and Hall report that all matters in connection with the closing of said roads have been satisfactorily performed by the City."

Fall gave way to winter and winter to spring. The Council of Assiniboia finally relented. Almost four years had elapsed between the start of negotiations to close the park highway and the opening of Corydon Avenue. The municipality had deployed the road closure issue as a means of expressing its displeasure over the loss of taxation revenue on lands comprising Assiniboine Park. In November 1908, the Public Parks Board finally authorized its chairman to complete road closure arrangements.

Planning the Park

Upon acquiring the lands for the suburban park, the Parks Board immediately set out to transform the woods and cow pastures into a pleasure playground. On May 25, 1904, Parks Board Secretary Henry B. Thompson wrote to Theodore Wirth, the parks superintendent in Hartford, Connecticut. In glowing terms, he described the lands purchased for the future Assiniboine Park. He asked if Wirth would undertake the task of planning the new park.

Thompson sent identical letters to landscape architects Frank H. Nutter, A.W. Hobert, Price & Snyder and William M. Berry of Minneapolis. Further afield, O.C. Simonds of Chicago, John C. Olmsted of Brookline, Massachusetts, and R. Denison of Ludlow Mills, Massachusetts received identical letters. The individuals contacted represented the elite of America's park and cemetery planners. Among the group, Wirth, a leading park administrator and planner, would soon relocate to Minneapolis and over a lengthy career design that city's park and driveway system. John C. Olmsted, nephew of Frederick Law Olmsted, succeeded his illustrious uncle in his successful practice. O.C. Simonds, a founding member of the American Society of Landscape Architects, had garnered recognition as one of America's leading cemetery planners.

The Parks Board did not approach young and unknown Montreal landscape architect Frederick W. Todd. He received no invitation. However, an unsolicited approach from Todd led to a

FREDERICK G. TODD, F.A

Frederick G. Todd, Landscape Architect in Mid-Career
DR. C.W. PARKER ED., *WHO'S WHO AND WHY: A BIOGRAPHICAL DICTIONARY OF MEN AND WOMEN OF CANADA AND NEWFOUNDLAND,* VOLUME 5, INTERNATIONAL PRESS, VANCOUVER, 1914

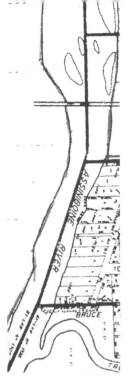

discussion on his possible role in the suburban park design. In a letter dated June 16, 1904 Todd informed the Parks Board of a planned trip to Winnipeg on private business. While in the city, he would welcome a meeting with Parks Board members. Secretary Thompson agreed that once Todd arrived, a meeting would be arranged. The meeting took place on June 24, 1904. Several Parks Board members drove Todd to the suburban park property "and together they went over the whole ground." On returning to the city, they discussed plans for the park's development.

Despite his limited park design experience, young Todd impressed the Parks Board members, who viewed his credentials as "the very best." Most importantly, "his terms they considered the most suitable and his chancing to be in the city at the time on other business seemed a fortunate coincidence." On June 30, 1904, the Parks Board selected Todd to plan the suburban park. Todd would be compensated $1,285 for his efforts. Struggling to keep pace with rapid expansion, Winnipeg had economized on its selection of a landscape architect. Best of all, Todd paid his own travel expenses from Montreal.

On June 30, 1904, the *Winnipeg Tribune* interviewed Todd prior to his return to Montreal. Enthusiastic with his first major park commission, he promised that "a most charming recreation ground…can be made out of the city's new suburban park owing to the natural beauties of the ground in the shape of trees and so forth. I will make as much as I possibly can out of natural advantages." But Todd faced a challenge. In his four years of independent landscape design practice in Montreal after apprenticing with Frederick Law Olmsted, the New Hampshire native had undertaken only a few small commissions: Trinity College grounds in Toronto; railway magnate William Mackenzie's spacious personal home yard; the Canadian Pacific Railway's station grounds in St. Andrew's, New Brunswick; several small parks in Sherbrooke, Quebec; as well as an unexecuted design for the Ottawa parks system. Todd's relationship with Winnipeg's parsimonious and cash-deficient Public Parks Board and city council would reveal a clash of two distinct park design philosophies.

In the confines of his Montreal office, Todd set to work penning plans for Winnipeg's new park. The Public Parks Board terms of reference were vague: "to make the new suburban park on the Assiniboine River effective as a broad landscape" without the use of flowers or plants. By September 30, 1904, rough sketches had arrived in Winnipeg. Todd proposed a main driveway thirty feet wide circling the park's perimeters, with the north section straddling the Assiniboine River. At the mid-point on the north side, public baths for adults and children would be located. Todd reserved the southeast corner for athletic grounds. In the northwest the park retained its natural features bisected by footpaths through the forest. By early December, Todd had transformed his sketches into preliminary plans (which have been lost). On December 7, 1904, the Parks Board discussed these first drawings. Some members expressed concerns. According to the *Telegram*, "some of the members seem of the opinion that the grounds were not laid out as well as they might have been in the selecting of certain portions for bathing places, etc." Todd requested and received an extension to revise his plan.

The revised plan of April 1905 revealed a contrast of philosophies between Frederick Todd and the Public Parks Board. Todd called for a complete rearrangement of the existing landscape and the removal of vast numbers of trees and shrubs. In the denuded 280-acre (113.3 hectares) spread, an Arcadian park of the imagination would rise. Todd's vision reflected the ideas of his mentor, Olmsted, and his design of New York's Central Park. But Todd did not consider the Winnipeg Parks Board budget, nor the time it would take to develop his ideas.

The Parks Board offered a more practical vision: enhance the natural environment with plantings and landscaping, but retain open areas, trees and shrubs. At modest cost, the park would open to the public in a year or two.

Todd's proposal earned not just the scathing criticism of the board, but also of the press. The *Free Press* commented that his plans "would be extremely expensive if adopted" and take too long to implement. The plan "does not accord with the general desire to produce a park effect as soon as possible. Some of the members of the board want to see the park in a developed condition before their grey hair is entirely white." Both the *Free Press* and Parks Board believed that Todd had ignored the site's natural advantages. The existing variety of trees and vegetation encouraged Parks Board members to "feel that a very beautiful place can be made which would be presentable to the citizens in the course of a year or so."

The Parks Board took immediate ameliorative measures. On April 20, 1905, they held an outdoor meeting at Assiniboine Park. Attendees consisted of Parks Board Chairman T.W. Taylor, and members F.W. Drewry, H.C. Stovel, R.D. Waugh, D.A. Ross, C.W. Sharpe and Chief Gardener D.D. England. They ordered an outline proposal to be

The revised plan of April 1905 revealed a contrast of philosophies between Frederick Todd and the Public Parks Board.

prepared showing the main features of Todd's plan and "the location of bluffs and low places that would readily lend themselves to the making of waterways, swimming ponds and canals." A local public land surveyor named H. (name unknown) Patterson was hired to prepare the sketch.

And it was back to the drawing board for Frederick Todd.

In late October 1905, Todd travelled to Winnipeg and presented his second revised plan. Again, it failed to retain many existing park features. At its October 30 meeting, the Parks Board instructed "Mr. England [to] confer with Mr. Todd and report to the Board with a view to having his plan modified so that as many of the trees and open spaces now in the park can be utilized as far as possible." Two days later, the chief gardener and Todd visited the park and reviewed the plans. Todd agreed to the changes and the relocation of the main entrance to the park's southeast corner. On November 3, 1905, the Parks Board considered and approved the changes. The *Free Press* noted

that the amended drawings embodied the recommendations of D.D. England and would "preserve as far as possible the natural advantages of the property and promise a fine recreational ground for the citizens."

Back in Montreal, Todd added the finishing touches to his plans. By December 23, 1905, the final drawings arrived in Winnipeg. On January 3, 1906, the Public Parks Board adopted the plans. The package contained several immense blueprints, a bird's eye park sketch, and a detailed explanatory letter. According to the *Telegram* the plans showed "a profusion of groves or bluffs punctuated or skirted by two or three drives and many smaller drives." The main entrance at the southeast corner featured an oval comprising seven and a half acres (three hectares) and concentric aisles of trees. A drive skirted the Assiniboine River and highlighted an island at the park's centre. Several ranges of trees bordered east, west and south boundaries.

Todd allocated the northwest section of the park to zoo purposes. Here the buffalo, moose, elk and deer

would be kept in an area of eleven and a half acres (under five hectares). Within park boundaries, visitors would enjoy four and a half miles (seven and a third kilometres) of drives, over four miles (six and a half kilometres) of equestrian paths and more than six miles (ten and a third kilometres) of walking paths. While Frederick Todd's plans have been lost to posterity, the general park layout and features remain partially visible today.

The uneasy relationship between the Public Parks Board and Todd affected both parties. In a second but lesser park project, Kildonan, the city prepared its plans in-house. George Champion, who succeeded D.D. England as chief gardener (later known as the parks superintendent) designed Winnipeg's North End playground.

Frederick Todd benefitted from his Assiniboine Park learning experience. In a career spanning half a century, he penned plans for Wascana Park in Regina, the Alberta Legislative Building grounds in Edmonton, the Plains of Abraham restoration in Quebec City and a multitude of parks for Canada's municipalities and land developers. Assiniboine Park had launched his career.

The D.D. England Controversy

In 1905, the Public Parks Board possessed a simple organizational structure. At the top stood Parks Board members and their chairman. Reporting to the board was its secretary. Following Parks Board decisions, the secretary issued instructions to the chief gardener. Individual caretakers supervised the works in each park.

Until mid-1905, Henry C. Thompson served as Parks Board secretary. In early August of that year, he was promoted to the position of city treasurer. James H. Blackwood replaced Thompson as Parks Board secretary until his career ended in 1929. D.D. England occupied the position of chief gardener from 1894 until late 1906. His subordinate, Thomas Denton, served as park caretaker until 1906. Neither England nor Denton would oversee the development of Assiniboine Park in its formative years.

In 1905, irregularities surfaced on England's practices. At the Parks Board meeting of July 5, member R.D. Waugh asked if the chief gardener was permitted to accept contracts in competition with other landscapers and if he possessed authority to order supplies under the Parks Board's accounts for this purpose. The board struck a subcommittee consisting of Chairman C.W. Sharpe and Waugh to report on the matter. On August 1, the subcommittee presented its findings. Its report confirmed the allegations and was adopted unanimously. However, England continued to serve as chief gardener.

In November, there were more accusations. The charges included

George Champion, Park Superintendent upon his Retirement, 1935 "GEORGE CHAMPION WHO MADE THIS A TREE AND PARK CITY, RETIRES AFTER LONG SERVICE," *WINNIPEG TRIBUNE*, OCTOBER 1, 1935, P. 3

deploying employees for private work on Parks Board time and expense. Periodically, employees cut wood for England, cleaned his horse, picked and bagged potatoes and plowed, harrowed and manured his garden. A second charge accused England of using Parks Board paid feed for his horse while receiving a $30 per month stipend for this purpose. A third charge against England and his Assiniboine Park caretaker Denton entailed poor staff supervision. Both knew that their employees consumed intoxicating liquor while working. However, they took no measures to curtail the practice.

A second Parks Board committee to investigate the charges against England held hearings on November 16, 1906. Witnesses testified under oath. In his defence, England refused to swear to his evidence. The committee prepared a report on the matter. It was adopted on December 4, 1906. The report validated the accusations.

England refused to acknowledge the charges against him. In his first letter of resignation, he wrote that

"I understand that it is the desire of the board to effect a re-organization for the purpose of enabling a more efficient central control than has heretofore appertained." He admitted that he may "have erred in the matter of giving private assistance to public spirited citizens" – a reference to his private landscaping work. The Parks Board rejected England's letter. It ordered him to sign a simple letter of resignation or be dismissed. He accepted.

England was purged from Winnipeg's civil service, but he eventually secured re-employment in his profession. In 1908, he was appointed superintendent of parks in Victoria, BC. In March 1909, *Park and Cemetery* magazine reported that England had presented his first annual report in his new position. "Mr. England is preparing a plan for a continuous boulevard system to connect the different parks." He also took charge of the rehabilitation of Victoria's Beacon Hill Park. England had thrived.

However, England's underling Thomas Denton was not as fortunate. Like England, the Assiniboine

Park caretaker ordered Parks Board employees to work at his city-supplied residence in the park at Parks Board expense and on Parks Board time. As in England's case, staff cut wood, picked and bagged potatoes and plowed, harrowed and manured his garden. Denton was censured for his "loose and careless" job performance and "hiding irregularities and misconduct on the part of other employees" instead of reporting them to the Parks Board. Unlike England, Denton escaped dismissal. The Parks Board demoted him to caretaker for the smaller neighbourhood Fort Rouge Park. It was definitely a step down, but still a job.

The Parks Board needed a new parks superintendent and a caretaker for Assiniboine Park. On December 12, 1906, it placed advertisements in the *Montreal Gazette*, *Toronto Globe*, *Toronto Mail & Empire*, *St. Paul Pioneer Press* and *Minneapolis Tribune*. An advertisement also appeared in the Chicago-based trade journal, *Park and Cemetery*. Applicants were requested to list their experience, salary expectations and references. On March 23, 1907, George Champion, an employee of the Toronto Parks Commission was appointed parks superintendent at a salary not exceeding $1,500 per year. Champion would faithfully perform his duties until his retirement almost three decades later.

On April 19, 1907, Henry Ditchfield was appointed caretaker of Assiniboine Park at a salary of $75 per month and also given a free house. Both Champion and Ditchfield would oversee the development of Assiniboine Park in its formative years.

Access to the Park

In late 1905, plans for Assiniboine Park had been finalized by F.W. Todd with much input from the Parks Board and its chief gardener. Only one major issue remained unresolved: access to the park by public transit for the multitude of anticipated visitors. Almost everyone relied on the Winnipeg Electric Railway Company for public transportation. Only merchants and wealthy individuals possessed their own horse-and-buggies or automobiles. A means to transport thousands of people quickly to the park was needed.

At first a joint railway/traffic bridge over the Assiniboine River was constructed at St. James. Its single track proved incapable of handling the large volume of passengers reaching the park by streetcar. In 1911, a seasonal pontoon bridge at the site of today's footbridge was erected. It provided a temporary solution for two decades. A permanent highway bridge near Assiniboine Park was discussed; as a result of funding issues, it never came to be. Easy year-round access to the park would remain unresolved until the onset of the Great Depression.

The first bridge over the Assiniboine River was a combined steam train, street railway and traffic bridge. Politicians and Parks Board officials considered a multi-use structure the least expensive option to provide access to the new Agricultural College (now the Asper Jewish Community Campus just east of the park), Assiniboine Park, and to enable Assiniboia residents living on the south side of the river to reach Portage Avenue.

Abandoned Steam Train / Passenger / Street Railway Bridge, 2017 PHOTO BY AUTHOR

In February 1905, representatives of the Canadian Northern Railway, Municipality of Assiniboia and the City of Winnipeg began to discuss erecting such a structure. There were the inevitable differences in

The *Free Press* demanded that city council "place the Park at the disposal of all the citizens by making it more accessible and to do so immediately."

objectives. Assiniboia preferred a bridge in St. James near today's Polo Park. The Public Parks Board objected to that site, arguing that it would serve the new Agricultural College well, but not Assiniboine Park. The *Free Press* commented that the Parks Board members were "anxious that the bridge shall be opposite either the east or west entrance to the park so that a loop line may be run out by Portage Avenue and back by River Avenue passing the park gates."

By fall 1906, a compromise had been reached, and a new multi-use bridge was built near Polo Park. On October 31, 1906, streetcars began running from St. James over the bridge to the Agricultural College. According to the *Free Press* the streetcar line "has been completed to the suburban park but will not be run until the Parks Board has the park ready for the use of the public." The streetcar line reached the park at its southeast entrance. There, a hundred-foot long (more than thirty metre) shelter was constructed in 1910.

Within a few years of its completion, the bridge and streetcar line

proved inadequate. In September 1908, Assiniboia Council passed a motion denying the Canadian Northern Railway its full subsidy for the bridge. The driveway on the bridge, Assiniboia Council concluded, measured only nine feet, or two metres, wide – too narrow to meet traffic requirements. Upon the official opening of Assiniboine Park in 1909, the newspapers expressed similar concerns. On April 20 of that year, the *Free Press* commented that only a single track extended from Portage Avenue to the Agricultural College, then west to the park. The service was too slow for extensive park patronage. Moreover, streetcars and trains shared the same tracks over the bridge – a recipe for disaster.

A month later, the *Free Press* dwelled further upon the park's inaccessibility. The streetcar line, it noted, unloaded passengers half-a-mile from the pavilion and the riverbank. "Under such circumstances it is only those citizens of leisure and means that can enjoy the use of the addition to the city's advantages." The *Free Press* demanded that city council "place the Park at the disposal of all the citizens by making it more accessible and to do so immediately."

As a temporary fix, it suggested laying a pontoon bridge over the Assiniboine River until a permanent structure was completed. *Town Topics* echoed similar views. In February, 1910, it recommended that "right now Council should take action with a view to secure the streetcar facilities requisite to make Assiniboine Park easily accessible by the citizens. What is the use of having Assiniboine Park if the people of Winnipeg cannot get to it easily?"

Clearly, visitors deserved better access to the park.

As an alternative to the inadequate railway/traffic bridge, the Public Parks Board followed through on the idea of a pontoon bridge. On April 8, 1909, the Board appointed a special committee to study the issue

Park Visitors crossing the Seasonal Foot Bridge, c. 1911–1914 CITY OF WINNIPEG OF ARCHIVES PHOTO

and submit a cost estimate. Six days later, Assiniboia's reeve appeared before the Parks Board in reference to the proposed bridge. He stated "that he was not prepared to say whether the (Assiniboia) Council would be willing to bear any portion of the expense or not and that he was sure the Council would raise no

objection to the Board building the bridge." Winnipeg's bridge committee recommended that a plan for a small footbridge be procured. If Assiniboia shared the expense, construction would proceed. The Parks Board approved the motion and the Municipality of Assiniboia offered no financial contribution. The pontoon bridge was not built.

In March 1911, the Assiniboia-based St. James Improvement Association stepped into the breach and offered to construct the pontoon bridge. On March 29, 1911, the Parks Board referred the organization's proposal to the city solicitor with instructions to prepare an agreement between the two parties. Parks Board Minutes indicated that the terms "will give the citizens of Winnipeg equal rights with residents of the Municipality and will protect the City of Winnipeg from damages from all manner of accidents, the bridge to be free to the public." Bridge plans were prepared by the association, submitted to the Parks Board, and forwarded to the city engineer for approval. He did so with minor alterations.

On June 22, 1911, the privately-funded seasonal pontoon bridge opposite Deer Lodge opened to the public. The *Free Press* proclaimed that "visitors going to Assiniboine Park will not have to change cars as all of them will pass right by [Assiniboine Park] including the Headingley, Kirkfield, Deer Lodge and Country Club cars. This will be of great convenience to the public, as by the old route it was necessary to change streetcars at St. James and sometimes change again at the Agricultural College" (to complete the journey along Corydon Avenue to the park).

The St. James Improvement Association funded the installation and operation of the bridge for only one season. In May 1912, it offered the bridge to the Parks Board free of charge. The Parks Board accepted the offer.

Year after year, the Parks Board erected the pontoon bridge crossing the Assiniboine River from Deer Lodge at an annual cost of $2,000 to $2,800. During seasons with normal water levels, the bridge provided adequate visitor access to the park.

Rustic Bridge, c. 1915
MANITOBA ARCHIVES PHOTO

In 1912, the *Free Press* noted that the Tuxedo Park streetcar line had almost been abandoned as a result of direct park access from the pontoon bridge.

However, the pontoon bridge presented only a stop-gap solution to Assiniboine Park's problem. On the Victoria Day weekend of 1913, the bridge could not be swung into place as a result of high-water levels. Only a limited number of passengers could be transported by streetcar across the railway/traffic bridge. According to the *Free Press* "thousands had to walk to the park from the [south side] of the St. James Bridge."

The Parks Board aimed to permanently resolve the access issue to Assiniboine Park. Year after year, while workers moved the pontoon bridge into place in the spring and removed it in autumn, the Board formulated plans to erect a permanent bridge in the park's vicinity. The first attempt in 1910 entailed re-erecting the old Louise Bridge at a point immediately west of park boundaries. In 1913, the Board abandoned its lofty goal. It modestly proposed to replace the seasonal pontoon bridge with the old Osborne Street bridge superstructure. Neither plan met with success.

The offer of the old Louise Bridge to the Municipality of Assiniboia became public knowledge in 1911. A letter from the Parks Board to Assiniboia dated February 17, 1911 reveals that the Parks Board would convey the superstructure "if they will assume the responsibility for erecting the bridge in accordance with plans and specifications prepared by the City Engineer and arrange with the Provincial Government and the Winnipeg Electric Railway Company for such assistance as they are willing to contribute towards the erection of same."

On March 1, 1911, Assiniboia council considered the offer. It was read, filed and promptly forgotten. Unable to finance its share of construction costs, on April 1, 1912, Assiniboia council finally declined the offer of the old Louise Bridge.

The matter refused to die. In November 1912, Assiniboia council proposed the construction of an entirely new bridge west of Assiniboine Park. At a special meeting held on November 21, Assiniboia council carried a motion to prepare a bylaw raising debentures for the project. In 1913, a severe recession hit Canada and Winnipeg. Municipalities operated with reduced revenues and the bridge remained unbuilt.

In spring 1913, the Public Parks Board made yet another attempt to erect a permanent bridge over the Assiniboine River. This time it scaled back its expectations. Proposed was a permanent bridge at the site of the pontoon structure. Parks Board Chairman Thomas Wilson asked the city's Board of Control to exchange the old Louise Bridge (1880) for the more modest former and newer Osborne Street (1894) structure. Wilson also sought the participation of Assiniboia's Council in the project. They expressed no interest in a bridge beneficial primarily to Assiniboine Park. The Parks Board made no immediate decision. The pontoon bridge remained in service in 1913.

In autumn 1913, the Parks Board decided to erect the old Osborne Bridge at its own expense. On September 27, 1913, Secretary J.H. Blackwood instructed the city engineer to prepare an estimate for placing it on pile piers at the seasonal footbridge site. Quietly, the Parks Board purchased a right-of-way from the north side of the proposed bridge to Portage Avenue. In a letter to newly-elected mayor F.W. Heubach of the Town of Tuxedo (which had been excised from Assiniboia), Parks Board Secretary Blackwood wrote that "as soon as satisfactory arrangements are made an effort will be made to have the bridge erected this winter and opened for traffic in the spring of 1914." However, the bridge remained a distant vision. The recession had also reduced City of Winnipeg revenues and the Parks Board's budget. The pontoon bridge would be erected, removed and re-erected time and again until the Great Depression.

The Parks Board had spent considerable funds, time and effort purchasing and planning Assiniboine Park. Along with most Winnipeggers, the Parks Board wished to construct a wide, scenic and grand tree-lined parkway to access the new suburban playground. The route was obvious. It would begin at the south side of the Maryland Bridge and follow the Assiniboine River to the park's eastern boundary. In 1906, work began on the scheme to lay out "a magnificent 150-foot driveway" from Academy Road towards the park. However, the Agricultural College presented an obstacle. On July 8, 1906, the *Free Press* commented that "so far the provincial government has refused to give a right-of-way through the north side of the Agricultural College grounds for the driveway, but it is expected in the near future." But the *Free Press* was too optimistic.

Two years passed, and the Parks Board struck a committee to wait upon the advisory board of the Agricultural College "to impress upon the Advisory Board the necessity for having the road opened through the College Property." The Parks Board approach fell upon deaf ears. Almost five years elapsed. In May 1913, the Parks Board convened a special committee composed of its chairman and members Wilson and Drewry to wait upon Premier Rodmond Roblin and request that a roadway be opened along the Assiniboine River through the Agricultural College grounds. Until the province abandoned the Agricultural College for a Fort Garry property and until the Town of Tuxedo to the west transferred its road and adjoining riverfront to the city, the parkway, like a permanent bridge over the Assiniboine River, remained a dream.

Developing the Park's Infrastructure

From 1905 to 1913, the Public Parks Board developed the infrastructure of Assiniboine Park pursuant to the plans prepared by Frederick G. Todd. As work began in 1905, the Public Parks Board published a brochure entitled "Summer Outings Round Winnipeg." The brochure predicted that Assiniboine Park

> will be a great attraction to the residents as it is large enough to supply the desires of all. A large section will be set aside for athletic purposes, while a buffalo paddock and deer run will provide accommodation for the City herd of buffalo

and deer. A zoo will be another attraction which will not only amuse but educate the children. Lily ponds and a small lake for bathing are among the improvements. Beautiful drives, cycle paths, music pavilion, etc will also be provided.

By 1914, it came to pass that all these ideas, except the bathing beach, bore fruition. A centrepiece pavilion and conservatory anchored the park's attractions.

Laying Out Assiniboine Park, 1907 CITY OF WINNIPEG ARCHIVES, PUBLIC PARKS BOARD ANNUAL REPORT, 1907

The Public Parks Board set to work in a methodical fashion. Before his ignominious departure, Chief Gardener D.D. England expressed in rather convoluted language his philosophy for the park's development. In his 1904 parks report, England remarked that

it must be remembered that the success of our parks has been largely in the system of improving them which we employ, the object being to give the public the use of them or at least part of them as soon as possible in other words to put down as much grass and drives as quickly as may be then as the public have the enjoyment of what is done, the more laborious and slower work can be proceeded with.

The first steps, he wrote, entailed fencing the park and providing for a water system "as it is obviously useless to spend money on trees, shrubs, grass and flowers until we are prepared to protect them from drought." Despite his departure at the end of 1906, the Parks Board and its new superintendent George Champion scrupulously followed England's plan.

In 1905 to 1906, the Parks Board fenced the perimeter of Assiniboine Park. On April 1, 1905, the *Free Press*

published a tender call for the fencing work. The tender required samples of the fence to be submitted together with full particulars of the proposal. Twelve days later, the Parks and Boulevards Committee of the Parks Board met and declared Thomas Black the successful tenderer. Petty interjurisdictional wrangling between Winnipeg and Assiniboia delayed the construction of the fence until autumn 1906. The newly completed fence surrounding Assiniboine Park would stand for a generation.

From 1906 to 1909, the Parks Board spent a significant part of its budget landscaping Assiniboine Park and laying out roads and pathways. The first step lay in clearing the bush and planting trees. In September 1906, the *Telegram* reported that for some time, fifteen men under England's supervision cleared bush and planted hundreds of elm and spruce trees. By March 1907, the *Free Press* noted that trees and shrubs had been planted along the east, west and south boundaries of the park and at various locations within it – all irrigated by a temporary waterworks system.

Pathway Through
Riparian Forest, c. 1915
MANITOBA ARCHIVES
PHOTO

At the same time, work commenced on laying a system of roads, driveways and paths within the park. On September 25, 1906, Civil Engineer C.A. Millican was contracted "to lay out and supervise the work of grading and constructing the various roads and driveways in Assiniboine Park and to submit profile plans and estimates of the cost of the work." The Millican contract did not proceed smoothly. As he was frequently intoxicated, Millican only partly fulfilled the terms of his agreement. However, he audaciously submitted an invoice for $200 which the Parks Board filed without paying. By June 1907, the work had still not been done. In October, the Parks Board finally relented and offered Millican the $200 "without prejudice" in full settlement of his account.

Under the direction of the new park superintendent, Parks Board employees completed road and pathway construction on their own.

Much of the work in the park entailed the creation of lawns, playing fields, playgrounds, picnic areas, flower gardens and the excavation of a miniature lake. Up until 1908, workers laid grass seed for lacrosse, cricket and baseball fields and created a ten-acre children's playground facing the riverfront and boasting a merry-go-round and swings. To

supply all of Winnipeg's parks, in 1908 the Parks Board laid out a plant nursery in the northwest corner where gardeners cultivated hundreds of flowering plants, trees and shrubs. North of the pavilion under construction, workers excavated a duck pond, featuring two fountains throwing jets of water forty feet into the air. Initially gravel-bottomed, a cement floor was added in 1911 at a cost of $1,850. At the southeast corner of the park, a five-acre flower garden completed the landscaped portion of the recreation grounds. Announced in

The First Pavilion
facing South CITY OF
WINNIPEG ARCHIVES
PHOTO

1908, it provided an impressive entry at the corner of Corydon Avenue and Park Boulevard and one of several access points to the park.

The Parks Board authorized the construction of water supply and electrical systems. In February 1906, the Parks Board established a committee of C.W. Sharpe and R.D. Waugh to oversee the project. The committee instructed the city engineer to prepare plans for the work. In April 1906, the committee reviewed the engineer's plan and requested that he prepare specifications for a system costing $12,000. Contractors Harpell-Stokes submitted the lowest tender to install the park's water supply system. It utilized water drawn from the Assiniboine River, piped underground to a 16,000-gallon tank concealed by the tower of the newly constructed pavilion and distributed to the duck pond and fountains and various parts of the park. Within a foot-deep trench, electrical cables transmitted power to the water pump and also supplied electricity and illumination to all parts of the park.

On Victoria Day 1909, the park was almost complete. The lawns had been laid, roadways and paths opened, the children's playground, playing fields and picnic grounds ready to welcome the public. The zoo had been operational since 1906 and the pavilion was newly operational. The Parks Board had neglected other parks to finance the new suburban playground. In the prelude to World War I, improvements would continue to be undertaken, including a greenhouse and streetcar platform in 1910, a cricket pavilion in 1911, a bandstand in 1912, the conservatory in 1913 and a new pumping plant and picnic shelter in 1914. The general public at the time would have agreed with the *Free Press* assessment that "today the park is the wonder of the casual citizen."

The First Pavilion and Conservatory

Located north of the Assiniboine River in the central part of the park, a large pavilion constituted the focal point for Winnipeg's new suburban playground. Throughout North America during the early 1900s, pavilions with restaurants and take-out counters had been constructed to fulfil visitor needs of food and shelter from inclement weather.

Como Park in St. Paul comprised a typical example. In that city, a lakeside pavilion had been erected in 1895. In 1905 a new pavilion with a bandstand extending on piers into Como Lake replaced it. Enjoying close contacts with their American counterparts, Parks Board officials likely wished to emulate the

American example. Selected from a number of designs in an architectural competition, architect J.D. Atchison's structure served park visitors from its opening in 1909 until its destruction by fire in 1929.

In January 1908, the Parks Board proceeded with the construction of the pavilion. A Report of the Special Committee on Water Supply and Plans for a Pavilion and Shelter recommended that an architectural competition be conducted and that the Parks Board offer prizes of $75, $50 and $25 for the winning design and two runners up. The plans would embody the following: the building would measure approximately eighty feet by one hundred and twenty feet (24.4 by 36.6 metres) and feature a lunch counter, catering facilities, lavatories and a sixty-foot (18.3 metre) high tower capable of supporting and enclosing a 16,500-gallon (75,010 litre) water tank. The building would rest on substantial foundations and be finished in either wood or rough cast. On February 8, 1908, the Parks Board advertised the architectural competition. The Parks Board received plans – all under pseudonyms to ensure

John Danley Atchison

Architect of the first Assiniboine Park pavilion in 1910, John Danley Atchison led a storied career in early 20th century Winnipeg. Born in Monmouth, Illinois in 1870, he apprenticed under eminent Chicago architect William Le Baron Jenney, a pioneer in the development of the steel-framed skyscraper and the Commercial style of architecture. After practising in Chicago for several years, in 1905 Atchison relocated to Winnipeg. His achievements were many. At first designing warehouses, small commercial buildings, upscale apartment blocks and residences, his competition-winning Assiniboine Park pavilion drew the attention of Winnipeg's leading businessmen to his architectural prowess.

John D. Atchison, Architect of First Pavilion
MANITOBA ARCHIVES, *LEADING FINANCIAL, BUSINESS & PROFESSIONAL MEN OF WINNIPEG,* C. 1913

Plans for Winnipeg's iconic pre- and post-World War I buildings followed, including the Union Trust at Main and Lombard, the original Great West Life Building at Rorie and Lombard, the Boyd Building at Portage and Edmonton, the Bank of Hamilton at Main and McDermot and the Manitoba School for the Deaf (now part of the Canadian Mennonite University Campus).

In 1923, Atchison relocated to the sunny climate of Los Angeles and spent the twilight of his career designing mansions for Hollywood's tycoons and leading citizens. He died in 1959 at age 89.

Pergola fronting First Pavilion,
c. 1909–1914 CITY OF WINNIPEG
ARCHIVES PHOTO

impartiality of the judge, contractor James McDiarmid. On March 26, 1908, the Parks Board notified architect J.D. Atchison that his plan had won first prize. He was paid $75 for his efforts and instructed to prepare working plans for the pavilion with an open-air picnic annex to the north connected by a pergola. The Parks Board then called tenders for construction of the edifice. The lowest bidder, Claydon Bros., was awarded the contract for $17,360. James McDiarmid had unsuccessfully tendered for the contract – an obvious conflict of interest. Construction of the open-air annex would be deferred until the main building was complete.

The pavilion received favourable press coverage from *Park and Cemetery*. According to the June 1909 issue of the journal, the completed edifice followed the building specifications to the letter. The open pavilion stood on the edge of a natural terrace overlooking a fine survey of rolling park meadows and commanding an excellent view of the meandering Assiniboine River. The main building ascended two storeys. A large refreshment counter

and lunch room occupied the main floor. On the second floor, three dining halls and service rooms surrounded by wide covered balconies "commanded fine views of the park." The interior of the building boasted a finish of plaster and British Columbia fir stained in soft shades of brown. The exterior of the building presented a rough cast stucco-like and stained pine finish. To visitors, the building stood splendid in its beauty and stature.

To the north of the pavilion, the open but screened-in picnic pavilion was erected in 1909. The Parks Board called tenders in March 1909.

Duck Pond with First Pavilion and Picnic Shelter in Background pre 1929 MANITOBA ARCHIVES PHOTO

Despite its attractive appearance, the pavilion and attached annex constituted a cheap, uninsulated and poorly-constructed firetrap.

As the lowest bidder, S.R. Ritchie was awarded the contract for $5,182. The picnic pavilion would shelter visitors from the elements during Assiniboine Park's early years.

Despite its attractive appearance, the pavilion and attached annex constituted a cheap, uninsulated and poorly-constructed firetrap. At an expenditure of under $20,000, this huge wooden structure cost only the same amount as the typical small but sturdy brick branch bank constructed throughout suburban Winnipeg during this period. Upon its completion, the pavilion soon required extensive repairs. In 1911, the pavilion received structural upgrades. The Parks Committee of the Public Parks Board recommended "action in the matter of having the balcony floors made water proof to prevent water from pouring into the building at every storm."

Fire protection caused another concern. In 1912, the Parks Board requested Superintendent Champion to provide an estimate for fire-proofing the building. In 1912, the Parks Board Catering Committee recommended kitchen improvements consisting of

prevent collapse. In 1914, the Special Committee Report on the Pavilion Annex recommended the installation of concrete footings, jacking up the roof, and enclosing the building in glass. The Parks Board approved the repairs. On the eve of World War I, the Public Parks Board's showcase pavilion appealed to visitors with its attractive design. However, it constituted a poorly-designed and shoddily-built structure in need of yearly repairs. The pavilion annex manifested the same poor standard of construction.

The concept of Winnipeg's first conservatory dates from June 1912. In the Parks Board annual report, Chairman Thomas Wilson proposed building a conservatory "where southern and tropical plants and flowers might be propagated...It would be a great source of interest to visitors and citizens alike in addition to the educative value to students of floriculture." The Parks Board interest in a conservatory may have been inspired by the opening of the new conservatory in Garfield Park in Chicago in 1910. Within its confines, lemon,

Interior of First Conservatory before Construction of North and South Wings c. 1915 MANITOBA ARCHIVES PHOTO

a new oval counter and shelves, two soda fountains, electric cooker and range, plate racks and wash basin. The pavilion annex was constructed to the same shoddy standard. It required structural upgrades to fig and orange trees were planted. Pomegranate, olive, pineapple, coffee, mango, vanilla and hemp plants attracted visitors. Throngs of people visited the Chicago conservatory for flower and chrysanthemum displays, Easter exhibits and mid-winter shows. As the Chicago of the North, Winnipeg was eager to emulate its American counterpart.

The First Conservatory before Construction of North and South Wings c. 1915
MANITOBA ARCHIVES PHOTO

That autumn, the Public Parks Board proceeded with the project. Instead of a central location, the Board chose the wide-open spaces of Assiniboine Park. On September 17, 1913, a site between the pavilion and Corydon Avenue opposite the cricket grounds was selected. A month later, the Parks Board opted for a prefabricated structure on a concrete base.

The manufactured frame would be ordered from Lord & Burnham at a cost of $8,197.

Producing greenhouses since 1860, the company operated from its Chicago head office with a factory in Des Plaines, Illinois. The building would be substantial in size. Constructed of steel and glass, it measured fifty by eighty-five feet (fifteen and a quarter by nearly twenty metres), rose thirty-four feet (ten and a third metres) and was topped by a domed roof. Particular attention was paid to the vestibule. In a letter to Lord & Burnham Company, Parks Board Secretary J.H. Blackwood stated that "the vestibule to be provided must be large and roomy and that there must be at least three doors to pass through before final admission to the palm house. The severity of our climate in the winter season make this necessary." During the First World War, extensions measuring thirty-five by sixty-five feet (almost eleven by twenty metres) would be added on each side of the central structure. The annexes would present horticultural shows of various varieties. At the rear of the main

building, boiler rooms, two propagating houses and three greenhouses would rise. Each greenhouse would measure twenty-five feet by one hundred feet (almost eight by nearly thirty and a half metres).

Construction of the conservatory proceeded smoothly. Utilizing casual day labour, erection of the brick-faced concrete base commenced in April 1914. About two months later, the Parks Board accepted a quote of $2,262 from a McDiarmid company, Winnipeg Paint and Glass Company, to supply glass for the palm house superstructure. In July 1914, the time arrived to construct the steam heating plant. The Parks Board called tenders for that purpose. A month later, plumbers Partridge & Halliday, the lowest of seven tenders, received the contract. By the onset of World War 1, the conservatory had become a reality. The structure introduced Winnipeggers and visitors to the city to tropical plants for over half a century.

Winnipeg's Assiniboine Park Conservatory featured prominently in Lord & Burnham's promotional endeavors. A large photo in *Park and*

Cemetery in July 1916 depicted the conservatory before addition of the two wings. The caption beneath the photo reads:

> By the look of this Winnipeg isn't exactly what you would call a bad number. It comes pretty close to being a match for the big palm house at Delaware Park, Buffalo, which is generally conceded to be one of the first of its type in the country. But the Winnipeg one is not completed. It's only started. See that framework on the gable at the left – it's for a wing house and a duplicate to follow on the other end. Yes, Canada is doing things.

The Zoo

In the late 19th and early 20th century, zoos constituted the rage in North American cities including Winnipeg. The first major zoo, the Smithsonian Zoological Park, was established in Washington, DC in 1889. In 1895, the New York Zoological Society founded the Bronx Zoo. Opened to the public in 1899, the Bronx Zoo embraced a philosophy that "no animal shall be kept in confinement that is uncomfortable and that all efforts should be made to give them all the room required for proper exercise and comfort." Carl Hagenbeck's large private zoo in Hamburg, Germany (established for breeding export animals) adhered to a similar philosophy. According to *Park and Cemetery* of March 1908, all the animals

> look as if they were in their native land. Rocks and covers of cement or stone are placed about the runs of animals which frequent rocky lairs in their wild state. For the polar bears, seals, and the like imitation blocks of ice are fashioned. Then there are natural forests in which one comes upon deer and antelope. Streams and rock fences that are scarcely noticed until the attention is drawn to them serve to keep one kind of animal out of the domain of the other.

Ideals had been established for displaying animals in zoological gardens.

Smaller city zoos failed to live up to these standards. Established in 1897, St. Paul's Como Park Zoo consisted of a large free range for

Buffalo Herd at Zoo, c. 1907 CITY OF WINNIPEG ARCHIVES PUBLIC PARKS BOARD ANNUAL REPORT, 1907

animals native to its region – elk, deer, and bison. Smaller enclosures housed lesser animals donated by the public. In Winnipeg, the Winnipeg Electric Railway Company housed a menagerie of animals in River Park. The pamphlet *Summer Outings Round Winnipeg* explains that the park featured buffalo, elk, caribou, moose, deer, antelope, silver and red foxes, lynx, timber and prairie wolves, badgers, porcupines, cinnamon and black bears, Angora Goats, grouse, wild geese, pheasants and ringed doves, all in confined spaces. River Park and its sister Elm Park were privately held and would eventually be sold for housing developments.

The Public Parks Board planned a publicly owned zoo open to all Winnipeggers. It would serve as a status symbol boasting Winnipeg's success as a modern, growing city. Moreover, Henry Sandison's justification for Assiniboine Park in 1903 called for a zoological garden. The Assiniboine Park Zoo would emulate on a smaller scale the zoos in the United States, particularly in St. Paul. With limited funds at its disposal, the zoo would offer native buffalo a sizeable and inexpensive range. Smaller animals would make do with more cramped quarters. Welcoming visitors in 1906, the zoo preceded the official park opening by almost three years. As funding permitted, it expanded into a modest menagerie by 1914.

The beginnings of the Assiniboine Park Zoo date from 1905. In part, the Parks Board created the zoo to display the city's buffalo herd. The progeny of bison donated by Lord Strathcona (Donald A. Smith) to the Dominion Government, most of the animals had been relocated from Winnipeg to Rocky Mountain Park (now Banff National Park). Upon request from city council, four cows and one bull, all "pure blooded," had been left behind in Winnipeg. By 1904, the herd had multiplied to thirteen and made Silver Heights its home.

In January 1906, the city relocated the bison to their new Assiniboine Park enclosure. The Parks Board awarded the Munro Iron Works a contract to furnish the wire fence for a compound. The specifications stipulated that the fence must "be of a high standard to successfully withstand any possible stampede on the part of the herd." But all did not stand well with the herd. The animals suffered from diseases caused by years of inbreeding. Moreover, the pasturage within the new Assiniboine Park compound proved unsuitable – a swampy, uncleared corral which undermined buffalo health. On April 20, 1905, the *Tribune* noted that a trade with Banff Park would be undertaken. Several buffalo will be sent in exchange for "two hardy specimens."

Health issues continued to plague the herd for several years. In February 1907, Parks Board Secretary J.H. Blackwood wrote Winnipeg's mayor and council for consent "to introduce new blood into the Buffalo Herd either by exchange of males for females or by the purchase of one or two females. The Board feels that this action is necessary to perpetuate the herd and to guard against degeneracy by inbreeding." Two months later in April 1907, Parks Board officials freed the animals to graze over a larger section of the park. The buffalo escaped and crossed the Assiniboine River to their former Silver Heights grazing grounds. After a full day's chase, horsemen deployed by the Parks Board returned most of the herd to the park. Only when the Board resolved the issues of pasturage and inbreeding would the buffalo exhibit assume its rightful place as the showcase of the Assiniboine Park Zoo.

… in April 1907, Parks Board officials freed the animals to graze over a larger section of the park. The buffalo escaped and crossed the Assiniboine River to their former Silver Heights grazing grounds.

The Assiniboine Park Zoo represented far more than buffalo. The short-term vision called for development of a collection of native Western Canadian animals and the avoidance of exotics. Moreover, the Parks Board acquired the animals by donation – not purchase. The Province of Manitoba provided the bulk of the native animals. At the Parks Board's request in 1905, the province would convey to the zoo "wild animals for the park which have been taken in the close season." Other animals were acquired from private donors. When the zoo first opened, all of its animals represented donations from the province and private individuals.

Initially, the Assiniboine Park Zoo welcomed its first visitors while operating on a shoestring budget. The 1906 Public Parks Board estimates called for animal pens for $610, a bear pit for $375, a deer yard at $300, animal water holes for $250, and a maintenance budget including food of $450. The collection awaiting visitors comprised "wild animals peculiar to the West." In addition to bison, Assiniboine Park displayed one elk, "Tommy"; two moose, one male and one female procured from Riding Mountain who "are fully domesticated and are among the most interesting and affectionate of the animals in the city's collection"; two white-tailed deer, "Nipper" and "Lucy"; two bears; a kit fox; and two bald eagles. The zoo opened in the spring and welcomed visitors until late autumn. In November 1906, the *Free Press* reported that each Sunday throngs of people came to view the buffalo and other animals. In the early years, with streetcar service operating only to the Agricultural College, visitors walked over a mile to the park zoo.

From 1907 to 1914, the zoo experienced slow growth. While the Parks Board proposed transforming the zoo into the park's greatest attraction, funding restrictions limited its expansion. About 1908, the zoo's operating policy changed because of a desire to obtain non-native species. The Parks Board eagerly filled gaps in the collection with the purchase of animals from various suppliers. No longer confining itself to Western Canadian animals, the zoo acquired more exotic species. By 1914, Assiniboine Park boasted a respectable zoological garden for an expanding mid-size North American city.

The pre-World War I period witnessed some improvements in animal housing. In 1910, Parks Superintendent George Champion designed a large pheasant enclosure. The Parks Board allocated $600 for its erection. A year later, workers completed an enlarged bear enclosure. Even though black bears hibernate, the Parks Board bizarrely undertook research to determine "if it is possible to keep a stream of water running through [the enclosure] during the winter."

Yet some compounds remained cramped. The *Free Press* reported that the deer yard was far from perfect. The deer, it maintained, "would not object to more room to move around in, but as a whole they are to all appearances well pleased."

In order to populate the new enclosures, the Parks Board secured animals by various measures. In 1908, the zoo added wolves to its collection. Two years later, the Parks Board purchased new pheasants – one cock and two hens each of golden, silver, Bohemian and ring-necked varieties. Though not native to Western Canada, the Parks Board funded the purchase of two monkeys. Although available locally, beavers were difficult to procure. In April 1912, the Parks Board contracted provincial game warden employees to trap a pair of beaver for the zoo.

Procreation increased the size of the zoo population. In July 1913, the *Free Press* remarked that the "beasts are having excellent health. They are multiplying … for three jumping deer, four wolves, four ground hogs and two elk have been born in the zoo during the last month."

By summer 1913, the zoo had grown to a moderate size. It housed black bears, bald eagles, deer, badgers, prairie wolves, beaver, Angora goats, elk, monkeys and buffalo plus an array of birds including geese, swans and pheasants. From small beginnings, the menagerie had been transformed in a decade into a successful zoological garden.

In the decade following its acquisition, much had happened to the cow pasture that made up the former Munroe Pure Milk dairy farm. The Public Parks Board had transformed it into Winnipeg's showcase suburban park, complete with playing fields, picnic areas, playgrounds, a duck pond and a respectable zoo, all anchored by an attractive, if shoddily-built pavilion and a conservatory. Visitors would throng to the park by the thousands.

Chapter Four:
A Sabbatarian Playground, 1904–1913

From its official opening in 1909 until the beginning of hostilities in World War I, Assiniboine Park emerged as Winnipeg's preferred public playground for picnicking, official holiday celebrations, recreational sports, and relaxation. Thousands of visitors flocked to the park on weekends, holidays and weekday evenings. The park attracted numerous visitors for church and service club picnics and field days and Parks Board sponsored band concerts. The city entertained out-of-town dignitaries and conventioneers at official luncheons in the pavilion.

Picnic, c. 1909 - 1914 CITY OF
WINNIPEG ARCHIVES PHOTO

It may have offered something for everyone, but Assiniboine Park constituted a highly-structured playground. It operated under strict rules of personal conduct both in the park and in the pavilion. Above all, it functioned as a Sabbatarian playground. As a result of both provincial and Dominion Government Sunday observance laws (the so-called Blue Laws), Sabbath activities in the park were tightly circumscribed and regulated in the pre-war period. The Sabbatarian nature of the park met with widespread public approval.

The Legislative Framework

It has been argued by one historian that a rapidly industrializing, late 19th-century Canadian society required disciplined, rested and relaxed employees ready to face the challenges of the Monday workday. Politicians across Canada turned to rigid Sunday observance legislation to achieve this goal. Beginning a process of rapid growth and industrialization in 1898, Manitoba followed that pattern. Inspired by zealous Presbyterian, Methodist and Baptist Sabbath-promoting clergy, members of the Manitoba Legislature imposed the Lord's Day Observance Act in 1898 on an accepting electorate.

Among other terms, the provincial act stipulated that it was unlawful "to play any game in any public place in which opposing sides compete for any prize or reward of any kind." While undefined, prizes could be interpreted to include ribbons, trophies or plaques and even candies or chocolate bars for children. Moreover, it prohibited advertising "in any manner whatsoever of any match, game, theatrical or other public amusement to take place on the Lord's Day or to open on the Lord's Day." Therefore, promotion of any event via newspaper advertisements, fliers or billboards became illegal. Penalties for contravening the Act's provisions could be severe. Charges could be initiated "upon the oath or affirmation of one or more than one credible witness." Convictions resulted in maximum fines not exceeding $40 and if left unpaid, a maximum jail term of one month. Under guise of this legislation, Manitobans could spy and report to authorities on neighbours and strangers who had desecrated the Christian Sabbath by organizing picnics and playing baseball, soccer or lacrosse. Manitoba society had gone puritan.

In 1906, at the urging of Protestant clergy, the Dominion government passed the Lord's Day Act. Supplementing but not replacing provincial statutes, the federal Lord's Day Act implemented Sunday observance across Canada. Some of the statute's terms echoed those of Manitoba's Lord's Day Observance Act – no games or organized events on Sunday and no advertising of events.

However, the Dominion act went further. It prohibited paid excursions "by any mode of conveyance to any event" and imposed fines to any corporation including municipalities authorizing, directing or permitting its employees to engage in prohibited Sunday activities. Recognizing its intrusion into provincial jurisdiction, the Dominion Government restricted the enforcement of the Act. Should any province decide to prosecute under the Lord's Day Act, only the attorney general for that province could initiate proceedings.

Sabbath observance received general public approval. In the debate over provincial Sunday rules, on March 31, 1898, the *Free Press* editorialized that

the observance of Sunday as the Christian Sabbath is doubtless a religious question, but with this our legislators have nothing to do in regulating Sunday observance, except to give effect to the desire of a majority of the people in the selection of the day of the week. The selection of a day for common observance is necessary and its selection interfered with nobody's observance of another day as his Sabbath. It simply fixes a day for its general observance as the religious Sabbath of a majority of the people makes it convenient as the civil day of rest... [The Statute] provides only that certain forms of every day business and amusement which might interfere with its effectiveness as a day of rest shall not be undertaken.

Most *Free Press* readers of the time would have concurred in the assessment that compulsory Sunday observance offended nobody.

But not everyone supported Sunday rules. The Winnipeg Trades and Labor Council weekly, *The Voice*, accused the proponents of Sunday observance as being

worthy moralists not satisfied with making the rules of life for themselves [who] are determined to make it for all the rest of us...It looks ridiculous at first sight, but it is serious indeed when we find our fellow citizens busying themselves night and day, holding meetings conspiring for the express purpose of bringing all of us into the criminal code for doing nothing more than what our fathers did as within their just rights as British citizens.

Moreover, *The Voice* argued, Sunday observance laws discriminated against unbelievers.

To say to people, you cannot form a party and go on an excursion is we think transgressing on individual rights. Religion is purely a matter of conscience and no legislative enactment can be passed that will compel people to hold one belief or another."

J.S. Ewart, a leading member of Winnipeg's legal profession agreed with the position taken by *The Voice*. Ewart had represented the Roman Catholic community during the Manitoba Schools Question of the 1890's and argued their case for publicly funded Catholic schools in Manitoba before

John S. Ewart –
Anti-Sabbatarian
Crusader MANITOBA
ARCHIVES PHOTO

the Supreme Court and Privy Council. He found Sabbath observance laws repugnant. According to the *Free Press*, he strongly disagreed with the idea that amusing oneself on Sunday was sinful and unlawful and ought to be penalized by fine and imprisonment. He expressed amazement that considerable numbers of people thought it was possible to compel others to conform to their beliefs. Instead of listening to sermons on Sunday afternoons he found it more enjoyable to play golf.

Yet Manitobans dismissed the sound and reasonable arguments of *The Voice* and J.S. Ewart. In Assiniboine Park in particular, Sunday would be like no other day of the week.

Park Rules and Organization of Services

Upon the official opening of Assiniboine Park and its newly completed pavilion on Victoria Day, 1909, the Public Parks Board imposed a strict code of public conduct on visitors and the pavilion caterer. Approved on April 28, 1909, park and pavilion rules fell into two categories – common sense and morality. Least controversial of fifteen rules, those espousing common sense enhanced the park user experience and protected visitors from being harassed by undesirable individuals. Those rules included no swearing or obscene language, no intoxicants or anything approaching such, no gambling, no card playing, no spitting on floors, no games of chance and no loud talking or haranguing in or around the pavilion. To prevent park visitors from being approached by hucksters selling refreshments from tents or stands, the Parks Board restricted food sales to the pavilion. Once inside the new structure, no tipping was permitted. Initially, for a brief period and for some bizarre reason the Parks Board tolerated no merry-go-rounds – evidentially a social evil. In the pavilion, it enforced a strict ban on cigarettes, then equated with the rougher classes of society, while odoriferous cigars, the taste of upper classes, could be readily procured. In line with provincial and Dominion Sunday observance laws, the pavilion restricted Sunday hours to lunch and dinner times only. Less than three

Group Get-Together, c. 1910 MANITOBA ARCHIVES PHOTO

weeks after the park opened, a public clamor for Sunday snacks forced the Parks Board to permit the sale of refreshments in all daylight hours in July and August. Clearly, Assiniboine

Playgrounds, 1909 CITY OF WINNIPEG ARCHIVES, PUBLIC PARKS BOARD ANNUAL REPORT, 1909

Park presented a safe and welcoming, if not an over-regulated place for individuals and families seeking relaxation.

The Parks Board administered the food outlets directly. The concept of municipally-operated pavilion restaurants and takeout counters originated in the United States. At the American Parks Superintendents Convention in Minneapolis in 1908, J.T. Foster, superintendent of the South Park system of Chicago addressed his contemporaries on the matter, a transcript of which was printed in *Park and Cemetery* on October 1908. He argued that park restaurants and takeout counters should not be operated by the private sector: "Service is most generally inefficient, and the parks become, to a degree business centers and traffic is in evidence at every turn." The public appetite, he argued, should be suppressed so that visitors could enjoy the beautiful landscapes! The goal of publicly operated pavilion refectories lay in selling sufficient food and snacks to recoup operating expenses – not turning a profit.

South Chicago park commissioners had successfully operated their own restaurants since 1869 "to meet the reasonable needs of the people." They charged low prices to enable less affluent people to purchase food. Winnipeg Parks

Superintendent George Champion attended the 1908 conference and was likely impressed with Foster's presentation. Upon the opening of the Assiniboine Park Pavilion in 1909, the Parks Board adopted the Chicago model.

Throughout the Assiniboine Park pavilion's early years, the Public Parks Board managed the refectories as a public service. Each spring they held a competition for a married couple to operate the facilities from May to October. Remuneration consisted of a $100 per month salary and free room and board in the pavilion. Occasionally the Parks Board choices proved ill advised. In 1909, the pavilion's first caterers, S. Hannay and his wife, resigned after less than three weeks on the job.

The Parks Board micro-managed the restaurant operations. Each spring, the Board's catering committee issued tenders for seasonal supplies. 1914 was a typical year. In April, the Parks Board accepted bids from a multiplicity of suppliers including E.M. Miller for cigars, the Crescent Creamery for dairy products, Blackwoods Limited for mineral, aerated water and soft drinks and Spiers-Parnell Limited for the supply of bread. Some perishable items including fruits, confectioneries, ice-cream cones, meats, vegetables and soda fountain supplies were acquired without contract upon monthly instructions from the chairman of the catering committee. Operationally the system proved both unwieldy and bureaucratic.

Some bureaucratic practices extended to the consumer level. In the pavilion lunchroom, customers could not pay directly for desired food items. In order to secure snacks or light meals visitors pre-purchased tickets or vouchers in denominations of 5 cents or 25 cents. During peak periods they stood in long separate lines to purchase the voucher and to order the food. Although inefficient and cumbersome, the system prevailed during the pavilion's early years.

The Park and the Public, 1909–1914

The question invariably arises – who visited Assiniboine Park during its formative years? A review of visitor activities in the *Free Press*, *Tribune* and *Telegram* suggests that middle-class Protestant and Catholic Winnipeggers residing in Central Winnipeg, the West End, Fort Rouge and Crescentwood gravitated towards the park because it could be reached with a relatively short streetcar ride. Moreover, the middle class possessed the discretionary leisure funds for streetcar fares and snacks and meals at the pavilion. At

In terms of family enjoyment, Sunday was like no other day in Assiniboine Park. Strict Sabbath observance applied right down to the to the playground. Every Saturday evening Parks Board employees removed the ropes from the swings and placed a hobble on the merry-go-round.

Assiniboine Park, these individuals participated in formal church and informal family picnics, organized sports and attended Parks Board-sponsored band concerts.

Except for organized church picnics, most North End immigrants and working-class people chose to stay close to home. When Kildonan Park opened in 1911, North Enders flocked to the new leisure grounds. Every year on the August civic holiday, however, children from all classes and all parts of the city enrolled in the playground movement converged on Assiniboine Park for an afternoon and evening of organized song, dance and games. But for the most part, Assiniboine Park attracted mainly the middle-class mainstream.

Upon its completion, Assiniboine Park emerged as Winnipeg's choice location for both organized and family picnics. With the opening of the seasonal footbridge over the Assiniboine River in 1911, picnickers could reach the park on the Winnipeg Electric Railway's Portage Avenue routes. Most organized church picnics generally took place

on Victoria Day, Dominion Day, and above all on Saturdays. Protestant church and benevolent society groups including St. Stephen's Church Young People's Club, St. Andrew's Church, St. Paul's Christian Endeavor Society and Young Men's Club, Grace Church Young Men's Club, St. Matthew's Sunday School and many others held their annual picnics and field days in the park. Roman Catholic groups including St. Edward's Parish, St. Anne of the Immaculate Conception and St. Ignatius Children's Club preferred summer weekdays for their children's picnics.

Picnics followed a common format. Formally attired women congregants catered picnic lunches to the mass crowds. In the afternoon, team sports and track and field events followed. The picnic of St. Edward's Parish on Monday, July 17, 1911 was typical. A baseball tournament involving St. Mary's, St. Edward's and St. Boniface teams took place. Boys and girls boot races, running events, three-legged races and wheelbarrow races were held. The winners received suitable prizes while

Band Stand and
Concert, c. 1915
MANITOBA ARCHIVES
PHOTO

Lord's Day Act disallowed organized picnics on Sundays. Consequently, Jewish groups who observed the Saturday Sabbath could not enjoy the benefits of group activities on the weekend even though they paid property taxes like everyone else.

In terms of family enjoyment, Sunday was like no other day in Assiniboine Park. Strict Sabbath observance applied right down to the

congregants dispensed ice cream and candies to all of the children.

Unorganized family picnics took place on all days of the week. Nuclear families of mother, father and children enjoyed picnic lunches. The children played ball or other unorganized games or utilized the swings and merry-go-round. Frequently a visit to the zoo to see the buffalo, bears and monkeys followed lunch.

The Provincial Lord's Day Observance Act and Dominion

to the playground. Every Saturday evening Parks Board employees removed the ropes from the swings and placed a hobble on the merry-go-round. On Monday morning, Parks Board employees re-installed the ropes on the swings and unhobbled the merry-go-round so that children could once again use them. *Town Topics* expressed outrage at the practice. On August 2, 1913 it accused these adult men, ministers and acolytes of the Parks Board [of forcing children] to obey the will of the sour-minded Sabbatarians who believe in a sour-minded God who they have fashioned in their minds, after their own image, and who in their sanctimonious hatred of the joy of life and their mania for regulating the lives of other people would like to be able to draw a Sunday curtain over the world, shutting out the sunlight and cooping us all up...all day long to listen to sermons making childhood a misery and manhood and womanhood a servitude to sniffling puritanism.

The removal of the ropes from the swings and the hobbling of the merry-go-round, *Town Topics* concluded, "is a shameful wrong, a crime against civilization, a disgrace to Winnipeg in the sight of God and all right-minded human beings." Yet *Town Topics* sympathized with some Sabbath restrictions. It supported the prohibition of organized picnics on Sunday in Assiniboine Park while approving private picnics which permitted children to use swings and the merry-go-round on Sundays as on all other days.

Assiniboine Park emerged as a favoured location for organized sports activities in the pre-World War I period. Two sports dominated: cricket and lacrosse. At its annual meeting in October 1910, the Civic Cricket Club announced that Parks Board Chairman C. Sharpe promised to lay out a cricket pitch in the park. Within two years, the park possessed outstanding cricket facilities across from the future conservatory for the mainly British-born players. On March 23, 1912, the *Free Press* declared that "the Parks Board have laid out pitches and where they will lay out more if the cricketeers will show them that they want them. The park is the logical place for cricket now. It has everything and is easy of access." In August 1913, an interprovincial cricket tournament was held in Assiniboine Park. Teams representing Manitoba, Saskatchewan and Alberta competed with one another. Manitoba won and claimed bragging rights.

Lacrosse was also extensively played. The Parks Board granted individual lacrosse clubs locations to practise on weekday evenings. The governing body, the Winnipeg Amateur Lacrosse Association, organized its matches for Saturday afternoons.

By 1914, Assiniboine Park had become a mecca for cricket and lacrosse. Cricketeers indulged in their favourite pastime across from the conservatory for generations. Lacrosse remained popular until well after World War I.

During the four years commencing in 1909, the Public Parks Board tolerated snowshoeing during the winter. Snowshoers had been granted park use as an experiment, and the YMCA and the Manitoba Snowshoers' Association organized outings in Assiniboine Park.

In 1910, snowshoers seeking deep snow had destroyed hundreds of valuable shrubs. J.H. Blackwood, the parks board secretary, indicated that snowshoers "had destroyed shrubs and perennials by walking everywhere and anywhere... If the same results are proved this winter, it will mean the elimination of snowshoeing in Assiniboine Park."

Initially, the park's caretaker provided limited dining facilities for the participants in his private quarters and undertook catering "upon his own responsibility." In October 1910, H.R. Hadcock, the YMCA's physical director, enquired about provisions being made for snowshoers in the coming season in the pavilion. Blackwood responded that "the building is slightly constructed and is not intended for winter use."

Until the end of the 1912 season, organized snowshoeing continued in Assiniboine Park. In January 1913, a deputation from the Manitoba Snowshoers' Association waited on the Parks Board and requested that Assiniboine Park be opened to them for the coming season. The Parks Board carefully considered the request. In reply to Edgar J. Ransom, head of the Manitoba Snowshoers' Association, Blackwood wrote "as this would involve the opening of the park to the detriment of the newly planted shrubberies and perennial plants we regret therefore that we cannot accede to the request of your association."

The ban on winter activities including snowshoeing in

Assiniboine Park would remain in effect until the 1960s.

One activity which elicited absolutely no Parks Board support was automobile speeding on Assiniboine Park's driveways. At the time of the official opening of the park, the automobile had increased in popularity among Winnipeg's elite and upper middle classes. Young men in particular found Assiniboine Park's winding driveways alluring for testing their vehicle's speed capabilities and in the process terrorizing pedestrians. In May 1909, the Public Parks Board amended Parks Board Bylaw No. 3 to prohibit speeding in all of Winnipeg's parks. The amendment stipulated that "no person shall drive any automobile or other vehicle or ride or drive any horse at a speed exceeding ten miles per hour upon any road within any Park under the control of the Public Parks Board of Winnipeg." However, the bylaw amendment failed to control road racing in the park. Representing the majority of responsible automobile owners, the Winnipeg Automobile Club expressed concerns. On

Catching a Concert, c. 1915 MANITOBA ARCHIVES PHOTO

September 8, 1909, R. McLeod of that organization addressed the Parks Board regarding the issue. The Parks Board referred the matter to Park Superintendent George Champion. Two months later, the Board acted. A further amendment to Parks Board Bylaw No. 3 reduced the speed limit in the city's parks from ten to eight miles per hour for any motorcycle, automobile or horse. To ensure compliance, the Parks Board imposed fines not exceeding $100 for infractions. In terms of early 20th-century salaries, $100 represented a sizeable sum and a serious deterrent for young men trying to prove their virility. Parks Board Police enforced the speed limit.

Throughout its early history, the Public Parks Board organized and financed numerous band concerts in the city's major parks. Those in

Assiniboine Park proved particularly enticing. According to Parks Superintendent George Champion "the Sunday band concert at the city park had been found the most popular of all in the way of attendance."

The Parks Board employed numerous bands, including the Citizens Band, Cameron Highlanders Band, 108th Regiment Band, 100th Grenadier Band, Trades and Labour Council Band, Ninth Pipers Band and the Cambrian Male Choir. All bands were unionized and received fair wages for their endeavours. In 1913, the Parks Board scheduled eighty concerts for all Winnipeg parks, including nine in August for Assiniboine Park. Hundreds of people attended each concert.

The Public Parks Board exercised complete control over every aspect of a band concert. It decreed that all bandsmen must appear in uniform and that the number be fixed at twenty-five men in 1906 and thirty-one including band master in 1911. Even the duration of concerts was circumscribed – three hours for afternoon performances and two hours for evening events. The Parks Board rigorously controlled the content of each concert. Until 1913, only instrumentals could be played, and no vocal numbers were performed. Discouraging the attendance of unbelievers and Jews, Sunday afternoon concerts were limited to sacred music numbers. Before each concert, bandmasters submitted the day's program for approval. If the music proved unsatisfactory, the Parks Board cancelled the concert in advance. Public Parks Board members empowered themselves to be judges of good taste in music and enforcers of Sabbath legislation.

Typical of band concerts was the Winnipeg City Band's Sunday, June 19, 1913 performance in Assiniboine Park. The band played the obligatory liturgical selections – a sacred fantasia, "Providence" by Theodore Moses-Tabani and "Inflamatus," "Holy City" and "Heavens are Telling" from Cavalleria Rusticana. To retain audience attention, several secular numbers received an airing. Opera pieces like "Lohengrin" by Richard Wagner and Domenico Donizetti's "Lucia" entertained Winnipeggers. The Winnipeg City Band played selections from 20th-century composer Theo Bendix. The concert ended with a flurry of patriotism – "Canadian Patriot" by Williams, "The Maple Leaf Forever," and "God Save the King." Despite some secular elements, this Sunday concert proceeded as planned. Public Parks Board Chairman Thomas Wilson addressed the issue of the Parks Board contravening its own musical guidelines. By inference, he stated that "if there is any one department of the city that is doing more to make Sunday comfortable for the citizens than the parks board is doing, I have not become aware of it."

Not everyone approved of the repertoire and quality of band concerts. Residing on Inglewood Street in St. James and not paying Winnipeg property taxes, Reverend F.M. Bell-Smith nevertheless criticized Sunday band performances in Assiniboine Park. He commented that "there was a religious item occasionally to input a certain tone, but most of the items were far from bearing that character." Another individual complained of the poor quality of band performances. On

May 15, 1914, in a letter to the *Free Press* "A Natural" wrote that "there are one or two of our band organizations which have reached a very high standard fit to play the most difficult as well as the popular work of any composer with uniform excellence and good judgment in their interpretation of the subject. There are others whose place is wholly in the department of rag-time and the cake walk and there is more than one 'band' which seeks the tolerance of Winnipeg's musical ear but whose performances are a ghastly joke, and the more so when offered in all seriousness." The criticism went largely unanswered. Band concerts continued unchanged.

Before World War I, Assiniboine Park excelled in hosting many official events – some desirable, others more questionable. Topping the desirability list, city council tendered luncheons at the pavilion to promote Winnipeg to visiting dignitaries. At a luncheon

Golf in Assiniboine Park?

Before World War I, the Parks Board recognized the need for a publicly-owned golf course in Winnipeg. In 1913, members of the local golf community pressed the Parks Board to act. The Parks Board instructed Superintendent George Champion to lay out a nine-hole golf course in the eastern part of Assiniboine Park. According to the *Free Press* of July 3, 1913 "the course would start at the northeast corner of the park and will follow a zig-zag route till it finishes about the middle of the park, near the car shelter." The course would cost about $2,500 to $3,000 to construct and employ twelve skilled workers. The design adopted possessed one fatal flaw. It crossed the road leading to the Formal Garden. In admiring Assiniboine Park's horticultural splendor, flower lovers would risk being hit in the head and other parts of the human anatomy by errant golf balls. In its instructions to Superintendent Champion on June 18, 1913, the Parks Board made clear "that no play will be permitted across the above-mentioned driveway."

The golf course was never laid out. Lack of funding forced the Parks Board to defer construction for a year. In 1914, the plans were formally abandoned. On June 17, 1914, the Secretary of Winnipeg's Board of Control wrote the Parks Board that a golf course in Assiniboine Park "was both impracticable and dangerous." But the need for a public course to serve golfers of modest means remained. In August 1920, the Kildonan Park Municipal Golf Course opened its fairways and greens to the public.

in 1912, city council feted a group of one hundred British manufacturers seeking Canadian investment opportunities. The city warmly received tourist promotion groups. In May 1913, the Twin City ticket agents from Minneapolis-St. Paul arrived in Winnipeg and were shown the city's sites culminating with a

civic luncheon in Assiniboine Park. Less than two months later, Mayor A.L. Lavallee of Montreal visited Assiniboine Park with delegates on their way to the Union of Canadian Municipalities convention in Saskatoon. On their Winnipeg stopover, the city entertained the visitors. Lavallee admired the planning and layout of the park. Once the city grows, he declared, the park will be near to the city centre and useful to the working classes for whom it was intended.

The Parks Board authorized various associations to hold events for their members in Assiniboine Park. In 1913, the Provincial Masons met in Winnipeg for their annual convention. The verdant and idyllic surroundings of the park proved ideal for their luncheon. On June 12, 1913, the *Free Press* reported that about forty automobiles loaned by local members of the lodge transported delegates and their wives to Assiniboine Park for a catered luncheon. "The proceedings at the park were quite informal, there being no speechmaking." Less respectable groups received grudging Parks Board approval to hold events. In April 1912, the Twelfth of July Committee of the Orange Order requested permission to hold a 'celebration' in the park. Afraid of stirring animosity between Protestants and Catholics in Winnipeg, the Parks Board delayed its response for three full weeks. Finally, J.H. Blackwood wrote to A.F. Booth, secretary of the Twelfth of July Committee, that the Parks Board had no objection "so long as you comply with the rules and regulations in force." Moreover, no goods could be offered for sale. The letter enclosed a copy of parks bylaws specifying proper conduct. The Parks Board offered catering services to the group and encouraged the organizer to arrange with the park superintendent for these services. If a sectarian group held an event in Assiniboine Park, at least the Parks Board could benefit from refreshment and food sales!

Assiniboine Park helped to fulfil a role in acculturating children from all ethnic backgrounds, classes and residential areas into disciplined law-abiding citizens embracing Anglo-Saxon values who took pride in their role as Canadians and members of the British Empire. Based in Winnipeg schoolyards and sponsored by the Winnipeg Playgrounds Association, the Playground Movement provided safe structured summer recreational activities for children. Playgrounds from all parts of the city participated – Lord Roberts, Gladstone, La Verendrye, Greenway, Mulvey, Pinkham, Central, Wellington, John M. King, Dufferin, Weston Park, Aberdeen, Norquay, King Edward, Argyle, Luxton, Selkirk, Machray and Strathcona. Every day in July and August, children could be found at individual playgrounds involved in informal games, organized sports, patriotic marches and dramatic plays. On the civic holiday, the children congregated in Playfest in Assiniboine Park for the grand season finale. Highly structured and attended by thousands of children,

their parents and activity organizers, Playfest epitomized for many the highlight of the school summer holidays. The daily newspapers covered Playfest extensively. A synthesis of newspaper accounts indicates that in mid-afternoon, children assembled in their respective playgrounds and embarked on chartered streetcars to Assiniboine Park. After crossing the Assiniboine River footbridge, the children marched in unison to their reserved spaces led by a cadets' band.

Massed folk dancing, singing, and the performance in plays such as the Red River Pageant with over one hundred actors, including adults, followed. Games played included volleyball, dodgeball, baseball and basketball. Flag drills, with the participation of both boys and girls, formed part of each year's program. The day's events concluded by singing "The Maple Leaf Forever" and "God Save the King."

Playfest attracted thousands of participants and spectators. During the August 1914 civic holiday, 3,000 children engaged in Playfest activities. An estimated 7,000 adults witnessed the spectacle. In its idyllic Assiniboine Park setting, Playfest performed a role

in developing good citizens for the Dominion and Empire.

From its official opening in 1909, Assiniboine Park quickly emerged as Winnipeg's centre for holiday celebrations. The warm weather festivities of Victoria Day, Dominion Day, the civic holiday and Labour Day drew multitudes of visitors to the park – most arriving over the seasonal footbridge. The *Free Press* remarked that the absence of amusement devices and free admission drew Winnipeggers in droves to Assiniboine Park. The *Tribune* pointed out that "thousands realized for the first time what a treasure the city possesses in the expanse of broad meadows and beautiful trees." Victoria Day 1914 celebrations typified the pre-War period and received extensive press coverage. Six thousand people visited Assiniboine Park that day. They picnicked, played baseball or tennis, watched a cricket match between Winnipeg and Brandon or enjoyed a concert by the Cameron Highlanders. The zoo proved popular. The *Free Press* remarked that "even the bears got enough life into their hulking bodies to climb to the top of the pole in their cement dug-out and reach lazily for tidbits thrown at them." Three Parks Board police officers spent the day locating children who had strayed from their parents.

summer. According to the *Free Press,* in 1912 almost 6,000 people "regaled themselves with games and idled along the riverbank enjoying the breeze. Throughout the long stretch of the park, girls and men in summer attire strolled aimlessly or rested on

matches. During the 1911 civic holiday in Assiniboine Park, food sold out at the pavilion; people purchased 115 gallons (522.8 litres) of ice cream, all in cones. Labour Day unofficially terminated the summer season and ushered in the beginning of autumn.

It also drew the largest crowds to the park. On September 3, 1914, the *Free Press* reported: Assiniboine Park was the objective point of thousands yesterday. Never since it has been a park have such a multitude poured into it. Parties were to be found everywhere… Automobile after automobile sped around the oiled roadway from 2 in the afternoon until nearly dark. A rough estimate of the number who visited the park yesterday would be at least 10,000. Picnic parties everywhere, crowds of boys and girls in every nook and corner, races, baseball, croquet, tennis, everything seemed in full swing.

During the 1911 civic holiday in Assiniboine Park, food sold out at the pavilion; people purchased 115 gallons (522.8 litres) of ice cream, all in cones.

Dominion Day, the civic holiday, and Labour Day activities followed a similar pattern. Dominion Day attracted large crowds partaking in the lazy days of the brief prairie

the benches." Many people enjoyed a concert of the Veterans Brigade Band.

The civic holiday was marked by organized Playfest activities and the usual band concert and cricket

Public transit could not handle the departing masses in the evening.

As summer 1914 gave way to autumn, Assiniboine Park's position as the focal point for warm weather holiday activities in Winnipeg stood unchallenged.

Alternatives to Assiniboine Park

In the pre-World War I era, Winnipeggers possessed many recreational alternatives to the new Assiniboine Park pleasure grounds. On the Victoria Day weekend of 1909, those staying within the city could still visit the commercially operated Elm Park for picnicking and River Park for sporting events. Kildonan Park opened its gates in spring 1911. It attracted many North Enders opting for a relatively short streetcar ride from their homes. However, it lacked one of Assiniboine Park's main features – a zoo.

Many families chose a lakeside excursion. In 1902, the Canadian Pacific Railway completed its line to Winnipeg Beach. Passenger service started in 1904, and by 1906 the CPR operated up to thirteen trains per day on weekends. By 1908, the train trip to Winnipeg Beach took only seventy-five minutes. According to historian Dale Barbour, Winnipeg Beach became known "for its commercial carnival tradition" and as a place where young adults could meet and court. Grand Beach opened later. Following completion of the line from Winnipeg, it would welcome visitors near the end of World War I.

Many organizations sought lakeside locales for their annual picnics rather than the architecturally enhanced meadows of Assiniboine Park. According to Dale Barbour, by 1913, forty to fifty picnics per season took place at Winnipeg Beach for groups from all walks of life including social clubs, church organizations and employee associations. Labour unions in particular enjoyed the camaraderie of picnics outside the city and sometimes selected less popular locations. In August 1913, the Canadian Pacific Railway employees held their annual picnic at Gimli while the Plumbers Union selected Selkirk Park for their annual get-together. The Canadian Northern Railway employees outdid all others in their picnic plans. Taking place in June 1914, the employees travelled by train to Warroad, Minnesota, accompanied by city bands.

But all these picnics took place on weekdays or Saturdays. The Lord's Day Act of 1906 prohibited Sunday excursions. On Sundays, only the parks within Winnipeg's boundaries vied with Assiniboine Park for visitation. The provincial Lords Day Observance Act and federal Lord's Day Act rendered organized Sunday picnics illegal. Until 1924, Sunday train excursions to the Lake Winnipeg beaches and other locales were forbidden by law. Possessing few alternatives, individuals and families congregated in Assiniboine Park. They picnicked with friends and relatives, listened to bands playing religious music and perhaps visited the bears, buffalo and monkeys at the zoo. Children played – but not on the swings or the merry-go-round. In 1914, Assiniboine Park represented a true Sabbatarian playground.

Chapter Five:
World War I and its Aftermath, 1914–1919

In August 1914, hostilities broke out in Europe. Along with Great Britain, the British Empire and its allies, Canada went to war against Germany and the Austro-Hungarian Empire. On August 2, Prime Minister Robert Borden offered to send an expeditionary force overseas and on August 6, the federal cabinet ordered the mobilization of the first Canadian contingent. Despite unrealized hopes for a quick victory, the First World War dragged on for four years. It necessitated a total effort and the allocation of all of Canada's human, financial, agricultural and natural resources. The federal government placed all of Canada on a war footing. Assiniboine Park was at war.

Conservatory with North & South Wings, 1924 *WINNIPEG: KNOW YOUR CITY – SOUVENIR OF WINNIPEG'S JUBILEE, 1874-1924, C. 1924*

Assiniboine Park performed a supporting role in Winnipeg's war contribution – a place of peace and tranquility where citizens could picnic, visit the zoo, play sports, walk the nature pathways and temporarily escape the news of war casualties and the demands of a wartime economy. Despite budget cuts from 1915 to 1918, the Public Parks Board proceeded with several projects, namely the addition of north and south wings to the conservatory, construction of a new decorative southeast gate to the park, the expansion of zoo enclosures and the enlargement of the zoo – all measures intended to boost public morale. The Parks Board funded official celebrations of Canada's Jubilee in 1917 and the yearly ceremonies of Victoria Day, Dominion Day and the civic holiday. Following the armistice, Winnipeg sponsored Peace Day celebrations in Assiniboine Park. A popular and extensively reported visit of the Prince of Wales in 1919 brought closure to a difficult period for Winnipeggers.

Infrastructure and Collections

The First World War ushered in a period of reductions in the Public Parks Board budget. The cuts began in 1915. On February 16, Mayor R.D. Waugh addressed the Parks Board. He impressed upon that body "the necessity for keeping the expenditures of the Board down… to the lowest possible estimate and requested the Board to do no new work or anything they could possibly get along without." Accordingly, the Parks Board reduced its 1915 estimates by $22,235. Despite reduced funding, the Parks Board was determined to continue Assiniboine Park's development.

The construction of fifty-foot-long north and south wings to the conservatory constituted by far the largest project undertaken in Assiniboine Park during the war years. On August 16, 1916, the Parks Board appointed Chairman Henry Sandison and member James McDiarmid to a special committee to obtain prices for the supply of materials for each of the two wings.

Two months later, Sandison and McDiarmid presented their report. They recommended that the Parks Board erect the two wings in 1917 at an estimated cost of $13,000 and that an order be placed immediately with Lord & Burnham for the prefabricated steel superstructure. The erection of the building they proposed would be carried out by day labour under supervision of the Parks Board superintendent. The report also dealt with materiel procurement. The twenty-nine-ounce glass, the piping, and all construction materials would be "purchased in the local market to the best advantage." However, the Parks Board did not award all materiel contracts to local suppliers. Lord & Burnham tendered successfully for the supply of twenty-nine-ounce (.822 kilogram) hail resistant glass panels. Local Winnipeg firms Bowyer Boag Limited and Partridge and Halliday received contracts for the steam heating systems in the south and north wings. A year later, the Parks Board called tenders for a new upgraded boiler for the conservatory. By summer 1918, the expanded

Conservatory Interior, 1924
WINNIPEG: KNOW YOUR CITY – SOUVENIR OF WINNIPEG'S JUBILEE, 1874–1924, C. 1924

conservatory would welcome the public.

The conservatory offered war-weary Winnipeggers a free and temporary escape to a tropical paradise. On September 1, 1917, before the two fifty-foot (15.24 metre)

The conservatory offered war-weary Winnipeggers a free and temporary escape to a tropical paradise.

wings were completed, the *Free Press* described the glass structure with its high roof and tropical plants as "a little bit of heaven." It commented that "lovers of nature in all her abundance could spend hours in this lovely spot and find every second fascinating. Here grow lemons and oranges, and although bananas are

missing, another form of the banana plant rears its great leaves among the bamboos, Norfolk Island pines, Birds of Paradise plants… and the score of other varieties of plants not common to the north country." The completion of the north and south wings to the conservatory presented opportunities for year-round horticultural shows. Chrysanthemum displays proved particularly popular. On November 14, 1918, the *Free Press* reported that the north wing of the conservatory was "now ablaze with chrysanthemums of many varieties and colours." Winnipeggers could clear their minds from the ongoing war and enjoy the best of the tropics.

A year into the First World War, Assiniboine Park boasted a mid-sized zoo with a wide variety of animals. Numbering approximately 120 animals, the collection included angora goats, beavers, red foxes, buffalo, badgers, elk, tortoises, "jumping" deer, prairie wolves, elk, rabbits, black bears, alligators, monkeys and many species of birds. On December 11, 1915, the *Free Press* commented that "the zoo is annually being added to and has proved a great attraction ... to children who [exhibit] interest in the birds and animals and receive considerable amusement from the bears and monkeys." The *Free Press* continued that the cost of zoo maintenance "is comparatively low, amounting to a little over $2,000 per year."

Evidently, the Parks Board agreed. It continued to expand the zoo during the war years despite budgetary restraints.

Expanded animal accommodation constituted a Parks Board priority. In 1915, it allocated $250 for the construction of small animal cages. A year later, it authorized the erection of a new elk enclosure, bear pit and pigeon loft. The 3,000 square-foot (914.4 metre) elk enclosure proved the costliest, and the Manitoba Anchor Wire Fence Company was awarded a contract for $1,650 to fence the new corral.

At $1,100, the bear cage stood second in expenditure. The Parks Board instructed Superintendent George Champion to construct an iron cage twenty-four by twenty-four feet (7.31 by 7.31 metre) with a den and pool for the iconic Canadian animals. In 1917, the park's beavers benefited from improved housing. On May 16, the Parks Board passed a motion authorizing Superintendent Champion to erect an outdoor enclosure with an iron fence and concrete pool at a cost not exceeding $350. To populate the new and existing enclosures, the Parks Board expanded the zoo's collection. The zoo received several birds by donation – four young goshawks in 1917 and a snowy owl a year and a half later. But the zoo's collection grew mainly by purchases. During the war, a budget of $100 per annum enabled the Assiniboine Park Zoo to enjoy a modest growth and retain the interest of visitors.

The Public Parks Board sought to improve the quality of its collection. It achieved this goal by improved breeding techniques and by culling or disposing of surplus animals. The

health of an ageing bison herd long remained a Parks Board concern. In 1914, it secured on a temporary basis from the Dominion Parks Branch a young female buffalo for breeding purposes. The animal bore a healthy calf and thereby started the process of herd renewal. In March 1915, the herd consisted of six buffalo plus the loaner.

The Parks Board also dealt with an over-abundance of elk in its corral. In 1917, it donated six elk to the Province of Manitoba for release into the wild. On April 2 of that year, the *Free Press* reported that the somewhat difficult feat of crating six vigorous young elk and placing them in a box car was successfully accomplished by provincial government employees. The elk were shipped to "somewhere in the Spruce Woods between Brandon and Carberry."

Unwanted bears suffered a worse fate. On November 21, 1917, the Parks Board passed a motion "that the two large black bears be shot, the skins sold, and the carcasses used as food for the wolves and eagles." The measures undertaken ensured in part that Assiniboine Park would display

to the public a healthy menagerie of animals.

Yet the Assiniboine Park Zoo remained a work in progress. In August 1917, Mayor F.A. Davidson received a letter from visitor G.S. Decatur complaining that animals in the zoo had an insufficient water supply and that the water was "hot and dirty." Responding to a request from the Parks Board chairman, Superintendent George Champion reported that the animals drank from a plentiful supply of Assiniboine River water. Taking an unctuous and sanctimonious stance that he adopted periodically under criticism, Champion concluded "that the statement by Mr. Decatur was not in accordance with fact." Until the completion of the Shoal Lake aqueduct, problems with Assiniboine River water would persist.

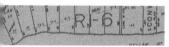

During the war years, minor improvements to Assiniboine Park continued, albeit at a reduced pace. The relocation of public washrooms from the pavilion to the picnic grounds and the construction of a monumental gate at the park's southeast entrance comprise such upgrades.

Approved in September 1915, the new washrooms were constructed by park staff the following spring and proved a great convenience to the picnicking public. The monumental entrance at Park Boulevard and Corydon Avenue assumed greater visibility. Initially, Parks Superintendent Champion submitted plans for the structure. However, Parks Board members were unimpressed. Consisting of chairman Henry Sandison and members James McDiarmid and J.G. Dagg, the board struck a subcommittee to accept suitable designs, procure tenders, award a contract and oversee construction. In March 1917, the Parks Board accepted the design of architect John Manuel and the tender of the Schmidt Brass & Ironworks of Winnipeg for a cost of $1,000. Parks Board Secretary J.H. Blackwood instructed the latter to proceed with construction immediately. In late summer, the *Free Press* reported that Assiniboine Park has "new handsome gates at the south entrance."

The Parks Board improved access to Assiniboine Park from River Heights. It had long been a goal of the city to extend Wellington Crescent through the Agricultural College grounds and along the Assiniboine River to the park. The provincial government had spurned City of Winnipeg approaches to bisect the college campus, in use since 1906, with a roadway. The completion of the new agricultural college in Fort Garry during the war years led the province to reconsider its position. In November 1916, the province agreed to open up "River Drive" through the old agricultural college grounds then being used by the School for the Deaf. The Parks Board responded by instructing the city solicitor to arrange a property transfer to the City of Winnipeg or the Municipality of Tuxedo and "have the same opened up for traffic at the earliest date."

In 1916, the city also established a buffer zone on its eastern boundary. The developers of Tuxedo, Heubach and Finkelstein, desired a wide road separating the grandiose newly constructed homes on Park Boulevard from Assiniboine Park. In August of

During the war years, minor improvements to Assiniboine Park continued, albeit at a reduced pace.

that year, the Parks Board passed a motion instructing the city solicitor to prepare a bylaw deleting forty-three feet from the park's eastern boundary between Wellington Crescent and Corydon Avenue and dedicating it as a public highway. A wider Park Boulevard became a reality and the city possessed a buffer zone and a connector route between the two arteries.

Military Activities in Assiniboine Park

Throughout the war years, Assiniboine Park hosted various military related activities. These events can be divided into two categories – first, drills, recruiting, military field days, troop luncheons, and secondly, picnics for the wives and children of troops serving overseas. Upon request from the military, the Parks Board periodically passed motions authorizing activities in Assiniboine Park that supported the war effort.

Direct military activities were by far the most numerous. Clearly in contravention of the Federal Lord's Day Act and the Provincial Lord's Day Observance Act, the Parks Board permitted the 34th Fort Garry Horse to drill in Assiniboine Park on Sunday mornings in 1915 "provided of course that no horses or artillery of any kind is taken into the Park and that [the regiment]… take the very best care of the lawns." Military field days received Public Parks Board support.

In 1915, the Minto Armouries-based 79th Cameron Highlanders requested and obtained Parks Board permission to hold a field day in Assiniboine Park. The Parks Board expressed "much pleasure in granting your request and we sincerely trust … that you may have a pleasant and profitable day." The Parks Board permitted military recruiting in the park. In June 1917, it authorized a military unit to erect a recruiting tent at the south end of the footbridge for that purpose. Troops passing through Winnipeg en route to the European front received the city's attention. On June 24, 1918, two trainloads of American soldiers from the 363rd Regiment US Infantry stopped in Winnipeg. In the city, they marched from the CPR Depot to the downtown University of Manitoba campus on Broadway. From there, streetcars transported them to Assiniboine Park where the city feted them with a luncheon. In a small way, Assiniboine Park contributed its part to Canada's effort in the conflict.

A second activity entailed support for families of the men serving abroad. On June 28, 1917, women's auxiliaries of the 61st Battalion and the 184th Battalion hosted picnics in Assiniboine Park for the wives and children of troops overseas. The *Free Press* account of the two picnics is particularly poignant and touching. It commented that among the 500 people assembled

> on the grass frolicked their little ones of every age from toddling midgets of 10 and 11 months who have never yet seen 'Daddy' to tall boys and girls of 15 who in… Daddy's absence are assuming responsibilities far beyond their years. Here were a few of the brave families of Winnipeg's brave men. One bright faced little woman was there with eight of her children. Two more had been unable to come.
>
> Over in the picnic shelter exactly 2400 sandwiches awaited the picnic throng and after the races had been run for all ages the party flocked to the long, heavily-laden tables where great jugs of lemonade and steaming tea stood at intervals down the centre of each. Ice cream and cake abounded, the entire supper having been provided by the battalion auxiliary and friends. At the other end of the shelter the 184th party gathered for tea and here again were happy children and patient mothers being ministered by the auxiliary's committee. All sorts of races were indulged in after supper by the youngsters whose fathers and brothers left Camp Hughes last September with the 184th Unit.
>
> Conspicuous among the women and children of both groups were several returned men who have already done their bit and have been returned to health and to their families. As twilight fell the happy voices of children, laughing and shouting could still be heard throughout the park and sweet-faced women, many wearing mourning for brave, loved ones who have gone on ahead smiled as they at least found temporary happiness in the enjoyment of the young.

The brutal reality of war – separated families and mass carnage – had reached Assiniboine Park.

Band Concerts, Public Celebrations, Picnics

Band concerts, public celebrations and organized picnics boosted public morale during an excruciatingly difficult war period for Winnipeggers. Performing patriotic tunes, band concerts sponsored by the Parks Board and the Winnipeg Electric Railway Company infused an aura of hopefulness in the assembled public. Official celebrations continued much as they had in the pre-war period. Throngs of people visited Assiniboine Park for Victoria Day, Dominion Day and civic holiday for speeches, band concerts, and sports events. Yet the park remained predominantly a white Anglo-Saxon bastion. Speakers at Assiniboine Park events promoted the war as a project of English-speaking people, even though the empire had entered the war in defence of Belgium and France, and the German Kaiser himself was Queen Victoria's grandson and spoke fluent English.

With many husbands and fathers off to war, fewer people visited Assiniboine Park than in the pre-war years. Streetcar usage declined, and the Winnipeg Electric Railway Company's profits suffered. The streetcar company attempted to increase ridership by organizing band concerts. In August 1916, the company sponsored a free Sunday concert in the park and advertised the event in the city's newspapers including the *Free Press*. Its advertising blatantly promoted streetcar use:

> What is the Band Doing? Why it is practising up some new tunes for the big concert out at Assiniboine Park on Sunday Afternoon from three to five o'clock. A gladsome afternoon for everybody. The band will play under the trees, plenty of room in the shade or sunshine; No long walk. The band will blow you to a good tune and right as you step off the bridge. And just one other point: We of course are supplying the band for your entertainment. There will also be lots of extra cars to take you to the park and back home again. All Car Lines lead to the Park.

The Parks Board continued its sponsorship of summer concerts – but in a more subtle and discreet manner. Bands including those of the Army & Navy Veterans, 184th Battalion, 144th Battalion Bugle, 100th Regiment and First Depot Battalion bands all performed for the public. The Parks Board relied on brief announcements in the newspapers with no glowing and self-promoting advertising.

Much as it had in the past, Assiniboine Park hosted official celebrations of Victoria Day, Dominion Day and the civic holiday. Victoria Day 1917 was typical. Throngs of people visited the park for the events and utilized the streetcar service to the limit. The zoo was a particularly popular escape from war-time realities for young families. According to the *Free Press* "the lazy black bear consumed more peanuts …than in the previous seven months. The swans at the fountain looked their very best for the pleasure of the wide-eyed kiddies and even the little black bear cub indulged in a few original hand springs for the benefit of the visitors."

Lieutenant- Governor
J.A.M. Aikins, 1913
MANITOBA ARCHIVES
PHOTO

The highlight of the war years was undoubtedly Canada's fiftieth birthday celebration in 1917. The Parks Board sponsored a program which included patriotic addresses, martial music and folk dances. Speeches interspersed with music by the Salvation Army band were delivered by Lieutenant-Governor Sir James Aikins; Premier T.C. Norris; Paul Nesbitt of the Oklahoma State Legislature; and William J. Tupper, son of Sir Charles Tupper. Ignoring his role as the impartial Queen's representative, Aikins' speech bordered on racism and xenophobia. Commenting on America's entry into the war, he declared "we are sprung from the same blood as they and God help our enemies when the whole of the English-speaking countries are against them." Aikins railed against immigration and referred to "undesirable foreigners who have been permitted entrance to Canada... We ought perhaps to be a little more careful of whom we allow to colonize this great promised land of ours." Norris avoided the race issue. He welcomed the American delegation to the event. He declared that "this great world war will have the effect of bringing together Canada, Great Britain and the United States in a bond of fellowship that should have been binding many years ago." Folk dances by children representing the Playground Association followed the speeches. For the remainder of the day, visitors attended the Winnipeg Kennel Club dog show at the park entrance, watched cricket matches, played tennis, and visited the zoo. The jubilee ceremonies instilled pride in the war effort and offered an escape from daily life in a city at war – at least for the Anglo-Saxon attendees.

Organized picnics comprised another recreational release from war pressures. Ethnic groups joined the mainstream Anglo-Saxon majority and began holding these events. One group was Winnipeg's Chinese community. In early July 1918, the Chinese Nationalist League requested Parks Board permission to hold their event on a Sunday as members of the community tended their businesses all other days. The Parks Board response was blunt and negative. Secretary J.H. Blackwood wrote "that under no circumstances are public picnic's [sic] of any kind permitted on the Sabbath, nor are any regular sporting programmes permitted under the Lord's Day Alliance [sic] Act, therefore in view of these facts, the Board is unable to comply with your request." Conveniently ignoring Parks Board permission to the military to drill and consequently sin on Sunday and that the Chinese did not practice Christianity, Blackwood extended "with great pleasure" permission to the Chinese to hold a picnic on any other day of the week. Members of the Chinese community were likely offended. Instead, they picnicked at the privately-owned River Park. In complying with Sabbath observance laws, almost the entire Chinese community left their workplaces to participate in the Saturday get-together.

The picnic received considerable press coverage. With utter contempt and racial superiority, the *Free Press* previewed the event. It wrote that "laundry tubs and chop suey boilers will be forgotten by Winnipeg's

The jubilee ceremonies instilled pride in the war effort and offered an escape from daily life in a city at war – at least for the Anglo-Saxon attendees.

China Town" when the community assembled for its Saturday imposed event. It pointed out that the program included "races of various kinds, baseball matches… while several Chinese orchestras will dispense 'music'…The picnic promises to provide some novel entertainment for those citizens who visit the park [and] see for themselves that a Chinaman can forget his scrub board and culinary utensils and partake of the joys of the out of doors." The *Winnipeg Tribune*'s account of July 22, 1918 was more complimentary. After the event, it commented that "many of the contestants in the different sports proved themselves splendid athletes. All of the events were purely Canadian and the way they were handled showed the Chinese are adapting themselves to the Canadian customs quickly and thoroughly."

Children's Activities

The war years witnessed the militarization of children's recreation in Assiniboine Park. Initially in 1914 and 1915, the Playground Association continued its civic holiday Playfest celebrations, but promoted patriotic themes. Lack of funding or the absence of adult organizers led to the discontinuance of Playfest – a gap partly filled by Winnipeg Electric Railway Company field days in 1916. As the war dragged on, the more militarily-oriented Boy Scout movement began supplanting Playground Association activities. As a result of military enlistments, it too faced a shortage of adult leaders.

Much as it had in the past, in the early war years the Playground Association sponsored its annual civic holiday Playfest. The 1914 program differed little from previous celebrations. But in 1915, wartime patriotism made its debut. With a slogan "One King, One Flag, One Empire" and a program starting with a flag salute, dances and flag drills, activities displayed a pro-war orientation. Nevertheless, the children participated in distinctly recreational activities including maypole dancing, playground ball, basketball, dodge ball and volleyball, and for the youngsters, reciting nursery rhymes. About 4,000 children representing the playgrounds of Winnipeg's public schools were transported to Assiniboine Park in special streetcars. Including parents and siblings, on the civic holiday, Assiniboine Park attracted about 10,000 people.

In 1916, the Playground Association ended its Playfest sponsorship. The Winnipeg Electric Railway Company partly filled the void. In several trips, the company chauffeured children under the age of twelve to Assiniboine Park in streetcars for an afternoon of sports and games. The first to participate were nearly 2,000 children from North End playgrounds. Those from Lord Roberts, Gladstone, La Verendrye, Mulvey, Carlton, St. Mary's, Greenway and John M. King Schools and the remainder from Central, Dufferin, Pinkham, Wellington, and Argyle Schools visited Assiniboine Park in two additional trips.

The Playground Association did continue, however, to organize the odd activity. In 1917, children from the association performed folk dances at Canada's 1917 Jubilee celebration – the most popular and largely attended event of the day. At war's end, city council absorbed the Playground Association into the Public Parks Board. According to the *Free Press,* a new goal "will be a concentrated effort to get all children to play. This was the result of the lesson taught by the war."

Towards the latter part of the war, the Boy Scout movement took root in Winnipeg. Unlike the publicly-funded Playgrounds Association, scout groups were sponsored by individuals and churches. In summer 1910, the Boy Scouts commenced Canadian operations. At the request of his friend, Scouts founder Lord Baden-Powell, Governor General Earl Grey organized the first Dominion Scout Council and became the first chief scout of Canada. At the same time, another friend of Baden-Powell's, Colonel Sam B. Steele, established the Manitoba Scout Council.

Initially, the movement grew slowly in Winnipeg with a few scout troops organized by Protestant churches in 1912 and 1913. As the war continued, boys' recreation became more militarized. The Scout Movement offered boys an opportunity to emulate their big brothers and fathers who had enlisted by wearing uniforms, participating in military-like drills and learning outdoor survival skills. In December 1915, the scouting movement introduced the Wolf Cubs program for boys aged nine to twelve. The departure to the war front of male cub masters led the Wolf Cubs to recruit women to lead individual units. A continuous line had been created for boys – first the Wolf Cubs, next the Boy Scouts and finally the military.

Assiniboine Park emerged as a focal point of both Boy Scout and Wolf Cub activities. The first Wolf Cub rally in Winnipeg was held in the park on June 2, 1917, with two wolf packs attending– Deer Lodge and Sparling. As the war drew to a close and with the Playground Association in disarray, the scout movement partly filled the gap for boys' recreation. In September 1919, 900 boys comprising 500 Wolf Cubs and 400 Scouts paraded in Assiniboine Park. Flags were awarded for attendance, correctness of uniforms, cleanliness of person, general smartness and steadiness on parade. The flag presentation ceremony featured motivational speeches by the Provincial Commissioner of Scouts and Colonel J.A. Hesketh, one of the original Canadian scoutmasters who had returned from military service overseas.

Assiniboine Park and the 1919 Winnipeg General Strike

The end of the Great War ushered in a period of labour unrest in Winnipeg and throughout Western Canada. During the final years of the conflict, wages had not kept pace with the rising cost of living. According to historian A. Ross McCormack, the prices of staple items rose by thirteen and a half percent without corresponding wage increases. Moreover, many workers did not enjoy the right of collective bargaining and could not negotiate an improvement in their condition. Inspired by the Bolshevik Revolution of 1917, a group of radical British unionists attempted to usurp Winnipeg's long-established craft unionist movement. They organized workers into the One Big Union and seized control of the Winnipeg Trades & Labor Council. A sympathy strike in support of striking metal workers shut down all commerce in Winnipeg, including municipal government services, for six weeks in 1919. The strike affected Assiniboine Park in terms of lack of maintenance, lower visitation, and reduced revenue from pavilion food services.

The Winnipeg General Strike began on May 6, 1919 and ended on June 21, 1919. At its height, between 25,000 and 30,000 workers including postal employees, taxi drivers, newspaper staff, telegraphers, telephone employees, janitors and elevator operators walked off their jobs. Although many of them had collective agreements, civic employees joined private, provincial and federal sector workers in sympathy. Among others, firefighters struck on May 15, 1919, despite having signed a contract with the city just two weeks earlier. The case of waterworks employees was similar. They also struck and "are ready to shut off water supply if this becomes necessary" despite having their wage demands met after an acrimonious strike in 1918. At the height of the Winnipeg General Strike, municipal services stood in a shambles.

The relative remoteness of Assiniboine Park shielded it from the excesses of the general strike. Lack of streetcar service prevented picketers from reaching the park and disrupting those Parks Board employees who remained on the job. Without a compelling reason to lose wages, some Parks Board employees chose to carry on their normal duties. The zoo, conservatory and flower gardens were unaffected by the strike. According to the *Free Press* "flower beds have been planted, the conservatories have been [looked] after and the animals in the Zoo have received careful attention."

Yet walkouts by labourers elsewhere did affect Assiniboine Park. On June 27, 1919, the *Free Press* commented that "the Assiniboine Park as well as the Kildonan Park have had neglected appearances during the past few weeks owing to the roads being in a state of disrepair. Piles of gravel had been deposited on the roads at the time the strike was called and were therefore left until laborers could be obtained.

Grass grew along the edges of the road." On Dominion Day 1919, "the City park especially resemble[s] a big meadow evident to frequent coils of dried grass."

The strike adversely affected Assiniboine Park in terms of attendance and revenue. Lack of streetcar service deterred many families from visiting the park. Only wealthy individuals with automobiles, cyclists, and residents within walking distance utilized park facilities. Revenue from the pavilion restaurant and takeout counters declined. Only the end of the strike restored visitor attendance and permitted the city to recuperate lost revenues.

Winnipeg city council required all striking civic employees who returned after the work stoppage to sign a pledge of allegiance. On July 4, 1919, Parks Board Secretary J.H. Blackwood wrote the teamsters, the Assiniboine Park constable, and the Assiniboine Park foreman "that all regular employees of the Board who went out on strike or who worked on a strike permit or were members of the Civic Federation at the time of the strike shall be required to sign an agreement pledging loyalty and faithfulness to duty in the future." Three weeks later, Parks Superintendent George Champion wrote the city solicitor concerning relations between the Parks Board and its workers. He indicated that only one unnamed employee who struck had been fired. While many cases of intimidation of parks, cemetery and boulevard workers occurred, he considered none sufficiently serious to warrant action. The Parks Board's

The strike adversely affected Assiniboine Park in terms of attendance and revenue. Lack of streetcar service deterred many families from visiting the park.

only concern were members of the Civic Federation who had struck on Labor Council orders. Champion concluded that "according to personal testimony of many of our employees, they had no grievance whatever, did not vote for a strike and had no wish to go out." At the strike's conclusion, Superintendent Champion only desired a return to normality.

Post-War Celebrations, 1919

Summer, 1919 had arrived. The general strike had ended. Winnipeggers decided en masse to celebrate the war's end and move on with their lives. A massive Peace Day celebration was held in Assiniboine Park on July 19, 1919. A visit and luncheon in honour of the Prince of Wales the following September put closure to the difficult and trying war years and strike months.

Peace Day celebrations enabled Winnipeggers to honour the veterans who had contributed so greatly to the war effort. Thousands of people travelled to Assiniboine Park by streetcar from all parts of the city. The *Free Press* reported that "the pontoon bridge fairly groaned under its burden of humanity, but despite the rumor to the effect it had broken down, the bridge stood the strain and continued to do its duty." Wealthier citizens arrived in their automobiles via River Heights and Tuxedo. Under the auspices of the Welcome Home Fund, veterans and their families participated in organized sports activities. Union Jacks and ribbons fluttered on vehicles and throughout the park. Pipers of the Highland cadets entertained the veterans, their families and thousands of visitors. Multitudes frequented the conservatory with its tropical plants, the zoo, park pathways and picnic tables. The pavilion restaurant and takeout counters experienced a booming business. From nine to eleven in the evening, a noisy and colourful fireworks display capped the day.

The visit of the Prince of Wales to Assiniboine Park put closure to

Prince of Wales leaving Assiniboine Park Pavilion, September 9, 1919
MANITOBA ARCHIVES PHOTO

the war. On September 9, 1919, the city hosted a luncheon in the pavilion for the heir to the British throne. In attendance were Mayor C.F. Gray, Premier T.C. Norris, Lieutenant Governor Aikins, members of the provincial cabinet, the prince's party, and several returned officers. In his speech, the prince praised the work of Winnipeggers during the war, both women and men. Following formalities, the party sat down for a princely meal – roast lamb in mint sauce with celery, stuffed olives, green beans and potatoes, salad with cream dressing, ginger and pineapple cremes, ice cream cake, fruit, tea and coffee, followed by cigars and cigarettes. The luncheon marked a fitting end to years of warfare and labour instability.

The Rise of Grand Beach

Towards the end of the Great War, Grand Beach emerged as another summer alternative to Assiniboine Park. Experiencing financial difficulties, the Canadian Northern Railway foresaw Grand Beach as a money-making proposition capable of alleviating its woes. The site selected offered spectacular scenery – a large sheltered harbour, great expanses of sand beach and sand dunes rising to heights of twenty feet or more. In 1915, the Canadian Northern laid a fifty-eight-mile (93.34 kilometre) line from Winnipeg to Grand Marais (Grand Beach). On March 24, 1915, the *Free Press* predicted that Grand Beach was "destined to become Winnipeg's choicest summer resort."

The Canadian Northern Railway advertised Grand Beach as featuring the largest and safest bathing beach in the West. It boasted about the facility's dance pavilion, refreshment booths, bath houses and beautiful walking trails under a canopy of immense birch, spruce, oak, elm and ash trees. It offered visitors athletic grounds, baseball diamonds, and rental canoes and boats. For Dominion Day 1916, the Canadian Northern Railway operated excursions leaving Union Station three times that day. Single day return excursions for $1.00 and a moonlight return of 50 cents stood well within the reach of many Winnipeggers. By 1918, Grand Beach equalled both Winnipeg Beach and Assiniboine Park in terms of summer holiday and Saturday popularity. During the civic holiday of that year the *Free Press* reported that nearly 15,000 people visited Grand Beach. "Many crowded trains left Union Station at all hours of the morning and the 'moonlight' added the usual quota of pleasure seekers." At the height of the short prairie summer, the popularity of Grand Beach eased the weekend congestion at Assiniboine Park at the end of the war and would continue to do so for over four decades.

Assiniboine Park had offered Winnipeggers a place of peace and tranquility where citizens could seek temporary solace from the stresses of the war. The zoo, conservatory, picnic grounds, playing fields and pathways all performed their part. At the same time, Winnipeggers converged upon the park for the traditional Victoria Day and Dominion Day holidays featuring patriotic speeches promoting the war effort. Towards the end of the war, the development of Grand Beach complemented Winnipeg Beach in offering alternatives to Assiniboine Park.

Chapter Six:
Towards A Modern Park, 1920–1938

On January 1, 1920, as the brutally cold prairie winter continued its icy grip, Winnipeg turned the calendar on a period of war and labour unrest. For the next ten years, the city enjoyed prosperity, followed by a decade of the worst depression Canada had ever experienced. Through these years, Assiniboine Park continued to attract Winnipeggers seeking a nearby escape from the stresses of city life.

Duck Pond Facing
Second Pavilion
after 1932 RANDY R.
ROSTECKI COLLECTION

Whether born inside or outside the country, everyone was Canadian and began appropriating Assiniboine Park as their own.

Change happened both to and in the park. Both in the prosperous 1920s and the financially challenging Great Depression, the road and building infrastructure was upgraded. During this time, the old notion of Canada as a component of a greater British Empire gave way to the emergence of a distinct national identity. Whether born inside or outside the country, everyone was Canadian and began appropriating Assiniboine Park as their own. The park began attracting residents from all walks of life – not just the middle-class Anglo-Saxon majority. By 1939, what was generally known as "city park" emerged as a modern and welcoming destination for all.

The Concept of Assiniboine Park

In 1921, the Parks Board re-stated the prevailing and longstanding concept of Assiniboine Park as being free to all, undisturbed by profit-making amusements, a sanctuary where the public enjoyed fresh air in idyllic surroundings. A proposal by businessman Charles Vanderlip prompted the Parks Board to take the unusual step of reaffirming Henry Sandison's original plans from 1903. In April 1921, the Parks Board received a request from Vanderlip applying for a concession to operate miniature sightseeing trains in both Assiniboine and Kildonan Parks. The park committee of the Public Parks Board reviewed the proposal and prepared a report. They concluded that any service device or amusement feature necessary in a public park should be installed and operated by the Parks Board for the benefit of the public. Furthermore, the Parks Board should discourage applications for amusement concessions by private operators in public parks "particularly because of the children and the temptation to spend money that the parents cannot afford." The report concluded that "outdoor season in Winnipeg is short and more and more each year the people are beginning to appreciate the value of the open air and beautiful surroundings in which to seek recreation...To operate any catchpenny device...is to admit that the parks are not fulfilling the functions for which they are intended." For the 1920s at least, the

Man Posing on Dilapidated
Seasonal Foot Bridge before
its Dismantlement, 1930
RANDY R. ROSTECKI COLLECTION –
PHOTO OF K. ROSTECKI

Parks Board held steadfast in upholding this vision of the park.

Infrastructure Improvements

During the interwar period, Assiniboine Park underwent many physical improvements. The Parks Board completed successful negotiations with surrounding municipalities for the long-sought permanent connection over the Assiniboine River, the extension of Assiniboine Park on the north side of the river and a scenic riverfront parkway linking the east boundary with River Heights. Within the park, a picturesque and fire-resistant new pavilion welcomed visitors after the original structure succumbed to fire. The precursor to the English Garden, the Informal Garden, drew multitudes of visitors with its colourful array of seasonal flowers and shrubs.

All these improvements marked the beginning of the modern park.

The construction of a vehicular traffic bridge over the Assiniboine River to the immediate west of Assiniboine Park had been a goal of the Parks Board since the park officially opened in 1909. Having failed to secure an agreement with the Municipality of Assiniboia before and during the Great War, the Parks Board attempted once again to move the project forward. As the portion of Assiniboia lying south of the Assiniboine River had been excised from the Municipality when the RM of Charleswood and the Town of Tuxedo were created, the Parks Board now negotiated with three municipalities. Moreover, the proposed location of the bridge lay outside City of Winnipeg boundaries

Winter Photo of First
Pavilion, ca. 1920s
MANITOBA ARCHIVES
PHOTO

did not need a road link to the largely residential Tuxedo or semi-rural Charleswood. A permanent foot-bridge over the Assiniboine River for year-round park access to its residents would suffice. A permanent structure would negate Assiniboia's need to establish its own park system.

Throughout the 1920s, the Parks Board negotiated with the Municipality of Assiniboia (later St. James), Charleswood and Tuxedo for the erection of a bridge. Lack of funding from the Parks Board, the municipalities and the provincial government prevented progress from being made. Moreover, the three parties could not agree on the location of the bridge or whether it would be multi-purpose or for foot traffic only. As an interim measure, each spring Parks Board workers erected the seasonal footbridge. In autumn they dismantled it. Alongside the city's right of way from Portage Avenue to the seasonal bridge, park visitors endured aggressive hucksters in ramshackle structures peddling confectionery and snacks – a distraction from the quiet Arcadian escape lying across the Assiniboine River.

and would abut on Assiniboia and Charleswood lands. Understandably, each municipality promoted its own interests. The Parks Board desired easy year-round vehicular, street railway and pedestrian access from Portage Avenue into the park. The municipalities of Charleswood and Tuxedo needed a vehicular bridge to Portage Avenue for their auto-mobile-owning residents. Assiniboia

In 1929, the Public Parks Board and St. James negotiated an agreement to extend Assiniboine Park from the north side of the Assiniboine River to Portage Avenue in exchange for a permanent pedestrian bridge over the Assiniboine River. The Municipality of St. James donated two land parcels comprising parts of River Lots 23 & 24, Parish of St. James fronting Portage Avenue to the immediate east and west of the 144-foot (nearly forty-four metre) right of way used as an approach to the seasonal footbridge. The property transferred possessed a frontage over 600 feet (182.88 metres) and with existing Parks Board property measured about 740 feet (225.56 metres) along Portage Avenue. With an average depth to the river of approximately 300 feet (just over ninety-one metres), the land parcel comprised five acres and was valued at over $30,000.

Ratified by Parks Board Bylaw and legalized by provincial statute, the agreement between St. James and the Parks Board dated March 21, 1929 incorporated a number of terms. St. James transferred the lands free from all future municipal, school and local improvement taxes. If St. James constructed a sidewalk alongside Portage Avenue park frontage, it would receive $500 from the Parks Board. When requested to do so, St. James would supply Assiniboine Park with metered water at the same rate paid by its residents. The agreement placed building restrictions on all Portage Avenue lands within 300 feet (91.44 metres) of the park. It required St. James to enact a bylaw outlawing buildings "which would be detrimental to the use of the said lands for park purposes." The Parks Board also adhered to specific terms. It agreed to prohibit "hawkers, peddlers or transient traders" from engaging in any business on the properties or "permit the operation of any catch-penny devices, circus features," or anything detrimental to park purposes. Foremost among terms, within seven years of the agreement, the Parks Board would erect a permanent pedestrian bridge across the Assiniboine River.

For almost three years, the Parks Board unsuccessfully sought funding for a permanent bridge over the Assiniboine River. The Great Depression settled in and reduced economic activity in Winnipeg to a fraction of its former level. To alleviate hardships among workers, the Dominion, provincial and municipal governments began financing local public works projects. On August 14, 1931, the Parks Board voted to proceed with the pedestrian bridge.

The Parks Board instructed the city engineer to prepare plans for submission to the Special Committee of Council on Unemployment Relief Work. Designed by the city engineer, final plans called for a "handsome ferro concrete structure" of cantilever design measuring 576 feet long (175.56 metres) with a twelve-foot (nearly four metres) walkway brightly illuminated with twenty lamps on concrete standards. The city awarded the construction contract to the lowest tender, Carter Halls Aldinger. The $47,000 cost was divided between the three levels of government with Canada paying fifty percent of the total.

On Saturday, May 21, 1932, the permanent pedestrian bridge to Assiniboine Park opened with

great fanfare. Bunting and flags festooned the sides of the structure. Winnipeg Mayor Ralph Webb cut a ceremonial tape across the centre of the bridge. Parks Board Chairman W. Percy White, St. James councillor Ronald Hooper, provincial Minister of Health & Welfare Dr. E.W. Montgomery and architect George W. Northwood, supervisor of Unemployment Relief Work, delivered short laudatory speeches. For the first time, pedestrians could reach Assiniboine Park year-round from Portage Avenue.

Second and Permanent
Footbridge over
Assiniboine River, 2018
PHOTOS BY AUTHOR

Throughout much of its time, the Parks Board dreamed of the construction of a scenic, riverfront driveway with panoramic river and riparian forest views open to cars and bicycles linking the old agricultural college to Assiniboine Park. On April 19, 1928, the Parks Board recommended that Tuxedo carry out the project with funding from that municipality, the city of Winnipeg, and the Dominion government. While wishing to reap the benefits, Tuxedo expressed little interest in participating in the project. Six months elapsed before Tuxedo issued a counterproposal. It offered to convey to Winnipeg for park purposes a 300-foot (91.44 metres) strip of land from the Assiniboine River to what is now Wellington Crescent between the old agricultural college and Assiniboine Park. The onus would be on the city to undertake construction. The Parks Board accepted the offer.

Ratified by City Bylaw No. 13123 and legalized by provincial statute, the agreement between the City of Winnipeg and the Town of Tuxedo dated February 19, 1929 established terms for the land transfer.

The lands would be exempt from all taxation, whether municipal, school or for local improvements. Tuxedo retained an easement to repair, maintain or construct sewers, hydrants, electrical and telephone poles and police boxes on the property. Most importantly, the city was required to construct and maintain a gravelled roadway to Assiniboine Park by December 31, 1930 without, peculiarly, resorting to the use of oil or tar. Prior to the same date, the city agreed to complete all under brushing, grass cutting, and tree trimming on the property while maintaining it to Assiniboine Park standards.

Tuxedo also wished to maintain its exclusivity as a residential neighbourhood. Therefore, the agreement prohibited the construction of visually distracting streetcar lines along the roadway without the town's consent and totally banned

Tuxedo also wished to maintain its exclusivity as a residential neighbourhood … and totally banned picnicking, loitering or vehicle parking on the lands.

picnicking, loitering or vehicle parking on the lands.

As warm weather ushered in spring 1931, Winnipeggers could drive or cycle along Wellington Crescent from the Maryland Bridge to Assiniboine Park. In Tuxedo, however, they could not stop, park their cars, dismount their bicycles, enjoy the view and picnic. Tuxedo was an exclusive place.

Since the park's opening in 1909, it had been a desire of city council and the Public Parks Board to possess a lake and public bathing beach within Assiniboine Park's boundaries. But nature did not bless Assiniboine Park with a natural lake. So the Parks Board turned to man-made means for inspiration. The Parks Board reasoned a dam across the Assiniboine River near the park's eastern boundary would flood the deep river valley upstream, create an artificial lake and permit the construction of a sandy bathing beach within park limits. Evidently not considered were the damages flooding might inflict on private lands on the north side of the river

for which the Parks Board would be financially liable. Moreover, the Dominion government exercised administration and control of the Assiniboine River pursuant to the Manitoba Act and Navigable Waters Protection Act. The latter statute explicitly stated that "No work shall be built or placed…across any navigable water unless the site thereof has been approved by the Governor in Council, nor unless such work is built, placed and maintained in accordance with plans and regulations…made by the Governor in Council." It remained unlikely that the Dominion Government would issue Privy Council approval for a structure intended solely for recreational purposes.

Nevertheless, the Parks Board decided to act. At a meeting on July 16, 1931, Chairman H.H. Cottingham spoke about the proposed dam across the Assiniboine River. He pointed to the possibility for provincial and Dominion government assistance utilizing unemployment relief funds. The Parks Board passed a motion requesting the city engineer take necessary

borings and levels on the Assiniboine River frontage, prepare preliminary plans and a cost estimate.

A month later, the Parks Board received blueprints from the city engineer and bacteriological and chemical analyses of Assiniboine River water. Parks Board passed a motion to submit the scheme to city council for funding under "Unemployment Relief."

In October 1931, the ill-conceived and poorly-concocted proposal which would have wreaked havoc to Assiniboine Park's riparian forest, drowned its woodland walking paths, and flooded lands on the north side of the river, died a fortunate death. While funding the Salter Bridge and the pedestrian bridge over the Assiniboine River, the Dominion government's representative on unemployment relief in Manitoba, architect George

W. Northwood, rejected the $87,500 Assiniboine Park dam and bathing beach proposal. The scheme would never be resurrected.

At 3 AM on May 27, 1929, the attractive but shoddily built twenty-year-old pavilion succumbed to flames. According to the *Free Press* account, even from far away downtown "the blaze was most spectacular, lighting the sky with a vivid glow." At 3:45 AM "the tower fell with a loud crash sending showers of sparks flying through the morning air." Efforts to save the building proved futile. The *Tribune* remarked that when firefighters finally arrived from the distant Dorchester and Wilton Avenue fire hall, the building was "doomed."

Ruins of First Pavilion after Fire, 1929
CITY OF WINNIPEG ARCHIVES PHOTO

Much guessing ensued on the cause of the conflagration. Parks Board Secretary J.H. Blackwood hypothesized that the building had been burglarized, because goods found scattered throughout the park appeared similar to those sold

New Pavilion after its Construction, 1930s
MANITOBA ARCHIVES PHOTO

in the pavilion. In his 1929 annual report, Parks Board Chairman John Easton attributed the fire to "boys breaking in to obtain supplies of candies, cigarettes, etc. and for lack of lighting facilities used matches that were carelessly thrown down."

No accounts of criminal charges or convictions were published in the daily press. However, the building's demise passed unlamented. Parks Board Superintendent George Champion noted that the pavilion "was in all respects except appearance out of date and inadequate."

With uncharacteristic haste, the Parks Board initiated construction of the new and current pavilion. On the day of the fire, the Parks Board authorized erection of a new structure. Avoiding the niceties of a competition, the board appointed veteran architects Northwood and Chivers to prepare plans. The board struck a committee comprised of Chairman John Easton, member and contractor James McDiarmid, Secretary J.H. Blackwood and Superintendent George Champion to assist the architects in planning the overall design. Less than two weeks later, Northwood & Chivers submitted

their plans which the board readily approved. To save funds, one key element was left out – a heating system. According to Public Parks Board minutes "the heating of the building [is to] be omitted but in putting in the foundation and cellar provision [is to] be made for the installation of a heating plant if found necessary at some future date." On July 18, 1929, the Parks Board awarded J.A. Tremblay the construction contract for a total of $77,800.

Constructed that year, the pavilion constituted an imposing structure. Measuring seventy by 110 feet (twenty-one and a third by thirty-three and a half metres) it reputedly projected an "early English style, half timbered and stucco." The foundation rested on piles driven to the bedrock. The superstructure utilized steel and timber, heavily insulated and fireproofed with concrete basement and floor slabs. Northwood and Chivers retained the pergola, garden and pool features of the former pavilion. They extended the pergola on each side of the building around the north end of the pool where the annex to the former structure stood.

Northwood & Chivers, Architects

The current Assiniboine Park Pavilion comprises the effort of two of Winnipeg's veteran architects, George W. Northwood and Cyril W.U. Chivers. Both had prospered in Winnipeg for decades before partnering in the mid-1920s in the latter part of their careers.

Northwood was born in Ottawa in 1876. Graduating from McGill University in 1900, he was one of the early Canadian university-trained architects. After practising in Ottawa for a few years, he relocated to Winnipeg in 1906. In the pre-World War I period, he specialized in designing branch banks for Canada's rapidly expanding financial institutions throughout the Western provinces.

The First World War interrupted his career and he served overseas briefly before being captured by the Germans and surviving three years in a prisoner-of-war camp. In 1918, he returned to Winnipeg and resumed his architectural career.

George W. Northwood, 1915 – Co-Architect of Second Pavilion "MISSING OFFICER," *MANITOBA FREE PRESS*, MAY 8, 1915

Chivers was born in England in 1879 and arrived in Manitoba with his family in 1897. He obtained an architectural education by apprenticing under Winnipeg architects S. Frank Peters and George Browne and working as a draftsman for the Canadian Pacific Railway. Starting in 1908, and interrupted by a wartime stint in Europe, his architectural practice concentrated on the design of apartment blocks and residences.

In 1926, Northwood formed a partnership with Chivers. Northwood focussed on securing clients and managing the business while Chivers drafted plans for many of the city's iconic 1920s and 1930s edifices, including the Wheat Board Building on Main near McDermot, the Dominion Public Building at Main and Water, and the Winnipeg Civic Auditorium (now the Manitoba Archives Building) at Vaughan and St. Mary. The Assiniboine Park Pavilion of 1929 constitutes one of the firm's most visible and admired creations.

Cyril M.U. Chivers, 1918 – Co-Architect of Second Pavilion "MILITARY CROSS FOR WINNIPEGGER," *MANITOBA FREE PRESS*, JANUARY 8, 1918

In his 1929 annual report, Superintendent Champion predicted that the new pavilion would last a century. Thirty-six years after its completion, architect Cyril Chivers reflected on his design. His goal, he declared, embraced all European cultures. Punctuated by deliberately defaced timbers, the building's rustic appearance represented an "English country club" with elements of a "French" continental flavor. The tower imitated a Bavarian town hall and the influence of "German discipline." The "lover's walk garden" at the north side of the building imparted American values. In short, the pavilion would welcome all peoples of European ancestry regardless of culture.

Thirty-six years after its completion, architect Cyril Chivers reflected on his design. His goal, he declared, embraced all European cultures.

Today's English Garden dates from the interwar period; it was the idea of then superintendent George Champion. Trained as a landscape gardener in England, Champion penned plans for Kildonan Park, St. Vital Park, Kildonan and later Windsor Golf Courses after succeeding D.D. England as the Parks Board's superintendent in 1906. Champion proved determined to leave his mark on Assiniboine Park. In May 1927, he proposed converting the plant nursery north of the zoo into an elaborate flower garden. The Parks Board authorized Champion to proceed over a several-year time frame. By season's end of 1931, planting had advanced to the final stage and the tree nursery relocated to an unused corner of the Windsor Golf Course. Soon the completed garden displayed artistic enhancements. In June 1935, E.H. Macklin donated a sundial in memory of his late friend, journalist Harry Sifton, the son of Clifford Sifton. Erected at the northwest corner of the acreage with the woods as a backdrop, the structure was mounted on a pedestal designed by architect Cyril Chivers.

From its inception, the Informal Garden, as it was known, drew large crowds. On Labour Day 1934, the *Free Press* reported that "the big attraction at Assiniboine Park was the perennial garden by the riverside which was thronged all afternoon by lovers of flowers who streamed in steadily to feast their senses on the gorgeous floral bouquet." The English Garden, as it was dubbed in the 1950s, has continued to delight the children, grandchildren and great-grandchildren of these first visitors.

At the height of the Great Depression, the Parks Board continued to spend scarce funds on park infrastructure. One such expenditure (which also resulted in cost savings) lay in consolidating greenhouse operations from several locations scattered throughout the city into Assiniboine Park. In July 1934, the Parks Board approved the erection of two prefabricated steel frame greenhouses each measuring twenty-five by 100 feet (seven and two thirds by thirty and a half metres) to replace those in Notre Dame Park. The $3,000 for steel frames from Greenhouses and Conservatories Limited at Humber Bay, Ontario comprised only the beginning. Walls, benches, drains, window glass, heating plant, coal storage bins, and a service corridor, in addition to the cost of day labour raised the total five-fold. City council withheld funding and two years elapsed before completion of the structures.

At the end of 1936, Parks Board Chairman John A. Flanders wrote that the board's greenhouses had been concentrated to the east of the conservatory and a new boiler and self-feeder installed to heat the combined plant. Having all greenhouses in one location enabled the Parks Board to achieve continuous savings in labour and transportation costs.

Administration of Food Services

In the late interwar period, the Public Parks Board abandoned its three-decade-old iron-fist grip on food outlets. Instead of running them itself, it leased all concessions in Assiniboine, Kildonan and Sargent Parks and Kildonan and Windsor Golf Courses for a fixed return. It took this step in an effort to generate revenue for a financially challenged city council.

The self-administered food system had also proved to be time consuming, labour intensive and unwieldy to maintain. Each spring the Parks Board called tenders for the food items it stocked or utilized in its restaurants – all food and drinks, as well as cigarettes, cigars, tobacco, camera film and chewing gum. The Parks Board stringently controlled quality and set prices. In 1929, the refectories accepted only certified milk containing five percent butterfat. Milk sold for ten cents per bottle while bottled soft drinks also commanded ten cents and fountain drinks half that amount. Secretary James H. Blackwood summed up Parks Board philosophy by writing that "our motto has always been that we operate to supply the demand but not to create it and therefore the health and wellbeing of the public and not profits are our first consideration."

At the height of the Depression, the need to generate revenue for the city overrode philosophical considerations. Therefore in 1936, the Parks Board privatized the food outlets in Assiniboine, Kildonan, and Sargent parks and the two public golf courses. In his 1937 annual report, Parks Superintendent F.T.G. White, successor to the retired George Champion, described the move as "a departure from the general policy." But the new leases yielded solid and welcome returns – $2,150 in 1936 and $5,500 a year later. Moreover, White was able to report "the Lessee gave satisfactory service, only a few minor complaints being

recorded." The experiment with privatization proved highly successful. In 1938, all park and golf course food concessions were leased to one tenderer for a three-year term of $13,500 payable in three instalments. Superintendent White concluded that "services were maintained in a very satisfactory manner and these premises kept in a clean and orderly condition." The move to modern privately-operated food concessions had been permanently established and would continue for the next seventy-five years.

Towards a Modern Zoo

During the Great Depression, the Parks Board took its first slow, halting and tentative steps in transforming the zoo from a popular but haphazard confined animal menagerie into a modern zoological garden. At the worst economic period in its history, and with little funds at its disposal, the Parks Board confronted a confident, strident and newly emergent conservation and animal welfare movement. Animal welfare advocates sought to shut down zoo operations – or at the

Bear Pit, Assiniboine Park Zoo, 1930s
MANITOBA ARCHIVES PHOTO

very least to provide spacious and comfortable quarters for animals to replicate their lives in the wild (minus the predators!). A spirited public debate on the future of the Assiniboine Park Zoo ensued.

The zoo of the late 1920s and 1930s resembled the menagerie of the pre-World War I period and had changed little in fifteen years. Its primitive quarters housed black bears, elk, foxes, badgers, beavers, raccoons, buffalo, monkeys, deer, squirrels, wolves, alligators and a wide variety of birds. Throughout the interwar years, the few additions were acquired mainly by donation – bighorn sheep from the Calgary Zoological Society, two young lions from Winnipeg members of Khartum Shrine, a young polar bear from a trapper on Hudson's Bay, alligators from a Jacksonville, Florida game farm, and a raccoon that had been terrorizing a Norwood chicken coop and had been captured by the coop owner while it was napping after a meal.

Beside the donations, the zoo had a prolific breeding program. In 1934 alone, the Parks Board dispatched free of charge a pair of elk to the Fort Frances Parks Board, a young bighorn sheep to the Toronto Parks Department and five bears and three white-tailed deer to Riding Mountain National Park to be released into the wild.

Yet the Parks Board erected no new animal enclosures for the additions. Only a new deer yard and buffalo corral were added to accommodate the growing collection. But multitudes of visitors entered the zoo's confines. In his annual report of 1929, Superintendent Champion remarked that "judging by the number of visitors this modest collection of live things is the most appreciated of all the amenities provided by the Board for the public."

Under his nom de plume, Grey Owl, conservationist Archibald Belaney initiated and led a spirited public discussion of animal welfare at the Assiniboine Park Zoo. Born in Hastings, England in 1888, Belaney emigrated to Canada at age seventeen and reimagined himself as the offspring of an Indigenous scout and an Apache woman. He learned

Grey Owl (Archibald Belaney)
1930s MANITOBA ARCHIVES
PHOTO

trapping from a woodsman in the Temagami region of northeastern Ontario and learned Indigenous culture from a series of women he married but never divorced. In Ontario, he married an Indigenous woman named Anahareo who inspired him to leave trapping and become a pioneering conservationist and writer. In 1931, Dominion Parks Commissioner James B. Harkin appointed Belaney as a conservationist in Riding Mountain National Park. His job entailed publicizing the National Parks system and reintroducing beavers, which had been trapped to near extinction, to the western parks. According to biographer Donald B. Smith, for the latter role "Archie was extremely nervous. Despite his years of trapping, he still knew relatively little about beaver." The welfare of beavers at the Assiniboine Park Zoo enticed Belaney to travel to Winnipeg and plead with the Parks Board for more spacious and humane accommodations for the giant rodents than the concrete pool they endured.

Belaney arrived in Winnipeg from Riding Mountain National Park in October 1931. In an interview with the *Free Press*, he warned Winnipeggers that a radical change in the housing of Assiniboine Park's beavers was required "to save the captives a slow death within a year." He also obtained an audience with Mayor Ralph Webb, whom he informed "that the present care accorded the beaver was only a refinement of cruelty." He offered Webb two options: the removal of the beaver to Riding Mountain National Park or the construction of more suitable enclosures.

Belaney's criticism drew a sharp response. He had made his comments from second-hand information before visiting the beaver enclosure.

Moreover, he failed to follow proper civil service protocol by first meeting with appointed peers before approaching the mayor and press. A few days after the *Free Press* article, Belaney met with Assiniboine Park Superintendent F.T.G. White and inspected the beaver enclosure. Later summarizing the meeting, White voiced barely restrained anger. He pointed out that the zoo's beavers "were in perfect health…The three present occupants have been there [Assiniboine Park] since 1926 and we are rather proud of their condition." He expressed surprise that in the newspaper article Belaney "had been talking about something of which he knew very little…My opinion was strengthened when in interviewing Grey Owl at the park he told me…that he was agreeably surprised that everything was in better condition than he had anticipated."

Once back in Riding Mountain National Park, Belaney wrote Herbert Cottingham, Parks Board Chairman, reiterating his earlier criticism of the beaver enclosure. Prefacing a description and sketch plan for more beaver-friendly quarters, Belaney declared that "if they are to serve for our pleasure, a term of life

[Belaney] warned Winnipeggers that a radical change in the housing of Assiniboine Park's beavers was required "to save the captives a slow death within a year."

imprisonment, let us at least make their incarceration as cheerful as possible thereby keeping them happy." He recommended the construction of a circular enclosure with a low fence six feet high (nearly two metres) on the river side to prevent the animals from escaping. Detailing the materials to be used, he recommended several truckloads of muskeg mud or peat clay or loose earth – not sand or gravel. Belaney stressed that beavers must be fed their natural diet – poplar leaves on the branch during summer, willow leaves, some dry chunks of spruce or balsam, particularly in the fall or winter. Belaney's comments made good sense. But Parks Board Superintendent Champion responded with a perfunctory thank you and that he would consider the matter in the next Parks Board's estimates. Facing scarce Depression-era funding, that was all Champion could promise.

Local conservationist and animal welfare advocate Tony Lascelles followed in Belaney's footsteps. A naturalist, writer for outdoor magazines, and a wildlife photographer, he had resided for thirty years in Western Canada and in Riding Mountain National Park and its antecedent, the Riding Mountain Forest Reserve, from 1924 to 1933. In 1933 and 1934, Eaton's Department Store employed him to introduce and explain films about beavers produced by the Dominion Parks Branch which the store aired free to the public. Lascelle's analysis of animal accommodation extended beyond

Big Horn Sheep, 1938
MANITOBA ARCHIVES
PHOTO

the beaver enclosure to the entire Assiniboine Park Zoo collection.

On June 14, 1933, Lascelles issued a scathing condemnation of zoo conditions. He declared that the pens housing the birds and animals "are little better than prisons to the unfortunate beasts confined therein." He decried the box-like cages of squirrels, owls, eagles and the concrete pond to which beavers were confined. He lamented the life of "wolves and foxes pacing in the manner of all caged things seeking their liberty." Lascelles made a passionate plea for freeing the animals – or at the minimum providing better living conditions. Animals, he argued, are more stoical than humans, "accepting their conditions and that food, water and shelter does not suffice to fill the natural requirements of existence. To breathe the fresh air and go an unhindered way is the heritage of all living things given by the Creator at the beginning of time." At the minimum, he concluded, if "we must cage wild things for the edification of a curious and seemingly unconcerned populace, we can at least provide a reasonably large environment simulating a nature home as is provided in part for the large species within paddocks and grassy enclosures."

A staunch advocate of the Assiniboine Park Zoo which he had been instrumental in developing, George Champion attempted to rebut Lascelle's criticism. He defended the major zoos for providing comfortable housing and care for all animals. In response to questions from the *Tribune* on the same day, he asserted that all leading zoo managers believed that wild animals enjoyed a more fulfilling existence in zoological gardens than in the wild. "In captivity they are safe from their natural enemies, and their average life is longer. The life of the ordinary wild animal is a fierce and continued struggle for existence and for sustenance against its natural enemies, including man."

However, Assiniboine Park Zoo was not without fault according to Champion. "We could add considerably to the pleasure of animals by spending money to make their condition a still more natural one. But we have done the very best with the limited funds at our disposal." Only limited Depression-era funding, Champion believed, prevented the zoo from meeting critics' demands for improved animal housing.

Inspired by professional conservationists like Grey Owl and Tony Lascelles, the public began advocating for animal welfare in the 1930s. Letters to the editor appeared in the *Free Press* criticizing conditions in the Assiniboine Park Zoo and recommending freeing the animals or constructing more commodious and improved enclosures. On June 30, 1931, "Animal Lover" wrote to the *Free Press*. He (or she) described the zoo as "a cruelty to animals" – but no worse than other zoos and certainly not one which tortured its denizens. In fact, the writer complimented the facility for its deer, bison and bird enclosures; the animals are "happy and well housed in large meadows and grassy pens." Such favourable conditions did not apply to the monkeys, bears, foxes, coyotes and porcupines. They endured sub-standard housing. "Animal Lover" questioned placing animals in captivity. "Animals in cages are not

"Animals in cages are not like animals in the woods. They are half dead while they still live."

A bear watches visitors from its pen at the Assiniboine Park Zoo c. 1930 MANITOBA ARCHIVES PHOTO

like animals in the woods. They are half dead while they still live. The caging of wild creatures is a mean and cowardly act unworthy of those who profess themselves human." Five years later on June 18, 1936, "Animal Lover" picked up the pen again. This time he (or she) complained about the condition of the bear enclosure. "The poor unfortunate bears were roasting under the rays of a tropical sun encouraged by the reflection from the hot concrete floor... Why not be humane to the animals and give each group a decent pen, with plenty of space? God never intended these denizens of the plain and forest to be crowded into enclosures for the benefit of amusing human beings... It would be a pleasure to watch the same animals after having been a month in pleasant surroundings. They would take a new interest in their location."

Letter writer Charles Goodyear expanded upon the woes of the bear enclosure. In a September 24, 1938, letter to the *Free Press* he asserted that "it is not a natural habitation. In this day four young ones were stretched out on the concrete floor panting for breath, with the hot sun streaming down on them and not a breath of air to cool them. They were rolling in their offal and presently got into their drinking pool in this condition. It was too disgusting for words." The writer recommended the bears should be housed in a large enclosure with room to roam and "sniff clear fresh air" and that they should be given running water to drink.

Soon the criticism from Winnipeg's citizenry of Assiniboine Park's animal enclosures would be too great to ignore. In his 1936 annual report, Parks Board Chairman John A. Flanders wrote that "it is to be regretted that through lack of suitable quarters for many of our animals they are not on view during the winter months. Shortage of funds has prevented the erection of even an initial unit of a zoo. This is a needed development. [Heated winter quarters] would greatly increase the popularity of Assiniboine Park during our long winters." A year later, Flanders lamented "the inadequacies of our zoo buildings." He declared that "the present buildings that contain our animals are a disgrace and a new building will have to be erected unless we dispose of some of our most popular animals."

The Parks Board dispatched newly appointed Parks Superintendent F.T.G. White to inspect the Brookfield Zoo in Chicago. Flanders and an unnamed Parks Board member also met with the superintendent of the Como Park Zoo to discuss and inspect that park's animal enclosures. With new enthusiasm, the Parks Board contracted architects Moody & Moore to design a new zoo building. A modest structure, plans called for an edifice measuring twenty-two by forty-five feet (almost fourteen by seven metres) of frame construction on a concrete foundation with partial basement for a heating plant and an external stucco and ornamental cement finish. The building remained unexecuted; no public funds were available.

In 1938, the Parks Board exerted pressure on city council to fund new animal enclosures. It threatened to dispose of Assiniboine Park's most popular assets – its two lions. On August 17, the Parks Board discussed the lions' fate. The Parks Committee of the Parks Board proposed that "the lions be disposed of by sale or gift or if necessary, destroyed." A week later, the Parks Board wrote Winnipeg Shriners, donors of the lions, for their suggestions. Not surprisingly, the Shriners expressed alarm. On September 21, 1938 a delegation from Khartum Shrine met with the Parks Board. The Parks Board appointed a committee to work with three Shriner counterparts on a solution to retain the beasts in Assiniboine Park. No action was taken. The lions continued to live temporarily in their concrete and barred enclosure.

In 1939, the first tentative and halting steps towards a modern zoo took shape. In April of that year, the Parks Board approved construction of a suitable zoo building for a maximum of $8,000. On May 4, 1939, the board awarded the construction contract to John Gunn & Sons. The board appointed members W.C. Birt, James Simpkin, and the superintendent to select a site for the building. As summer 1939 drew to a close, the parks board took possession of the new edifice. Designed by Parks Board employees according to Superintendent F.T.G. White's instructions, the visually pleasing building featured a reinforced concrete base, frame and stucco construction and housed the lions, other animals and birds. As the clouds of war descended once again upon Canada in autumn 1939, a modern

As the clouds of war descended once again upon Canada in autumn 1939, a modern zoo with spacious animal enclosures awaited more peaceful times.

zoo with spacious animal enclosures awaited more peaceful times.

Towards a More Inclusive Park

In the interwar years, Assiniboine Park evolved into a more welcoming place for all Winnipeggers, regardless of ethnicity or physical handicap. Religious minorities and people with disabilities chose Assiniboine Park's vast lawns and groves as the venue for their picnics and sports events. Secular organizations such as the Boy Scouts flaunted Sunday observance laws and at least on one occasion held a Sunday jamboree. City council hosted civic lunches in the pavilion for visiting sports teams, including the Hakoah soccer club of Vienna, Austria, which was comprised entirely of Jewish players. Of course, traditional recreational uses continued.

On summer Saturdays, Protestant church groups held picnics and field days much as they had since 1909. Gone were many of the religious aspects to recreational activities. On Sundays the bands hired by the Parks Board to entertain visitors confined their repertoire to secular music. In the interlude between the two world wars, Winnipeggers from all walks of life sought the idyllic Assiniboine Park surroundings as an escape from the city's hustle and bustle.

Interwar sporting events exhibited a diversity unheard of in Assiniboine Park's formative years. The boy scouts were the first to test the prevailing orthodoxy. In May 1921, the organization held its field day on a Sunday – a clear challenge to Sabbath observance laws. The program included the usual sprints, running, high jump, broad jump, shot put, and baseball throwing events. Absent from the program were marching drills and formations. The boy scouts had discarded their paramilitary training for more peaceful athletic pursuits. Jewish children participated in Boy Scout, Wolf Cub and Girl Guide activities. In early August 1928, a joint picnic of 300 children belonging to Young Judeans, 16th Girl Guides (Talmud Torah), 16th Brownies, 31st Brownies, 31st Girl Guides, 19th Talmud Torah Scouts and 19th Talmud Torah Wolf Cub Pack enjoyed baseball and football games and various races, including the three-legged race and wheelbarrow race. Despite residing mainly in the North End, Winnipeg's Jewish community chose Assiniboine Park for their field day – a clear indication that the park belonged to all Winnipeggers.

Blind people selected Assiniboine Park for their picnic and sports day.

People relaxing in front
of First Pavilion, 1920s
MANITOBA ARCHIVES
PHOTO

A Day Off, in the Park

In 1920s Canada, most married women stayed home, cooked and cleaned while their husbands worked at paying jobs. On weekends, couples and their children relaxed in the park. Saturday, June 19, 1920 was typical. The *Free Press* reported that picnics comprised the order of the day. "For one day mother knew a few hours of grace from the hot kitchen and was happy in spreading the table cloth on the grass in the shade of the trees, while dad and the children had the time of their lives feeding the bears and playing ball or running races." Upon the family's return home, the traditional roles resumed.

In July 1922, more than 175 people with visual impairments participated in a Canadian National Institute for the Blind get-together. Participants arrived at Assiniboine Park where races were held – blind men's race, blind women's race, blind men and sighted women's three-legged race, blind women and sighted men's race and a tug of war between blind married men and blind single men.

During this era, the park also witnessed a pronounced change of tone and emphasis in concerts and musical events in Assiniboine Park. In the 1920s, the Parks Board sponsored weekend band concerts in Assiniboine and Kildonan Parks. Sunday concerts such as the one performed by the 106th Battalion Band on August 24, 1923, contained no religious or liturgical selections. Lack of funding in the 1930s forced the Parks Board to cancel its weekend band concert program. The *Tribune* filled the gap by sponsoring community sing-songs. One such event took place on Wednesday, July 20, 1932. Held behind the pavilion, the sing-song attracted 18,000 parents and children. The *Tribune* wrote that "one song followed another with one effect – a response of melody from myriad voices that drifted across lawns, over the trees and winding park roads towards a sky still illuminated with stars." The crowds sang a medley of old favourites, all secular, including "Happy Days are Here Again," "Bring Back My Bonnie to Me," "Old Folks at Home" and "Old Black Joe." Many individuals reached the park by automobile. A special five-cent streetcar fare for park-goers enticed the less affluent to enjoy an inexpensive outing.

Winnipeggers launched their first attempts at multi-cultural celebrations in Assiniboine Park. Before an estimated crowd of 50,000 on Dominion Day 1927, Winnipeggers paid homage to the athletic prowess and music of the diverse nationalities comprising the city's make-up. Sports and picnics constituted a major part of the Diamond Jubilee festivities. Park authorities subdivided Assiniboine Park into twenty-five sections for separate sports activities and picnics for

Girl Guide Rally, August 28, 1928
CITY OF WINNIPEG ARCHIVES PHOTO

people of Scottish, English, Polish, Ukrainian, Welsh, Irish Protestant, Icelandic, Norwegian, Zionist (Jewish), Dutch, Swedish, Swiss, Danish, Finnish, German, Italian, Greek, Belgian, Hungarian and French ancestry, as well as Native Sons of Canada, the general public and the Boy Scouts. Conspicuously absent were Canada's Indigenous and people of Irish Catholic ancestry. In the early evening, winners of each group's sports events congregated for the championships pitting the ethnicities against one another. The winners of the races were announced by name only; they were, after all, all Canadians. More important was an afternoon stage show featuring performances by thirteen different nationalities – singing, dancing and acrobatics.

The *Tribune* praised the mingling of nationalities "from the songs of The Netherlands to the lilting melody for the Maypole dance of Merry England. The Polish choir was delighted when they were called to the stage to the sound of a Paderewski march." Ukrainians performed songs, "and the folk dancing especially of little children in native costume, was loudly applauded by the big crowd." Earning particular praise were exhibitions of Icelandic wrestling, Norwegian gymnastics and Scottish dancing. As a grand finale, groups of men and women in multi-coloured national costumes assembled on stage beside Hugh John Macdonald's daughter and sang the national anthems and "God Save the King." The *Free Press* aptly summed up the day's events – "They may have turned their backs on Europe, those thousands who surged into the park yesterday – some of them indeed knew the old countries only through the memories of their fathers and mothers but they had not utterly forgotten it. Their contribution to the new country was to give the best they had in the old and yesterday they put on their old costumes and sang their old songs and showed in a small measure what they had in them to give."

City council continued to fete visiting dignitaries with luncheons at the Assiniboine Park pavilion. The practice applied to members of internationally renowned sports teams. The luncheon for the Hakoah soccer team indicated that the city had become tolerant of religious minorities. The Hakoah sports club was created in 1909 to instill a strong sense of identity among East European Jews who had migrated to Vienna. In Austria, Hakoah (which in Hebrew means strength) engaged in a number of sports besides soccer – wrestling, skiing, hiking, climbing, handball, table tennis, field hockey, water polo, track and field and fencing. In soccer, Hakoah achieved its greatest success, winning the Vienna city championship in the 1924–25 season. In order to fund its operation, the Hakoah soccer team toured Europe, England, the United States and Canada.

As part of a North American tour, the Hakoah soccer team arrived in Winnipeg in late June 1927 and played an all-star Winnipeg team and a touring Scottish soccer club. On June 24, 1927, a day after its arrival, city council catered a luncheon for the club in the Assiniboine Park pavilion. One hundred sportsmen attended. Alderman John

Blumberg presided over the event and presented the key to the city to Hakoah team manager Arthur Baar. Mayor Ralph Webb delivered a welcoming speech. According to one attendee, Dr. Manly Finkelstein, the purpose of the Hakoah visit lay in creating better relations between Jews and Gentiles. The city's reception accentuated the transformation of Assiniboine Park as an inclusive place for all visitors.

Departures

The 1930s ushered in personnel changes at the senior management level of the Public Parks Board. Superintendent George Champion, who had taken over after the unplanned departure of D.D. England and who had been instrumental in the development of Assiniboine Park, retired in September 1935 after an illustrious career. He steered the formative development of Assiniboine Park and personally designed the duck pond and the English Garden. His accomplishments also included the design, layout and planning of Kildonan and St. Vital Parks and

[Blackwood] was convicted by judge and jury of stealing Parks Board funds; he accused colleagues of complicity in the act until his death.

Kildonan and Windsor Golf Courses. The *Free Press* called him "one of the outstanding horticulturalists and landscape gardeners of the city." In eulogizing him on the occasion of his death, the Parks Board concluded that "his many fine parks …will serve as a tribute to his memory."

Parks Board Secretary James H. Blackwood's departure was not as gracious. He went straight to Stony Mountain Penitentiary after he left the board. He was convicted by judge and jury of stealing Parks Board funds; he accused colleagues of complicity in the act until his death.

Blackwood was born in Scotland and emigrated with his brother to Canada at the turn of the century. After a few years in the Ontario building trades, he arrived in Manitoba. He secured employment with the Parks Board and was appointed its secretary in 1905. In a career spanning over two and a half decades, he executed the Parks Board's instructions, including

James H. Blackwood, Former Secretary of Public Parks Board
"BLACKWOOD TO SERVE 2 YEARS," *MANITOBA FREE PRESS*, MARCH 21, 1931, P. 4

overseeing the design and development of Assiniboine Park.

On March 10, 1930, the city audit department reported a shortfall in the Parks Board's ledgers totalling $3,056.20. The funds, which were found missing from the Parks Board's vault, resulted in an investigation. Searches located a portion of the cash in a box lying in Blackwood's desk. On March 31, 1930, police arrested him at a local theatre. Two days later, the Parks Board secretary was charged with two counts of theft and remanded in custody. He was committed to trial for stealing funds which the Imperial War Graves Commission had given the Parks Board for work done on soldiers' graves in Brookside cemetery. The Parks Board passed a motion suspending Blackwood from his duties. Blackwood tendered his resignation.

The trial was juicy news in the young city. The proceedings cost over $12,000 – a hefty sum in those days. The Crown called a total of thirty-eight witnesses. But their testimony was evidently not persuasive. On December 14, 1930, the trial ended

deadlocked. The jury voted nine to three for conviction; on not one of the thirteen counts did they reach unanimity. Faced with a choice of dropping the charges or proceeding with a new trial, the Crown chose the latter. On March 17, 1931 a new and more compliant jury convicted Blackwood.

The judge sentenced Blackwood to two years in Stony Mountain Penitentiary – a term both he and his lawyer considered harsh. Defence counsel W. Monahan pleaded unsuccessfully for a suspended sentence. He argued that Blackwood was no longer a young man: "the disgrace and humiliation that came from the jury's verdict…was already a terrible punishment" and that locking up Blackwood would serve no public good. Justice Adamson disagreed.

A day later, the *Tribune* published a scathing editorial on the conviction, suggesting blame for the theft could be spread:

It may be said that others share in some degree responsibility for this man's downfall … The general administration of the Parks Board was unbusiness-like, loose and inefficient. Transactions took place with the knowledge of members of the board that would not be tolerated in a well conducted business concern or in a well administered department of public affairs. It is not suggested for a moment that any of the irregularities known to members of the Parks Board were criminal in intent or that they put a dollar of public money improperly in their private pockets. But while there was no criminal intent and no dishonesty apart from Blackwood's own improper acts there were irregularities of a glaring character which threw the whole door open to one weak enough to flirt with temptation. It was in this loose business atmosphere that Blackwood went wrong… The lax system the Board permitted was, without doubt, a contributing factor in undermining Blackwood's moral character.

The *Tribune* called upon city council "to open up the methods of the Parks Board and let the public have a good square look at the system or lack of system under which an old public official fell into dishonest ways.

We have a right to expect our public officials to be honest even in the face of temptation, but we have no right to deliberately set temptation before them." In the *Tribune*'s view, Blackwood's conviction reflected far-reaching problems in the Parks Board's operations.

Two years later, Blackwood returned home from jail. In mid-August 1933, he demanded a judicial enquiry into the conduct of the Public Parks Board and its officials. Blackwood submitted a formal application to city council for the investigation. He noted that he had prepared a similar request in April 1931, but it had been rejected. He charged that "as a result the public and myself were done a grave injustice." Nobody, Blackwood wrote, believed "that he alone had been responsible for the irregularities…nor would they believe that a criminal trial dealing with specific charges would remove the necessity for an investigation." Surprised by the request, city aldermen read the request at a city council meeting and promptly filed it. City council took no action.

In February 1941, Blackwood died at the relatively young age of sixty-three. Ironically, he was interred in Brookside Cemetery whose burial funds he had stolen.

The taint from the Blackwood trial clung to the Parks Board for some time. New hires were to lift the Board out of the morass. Frank T.G. White was appointed Parks Superintendent in 1936 – after acting in the position for a year. Born in Scotland where he apprenticed as a horticulturalist, White arrived in Winnipeg in 1907 and promptly secured employment with the Boulevard Department of the Parks Board. Shortly thereafter he was transferred to Assiniboine Park where he managed the tree and shrubbery nursery. In 1918, the Parks Board appointed him foreman at Assiniboine Park, a position he held when Champion retired. White would guide the Winnipeg Parks system during the difficult World War II period and its immediate aftermath.

Chapter Seven:
The Park at War...
Again, 1939–1945

On September 10, 1939, following Germany's invasion of Poland, Canada declared war on the Nazi regime. As Germany continued its assault on European countries, Canada ramped up its war effort with emphasis on training Commonwealth troops and airmen and contributing combat personnel. After the Japanese attack on Pearl Harbour, the European war expanded into a world war. Like a quarter of a century earlier, Assiniboine Park went to war.

Games and races like this one put the grim realities of WWII in the background – for a little while, at least. MANITOBA ARCHIVES PHOTO

Assiniboine Park fulfilled a role as a military recruiting ground, a venue for military parades, military picnics and Victory Bond sales. The park emerged as a focal point for marshalling public support for the war effort

Rationing even applied to the animals in the Assiniboine Park Zoo, including carnivores.

by hosting patriotic Dominion Day celebrations, military band concerts and fundraising for the Community Chest (precursor of the United Way). At the same time, events in Assiniboine Park provided the public with escape from wartime stresses and realities. Businesses like the Winnipeg Electric Railway Company organized radio broadcasts from the pavilion. Parks Board staff continued to organize horticultural shows in the conservatory, including the ever-popular chrysanthemum exhibit. As the city's largest open-air meeting space, Assiniboine Park fulfilled multiple functions.

Wartime exigencies affected the operation of Assiniboine Park. Reduced public funding forced the Parks Board to maintain Assiniboine Park to only minimal standards and defer planned upgrades and maintenance until the end of the conflict. To ensure employee morale, the Parks Board demanded absolute staff commitment to the war effort. Two naturalized Canadian employees were dismissed for alleged membership in the Nazi Party.

Far-reaching federal government Wartime Prices and Trade Board regulations controlled the daily diet of both man and beast. In order to feed Canada's troops overseas, domestic rationing on a national scale limited meat consumption to several days per week. Rationing even applied to the animals in the Assiniboine Park Zoo, including carnivores. Even the lions, who enjoyed their new, improved enclosure, were only fed meat two or three days per week. On May 4, 1943 the *Free Press* wrote the "zoo lions lead sad lives as meatless Tuesday arrives."

Wartime restrictions on the use of rubber, gasoline and even railway transportation forced the public to spend their vacations at home. Consequently, Winnipeg's parks assumed an increased popularity. As a result of its appealing zoo and conservatory, Assiniboine Park witnessed increased visitation. It was in this environment of reduced public funding and regulatory restrictions that Assiniboine Park saw increased usage.

Military Activities

Assiniboine Park functioned as a venue for military activities in Winnipeg. The first major event took place on July 5, 1941. The *Free Press* previewed it in detail. In order to encourage the enlistment of 1,500 troops, a publicly viewed mock military battle would be held. A force of landed "enemy" parachutists would attempt to sabotage Winnipeg's public utilities. In a carefully scripted program, they would be annihilated in the Battle of the Park. The green space east of the conservatory became the battlefield, with active army soldiers portraying the attackers and Infantry Training Centre troops the defenders. Concealed in the woods, the enemy faced a lightning attack from two platoons of defenders. Both sides would fire blank ammunition including three-inch mortar shells. The *Free Press* advertised the event as a rally complete with military bands: Princess Patricia's Canadian Light Infantry, The Royal Canadian Air Force Band, a band of the Canadian Legion and a bugle band of the legion's General Monash branch. As in all military rallies, men and women in uniform marched through the park, past the saluting base in front of the pavilion.

A Victory Bond drive featuring a paratroop demonstration was held in Assiniboine Park on October 23,

1943. It attracted more than 50,000 spectators who encircled the forty-acre field east of the conservatory. The plan called for fifteen troops to parachute into the park from a height of 800 feet (243.84 metres). The performance would be repeated after the small Lockheed Lodestar returned from Stevenson Field with another fifteen airmen. The *Free Press* predicted that "spectators will hear every word spoken in the plane and by ground men. It will be a two-way radio conversation heard by all on the ground through a monster amplifying system which is being installed." Music accompanied the jumps. Scattered throughout the park, military bands provided entertainment and thereby encouraged the purchase of the bonds.

However, events failed to unfold as choreographed. During the second jump, a slight change in wind direction caused four paratroopers to drift into the woods and become entangled

Mock Military Battle in Park – Parachutists Entangled in Tree, October 25, 1943
WINNIPEG FREE PRESS, OCTOBER 25, 1943

received the salute in a march past by 1,400 troops in front of the pavilion. In the same year, 3,000 uniformed men participated in the largest military church parade in Winnipeg to the time. Protestant Chaplain A.A. Wells called the war a moral crusade for God, religion, humanity, justice, and decency. After a brief program of religious songs and prayers, the men marched past the pavilion where Air Commodore A.B. Shearer took the salute. Two thousand visitors witnessed the spectacle.

But all was not seriousness. The military required recreation. Picnics and dances fulfilled that function. In June 1941, more than 1,000 people including members of the civilian and air force personnel of No. 7 Equipment Depot enjoyed their first annual picnic in Assiniboine Park and participated in many sports events. On September 2, 1942, the Assiniboine Park pavilion became the venue for a dance by members of the Air Force Station No. 3 Wireless School and the Canadian Women's Auxiliary Corps who were in Winnipeg on a training course. The dance was a singular event. The pavilion's food concessionaire, F.L. Marks, reported that while participants behaved satisfactorily, the pavilion sustained damages to its floors. On September 16, 1942, the Parks Board passed a motion "that in future the policy of the Board will not permit dancing in the Assiniboine Park Pavilion."

in trees. One paratrooper, Sgt. Cecil Cavanagh, sustained a broken bone in his ankle and a wound to his left leg. The surrounding spectators escaped unscathed. The success of this particular bond drive is undocumented. The newspapers published nothing on the matter.

Throughout World War II, Assiniboine Park hosted many activities for military personnel. Events included both military and church parades. On July 11, 1941, Canadian Prime Minister Mackenzie King

Public Support of the War Effort

The public expressed its support for the war effort by holding holiday celebrations, attending military band concerts and Community Chest launches in Assiniboine Park. Dominion Day took on a particularly patriotic air. On July 1, 1942, the military held its Army Week activities in the park. The army presented long service medals and organized a march past of military reserve units. Premier John Bracken and local senior military officers took the salute. The Princess Patricia Canadian Light Infantry band performed. At twilight, the pipe band of the Second Battalion of the Queen's Own Cameron Highlanders sounded the retreat. About 10,000 people attended the event.

The public flocked to military band concerts. On Sunday June 1, 1941, the North Star Band performed. The program comprised largely of military marches and overtures with selections including "The Royal Highway," "Lights Out," and "Napoleon's Last Charge" being played. The concert was but one of many.

Labour Day activities incorporated a military component. In 1943, the No. 10 District Depot band opened the annual Labour Day event. Troupes organized to entertain the armed forces provided entertainment along with vaudeville acts and a sing song. While organizers solicited no donations at the show, the activities drew attention to the upcoming Community Chest fund drive. By attending the events at Assiniboine Park, the public indirectly voiced its support for the military.

Diversions

The war entailed a total commitment on the part of Winnipeggers and Canadians as a whole. To maintain a semblance of normality, some peacetime activities continued in the park. As in the past, children's events were held. At the war's height in 1942, the *Free Press* sponsored a school patrol picnic. The Winnipeg Electric Railway Company arranged transportation and the *Free Press* catered a buffet supper. The patrollers received awards for punctuality, attention to duty, personal appearance and general efficiency.

Adults were not forgotten. In order to encourage streetcar ridership, the Electric Railway Company sponsored recorded concerts on Saturdays and Sundays from loudspeakers placed outside the pavilion. Without interruption for three decades, Assiniboine Park employees organized the annual November chrysanthemum show. In November 1941, vast numbers of citizens attended the month-long display. In 1944, Parks Board gardeners exhibited 200 varieties of chrysanthemums – mauves, bright

yellows, whites, maroons, rusty reds and copper golds. According to the *Free Press* "there are mums as tall as a person; there are mums as big as footballs and Lilliputian varieties as small as a 50-cent piece." Civilian-oriented events temporarily diverted public attention away from the fighting overseas.

On April 30, 1945, Adolf Hitler committed suicide. Just days later, on May 8, 1945, the Allies formally accepted Germany's surrender. The war in Europe was over. Following the atomic bombing of Hiroshima and Nagasaki, on August 15, 1945 Japan surrendered.

Other than brief and spontaneous outbursts of joy in downtown Winnipeg on VE and VJ days, no one organized formal celebrations of victory or peace. A war-weary public craved a return to normalcy.

Assiniboine Park would resume its role as Winnipeg's suburban playground.

Chapter Eight: Professionalization and Multi-Culturalism, 1946–1960

In what would be the final decade and a half under Public Parks Board administration, Assiniboine Park evolved into a multicultural, recreational area with a professionally managed zoo and green space. The Parks Board purchased lands for a major extension west of the zoo for both zoo expansion and a buffer zone. The Parks Board initiated a process of professionalization to plan the zoo's future. A volunteer zoo advisory committee (later the Manitoba Zoological Society) proffered advice in preparing multi-year plans for the zoo's expansion and development.

Construction of Perimeter Road
on West Side of Park, 1962 CITY OF
WINNIPEG ARCHIVES

Operational practices at the zoo were professionalized – job descriptions, proper feeding, care and documenting of animals all took place. Equally important, the Parks Board employed a part-time zoo curator during the early 1950s before hiring a permanent director in 1958.

Social activities in the park continued much as they had since the original opening. The park now embraced multicultural activities; a public ethnic festival and an Indigenous powwow were among the examples. A visit by Queen Elizabeth II in 1959 highlighted the era.

Yet from 1946 to 1960, the park witnessed little development within its spacious green areas and zoo. Only new bear enclosures and the construction of a children's zoo, Aunt Sally's Farm, received funding. The Metropolitan Corporation of Greater Winnipeg (henceforth Metro) would face the challenge of improving Assiniboine Park's deteriorating infrastructure.

Park Expansion and Infrastructure Improvement

A major expansion of Assiniboine Park's boundaries took place in 1954 to 1955. As part of the zoo's master plan, the Parks Board decided to acquire the former subdivision known as "Rydal" adjacent to the park's western boundary. Not only would the lands provide for zoo expansion, they permitted the extension of the river road in Assiniboine Park westward and the construction of an additional park entrance on Roblin Boulevard near the zoo. Moreover, the acreage could be used for future parking areas to accommodate increased zoo visitation and to establish a landscaped buffer zone between the park and future residential development.

The Parks Board began the process of acquiring the land in 1953. It approached the Town of Tuxedo with the hope of buying the tract of empty land owned partly by the town and partly by eleven individual owners. However, Tuxedo was more interested in keeping the land on its tax rolls than in selling to the city. Coincidentally, Tuxedo claimed that

Extension of Park,
1954 Lands – 2018
PHOTO BY AUTHOR

Following World War II, Assiniboine Park's ageing infrastructure began experiencing maintenance issues.

a private party had started negotiations for the same property. That was an assertion that could not substantiated by Tuxedo council minutes. However, Tuxedo did set a price. It asked for $50,000 for its portion of the acreage alone and retention of its existing oil and natural gas rights.

The Parks Board agreed to Tuxedo's demands. However, some members of city council and the press were incensed. Winnipeg Finance Committee Chairman Alderman C.E. Simonite charged Tuxedo with "asking for the last dollar and all the frills." Alderman Stan Carrick remarked that "I personally don't like doing business with people with a gun in their pocket." Other aldermen supported the deal. Alderman George Sharpe said that "the matter should not be dropped. We should look ahead fifty years. When the park was bought in 1904 some thought it too big – now we have

a park second to none." Alderman Jacob Penner argued that "our only consideration should be whether $58,000 is excessive for 66 acres [sic]. We should consider that most people in Tuxedo do business in the city and pay some sort of tax. It is wrong to point out that we pay the shot for the park. We need the land. It is a generous offer and a reasonable price."

The *Free Press* expressed its opinion. It declared that "while a bigger zoo would be an excellent thing, the time has come to make sure that costs are fairly divided between the city and adjacent municipalities…On the whole, city council would do well to accept the recommendations of its finance committee and vote against the plan at the present price." On July 5, 1954, city council rejected the land deal by a narrow eight to seven vote. Presumably, the land deal was dead.

Two days after city council's decision, the Parks Board re-opened negotiations with Tuxedo. It appointed a sub-committee to meet with town representatives and negotiate a more acceptable deal. On July 22, 1954, Parks Board representative Alderman G. Sharpe and Parks Superintendent T.R. Hodgson met Tuxedo Mayor Lamont and Councillor H.B. Boreham. The Parks Board recommended offering Tuxedo $48,000 for the sixty-six-acre parcel. Several conditions applied. The land would fulfil park purposes only – no housing or commercial development. The city would create a treed buffer zone along its Roblin Boulevard boundary. To allay the sensitive nostrils of upscale Tuxedo residents "no smelly or noisy animals" would be housed within 300 feet of the park's southern boundary. Lastly, the city would incorporate the lands within its boundaries.

As cool September breezes ushered in the annual fall foliage display along Assiniboine Park's riparian forest, a draft agreement was reached between the city of Winnipeg and the town of Tuxedo. The Parks Board's annual report for 1954 highlighted the purchase of the spread minus the eleven privately owned lots. In January 1955, the Parks Board authorized the preparation of a topographical survey of the lands and an engineering survey of the riverbank. A Town of Tuxedo bylaw of August 16, 1955 closed the streets and lanes in the acreage conveyed to the City of Winnipeg.

In 1955, the Parks Board purchased the eleven privately owned lots within the land tract. But for almost a decade, development of the lands remained an unrealized vision.

Following World War II, Assiniboine Park's ageing infrastructure began experiencing maintenance issues. In particular, the forty-year-old conservatory showed signs of wear, tear and obsolescence. In 1952, the central palm house required and received $6,000 for repairs to its piling and walls. Equally severe was the condition of the conservatory's heating system. Long after most public buildings in Winnipeg had been converted to oil or natural gas, in 1960 a coal-fired stoker continued to keep the conservatory's tropical plants alive and flourishing.

Foreseeing difficulties, the Parks Board undertook a study. In his report of June 30, 1960, H.E. Sala noted that the stoker was "a very old type…The motor is in need of commutation, and if it were possible to obtain one it would require three or four weeks for delivery." "There is the one possibility this motor may not last very long." In case of a breakdown of one of the two boilers (the other was replaced in 1950), the furnace would need hand stoking with cord wood "of which we have no supply, and it requires three men to keep it going. Should this breakdown happen at below zero temperature and at night, this might create a critical situation, having no stock of cord wood and no men immediately available." In short, if the stoker failed, the conservatory's plants would freeze. The report recommended the installation of a gas heating system offering zoned heat throughout the greenhouse-like structure. Moreover, gas heating would eliminate the need for one full-time fireman. The Parks Board acted and in August, 1960 accepted a tender from the BurnOmatic Gas

Heat Company. For the modest sum of $4,775, the conservatory averted a disaster.

With the active participation of the Rotarians, the Parks Board turned its attention to the Informal Garden. In 1952, in return for renaming the popular destination as the International Fellowship Garden, the Rotarians offered to donate $825 for a new approach and contribute $100 annually toward garden maintenance. After consideration, the Parks Board approved the proposal in principle. Over a year elapsed and in 1953 a new circular approach to the garden was constructed from Rotarian-donated funds. The Parks Board renamed the garden the International Goodwill Garden "as a monument to good relations between Canada and the USA." Facing a parsimonious city council, the Parks Board had initiated a process of dedicating Assiniboine Park attractions to private financial donors.

Catering Concessions
In the years following the Parks Board exit from food outlet operations in 1936, the Assiniboine

Park pavilion had known only one concessionaire, Frank L. Marks. Through that time, Marks had delivered "trouble free satisfaction" and introduced "innovations and improvements at his own expense beyond the requirements of the contract." Marks had never tendered for his contracts; the Parks Board had sole sourced his services. But in the 1950s, when the notion of professionalization crept into parks activities, the Parks Board hired the accounting firm of J.D. Woods and Gordon to review the Marks operation. Their report recommended that "the concessions should in future be opened to public tender. If all other considerations are deemed to be equal the concession should then be leased to the highest bidder." The Parks Board deferred making a decision. Marks died in 1951, but his successor, the F.L. Marks Company, remained concessionaire until New Year's Eve 1957. Following an open bidding process, Kitchen Catering of Fort Street received a three-year contract in return for $13,001 per annum plus ten percent of gross receipts over $150,000.

The loss of their catering sinecure shocked the firm's principals, William J. and Patrick B. Marks. In March 1958, a letter from Barristers and Solicitors Newman, MacLean & Jewers reported that the Marks were preparing to remove certain fixtures from the pavilion and zoo which were understood to be Parks Board property. Among those items slated for removal from the zoo refreshment building were the freshwater lines including sink and faucet, florescent fixtures, and the 500-amp electrical service. From the Assiniboine Park pavilion the Marks company remained more modest and proposed removal of five to six feet (one and a half to nearly two metres) of florescent fixtures. The Parks Board responded by demanding that all fixtures remain untouched. But unwilling to pursue a concessionaire who had rendered over two decades of faithful service, the city

Pavilion Restaurant
c. 1940s UNIVERSITY
OF MANITOBA
ARCHIVES WINNIPEG
TRIBUNE COLLECTION
PC 18/399/118-032

compensated the company for their infrastructure expenditures.

Zoo Planning and Administrative Improvements

As the century reached its halfway mark, the Parks Board initiated a formal park planning process for Assiniboine Park Zoo to replace the hodgepodge development of earlier years. Highlighted by a plan for an expanded zoo for Western Canadian animals, the first phase ended with the defeat of a money bylaw in 1954. The second phase entailed a search for alternate funding and the preparation of a new ten-year master plan expanding the zoo into a world-wide sampling of animals.

The planning process for the Assiniboine Park Zoo started in 1949. Early that year, the Parks Board instructed Superintendent F.T.G. White to prepare a five-year development scheme incorporating new animal enclosures, improved polar bear accommodation and new aviaries. A year later, the Parks Board appointed a citizens advisory committee with representatives from the Manitoba Museum, Natural History Society, the University of Manitoba and the provincial government to assist the Parks Superintendent. This committee evolved into the Manitoba Zoological Society.

Professional consultants augmented the volunteers. University of Manitoba history professor Richard Glover played a lead role in the committee's deliberations and recommendations. From his unique perspective as Calgary Zoo curator, Tom Baines proffered advice to the Parks Board on zoo expansion in 1951. Zoo architect John E. Wallace transformed the recommendations of the citizens advisory committee into an overall zoo concept. Among others, these three individuals played key roles in finalizing a zoo management plan and concept.

Most prominent in the early stages of Assiniboine Park Zoo development was Richard Glover, chair of the zoo advisory committee. His expertise lay in the history of the Hudson's Bay Company and the fur trade era. A prolific writer and editor, in his professional life he edited the memoirs of fur traders Samuel Hearne and David Thompson and contributed to the Dictionary of Canadian Biography. In terms of zoo design and planning he was completely self-taught.

In contrast to enthusiastic amateur Glover, architectural consultant John E. Wallace could not have been more professional. He was one of North America's major zoo architects. Resident architect for the St. Louis Zoo in 1952, he collaborated with local firm Smith, Munn, Carter & Katelnikoff on the Assiniboine Park Zoo expansion. He had penned plans for zoos in Colorado Springs and Edmonton and consulted in New Orleans's zoo development. He believed in abandoning rusty cages and dilapidated sheds for a dry moat open air display system used in most modern zoos. In 1952, the Parks Board commissioned him at a fee of $1,000 to prepare a zoo layout showing the space requirements, relationship of enclosures, exhibit stations and paths for the proposed new development to be added to the existing facilities.

Glover led a zoo advisory committee composed of Manitoba

Games and Fisheries Director G.W. Malaher, Manitoba Museum Curator L.T. Norris-Glye, University of Manitoba Professor of Animal Pathology, Dr. Alex Savage and Zoology Professor R.H. Stewart-Hay. In December 1950, following a month of travel and meetings with zoo officials in England and the United States, he released his report. Glover called for a four-stage development of a zoo that would house a collection of Manitoba animals. Phase 1, "the Sportsmen's Zoo" would consist of grizzly bears, caribou, moose, and pronghorn to complete an existing collection of "big game animals." Phase 2, the "Businessman's Zoo" would gather together animals of high economic value – fur-bearing animals including mink, marten, fishers among others. Phase 3 would incorporate small mammals, while an aquarium would complete the development. A day after its presentation, the Parks Board approved the plan in principle. Upon recommendation of Parks Superintendent T.R. Hodgson (successor to F.T.G. White), a children's zoo was added. It would exhibit tame animals such as rabbits, guinea pigs and mice that children could pet. According to Glover, the plan offered a place "splendid and varied enough to provide an

[Wallace] believed in abandoning rusty cages and dilapidated sheds for a dry moat open air display system used in most modern zoos.

attractive drawing card." Above all, such a zoo "would be much cheaper to maintain than a collection of more delicate foreign animals from milder climates."

From 1951 to 1954, the Parks Board and zoo advisory committee

refined the proposed concept. Modern new enclosures would rise for native animals and better accommodation constructed for existing exotics such as lions and monkeys. The Parks Board hired a part-time zoo curator, Richard Sutton of the Manitoba Museum, to oversee the zoo's development.

Animal management procedures improved dramatically in these years. The first step lay in documenting the collection. By the mid 1950s, each animal received a unique identifier – copper ear tags for hoofed stock, tattoos for other animals, and leg bands for birds. Complete records were retained on the pedigree, health and feeding regimen of each species. The Zoo Advisory Committee proposed that animals should not be housed in view of their natural prey because it "causes too much fear on one side and frustrated tantalization on the other." Animals needed companionship but overcrowding resulted in fighting and bullying. Animals required special diets. For moose, Glover specified meals of carrots, sliced potatoes, rye bread, hay and willow.

Importantly, the public should be discouraged from feeding the animals. According to Glover "methods should be devised to prevent over-generous Winnipeggers from conveying to the moose those stale crusts." By 1954, Richard Sutton had successfully implemented the new procedures. The three zookeepers under his direction had adapted well to the changes. The animals benefited from proper diets devoid of junk foods.

The Parks Board also undertook a plethora of improvements in zoo personnel management during the 1950s. First and foremost, the Parks Board prepared new job descriptions from the lowest zookeeper to the position of zoo curator. Introduced in 1952, formal job descriptions enabled employees to understand their duties and responsibilities and provided management with the criteria to evaluate their performance. Zookeeper 1 constituted the entry level position and entailed cleaning cages and equipment and assisting with animal feeding. One level higher, Zookeeper 2 prepared rations and fed and watered the birds

Dominion Archery Championships, 1951
CITY OF WINNIPEG ARCHIVES

and animals. Far removed from the zookeeper's daily grind, were the responsibilities of the part-time zoo curator. Responsible for overall zoo operations, the curator identified and classified all zoo animals, maintained animal records, supervised feeding schedules, conducted research and prepared correspondence and promotional materials. Proper and formal job descriptions enabled employees to work harmoniously and in unison for the common good.

The improved zoo required substantial public funding. The goal could only be accomplished by a bylaw authorizing the issuance of debentures which were similar to municipal bonds. On September 1, 1954 the Parks Board estimated the capital costs of these facilities. Among others, items included new bear accommodations at $55,000, a Children's Zoo at $5,000, public washrooms, a concession stand and first aid room at $17,000, and a sewage treatment plant at $20,000. Assiniboine Park Zoo improvements comprised part of a greater scheme to be placed before ratepayers. Bylaw No. 17317 called for creating a public debt of $300,000 for extending the park system, including Assiniboine Park Zoo, erecting buildings and acquiring land.

The print media strongly supported the parks bylaw. According to the *Free Press* of October 19, 1954 the cost to homeowners was minimal. On a house assessed at $6,000, the yearly tax bill would rise a mere $2.30. "That is a small investment for large returns in terms of health and wellbeing in safety for children and in pleasure for leisure moments." Yet in Winnipeg's dated money bylaw approval process, which had not changed since 1902, a minority of electors could thwart the will of the majority. That is precisely what ratepayers did.

Winnipeg ratepayers approved public park and zoo expansion by a margin of 21,237 for versus 16,102 against. Yet the $300,000 money bylaw suffered defeat because it did not receive sixty percent of the vote. A minority had thwarted the will of the majority. In a letter to the *Free Press* on December 9, 1954, Alderman Jacob Penner blamed "the outmoded, undemocratic provisions in the City Charter which requires the approval of 60 percent of the ratepayers before a money bylaw becomes valid." Members of the Zoo Advisory Committee were "deeply concerned, distressed, and disappointed that anticipated improvements which have been the object of study and report for over three years are now indefinitely postponed." Although his term as part-time zoo curator expired, Richard Sutton expressed his dismay by formally resigning from his position.

Parks Superintendent T.R. Hodgson and members of the Zoo Advisory Committee considered options for salvaging elements of their years of hard work. Hodgson recommended that a special committee be formed to explore the advisability of establishing a properly funded Metropolitan Park District. Alternatively, he suggested that the Assiniboine Park Zoo be operated as a provincial park on condition that all native animals and hardy exotics were displayed. As an interim measure, Hodgson contemplated the disposal of wolves, coyotes and

Winnipeg ratepayers approved public park and zoo expansion by a margin of 21,237 for versus 16,102 against. Yet the $300,000 money bylaw suffered defeat because it did not receive sixty percent of the vote. A minority had thwarted the will of the majority.

cougars "pending available funds to provide proper accommodations." The Zoo Advisory Committee went further and recommended termination of the black and grizzly bear exhibits. As an immediate goal, both parties agreed to lobby municipal authorities to fund new black, grizzly and polar bear enclosures.

The Parks Superintendent and Zoo Advisory Committee eventually overcame their disappointment over the rejection of long-term zoo funding. In 1957, the Zoo Advisory Committee presented a revised approach to zoo development. In a May 1957 report to the Parks Board, it declared that the committee was solely interested in the development of the zoo as a public attraction and educational asset for both citizens and visitors. Furthermore, the Parks Board and Zoo Advisory Committee agreed that a conventional zoo was unsuited to Winnipeg as a result of high construction costs and a vigorous climate. Therefore, the committee patterned its concept after the Whipsnade Zoo near London, England, which substituted space wire fence and plantation strips for bricks, mortar, and iron bars. The report concluded that this category of zoo was rare in North America and its implementation would attract visitors to Winnipeg. The inevitable question arose – how would the zoo expansion be financed? The Zoo Advisory Committee offered a potpourri of suggestions – an admission charge, voluntary collections, revenue from miniature train and pony rides, vending machine and souvenir sales. Other ideas included the sponsorship of exhibits by private capital, a drive for public donations, and requests for grants from suburban municipalities. The Parks Board failed to adopt specific money raising schemes. The zoo continued to rely solely on the largess of city council.

The planning process at Assiniboine Park Zoo reached its apex with the hiring of a full-time zoo director (successor to the position of zoo curator) in 1958 and the preparation of a new and expanded zoo management plan two years later. In February 1955, the Zoo Advisory Committee first suggested that the Parks Board attract a full-time director to assume

The zoo would serve new purposes – a centre for "outdoor recreation" and "a haven of protection for animals threatened by extinction."

responsibilities for managing, guiding, and planning the zoo and organizing an educational program. Two years later, the Parks Board requested city council approval to negotiate a contract for a zoo director. The Zoo Advisory Committee recommended hiring Dr. Gunter Voss of Germany for the position. It was Voss who would prepare the new and expanded zoo management plan.

The parsimonious Parks Board delegated to the Zoo Advisory Committee the task of interviewing Voss. Knowing that one of the advisory committee members, R.F. Larcombe, lived in England, it suggested he travel to Germany to meet Voss. In June 1958, Larcombe reported to the Parks Board. He described Voss as possessing a pleasing personality and one who spoke fluent English. Voss had done

excellent work in developing the relatively small Klefeld, Germany zoo from practically nothing. The animals and birds he selected did not require heated quarters – an important consideration in Winnipeg. Best of all, Voss liked animals. "Even the camels, notoriously bad-tempered animals appeared to greet him with affection" wrote Larcombe.

Gunter Voss arrived in Winnipeg in January 1959. With the assistance of the Research and Advisory Committee of the Zoological Society

of Manitoba (successor to the Zoo Advisory Committee), Voss set to work preparing an expanded zoo management plan. The zoo would serve new purposes – a centre for "outdoor recreation" and "a haven of protection for animals threatened by extinction." Utilizing the new western park extension, the zoo would expand from ninety to 300 species. Abandoned were the days of a Manitoba-centred collection. Among mammals alone, foreign species would dominate by a count of III to fifty-two. Accessed by three large parking lots and two visitors' entrances, the zoo would boast a fish and reptile display as demanded by Mayor Stephen Juba, new animal enclosures arranged by habitat, a café, a boating pond, and new water and sewage installations. At a projected cost of $4.5 million, construction would take up to a decade to complete. Once opened to the public, the zoo would rank as number twenty-five to thirty among North American zoological gardens. The only thing remaining was long-term funding.

Zoo Animals and Enclosures

In the decade and a half following the war's end, the Assiniboine Park Zoo grew very little. With scarce funds at its disposal, the Parks Board relied on donations from government agencies and private parties to maintain its collection. Pursuant to the preliminary 1950 management plan, Assiniboine Park concentrated on acquiring Western Canadian

species. The year 1951 was typical. A consortium of breweries, Brewery Products Limited, donated $300 for the acquisition of pairs of martens and fishers provided that a plaque acknowledging their contribution be affixed to the appropriate cage. From the Hudson's Bay Company, the zoo received a white fox, from the Manitoba Minister of Mines and Natural Resources, the zoo added a male moose while de-scented skunks arrived courtesy of a private donor. Except for a grizzly bear and two badgers from the Calgary Zoo and one sika deer from the Memphis Zoo, the Parks Board spent no money on acquisitions. To an even greater degree, the year 1953 continued in the earlier pattern. Government organizations were major contributors – three bighorn sheep from the director of National Parks, one silver and one platinum fox from the provincial government Experimental Fur Farm and fifty-three native ducks, geese, and swans from the Delta Waterfowl

Research Station. Private individuals enhanced the Winnipeg Zoo with contributions of badgers, white-tailed deer, mink, raccoons, skunks, and bobcats.

Except for the purchase of pairs of Bactrian camels, wallabies, and Siberian tiger cubs in 1960, the Assiniboine Park Zoo focussed on a Western Canadian collection. In spite of almost non-existent municipal funding, provincial and federal government agencies and private individuals recognized the benefits of a viable Assiniboine Park zoological collection and eagerly donated specimens.

The final decade and a half of Parks Board administration resulted in few upgrades to animal enclosures. Public rejection of the park bylaw in 1954 curtailed all zoo improvements. Yet some enclosures, like the grizzly bear pit, did require immediate replacement. In November 1954, the Parks Board was told by the superintendent of Construction and Maintenance that the pit was "in a poor state of repair as the concrete walls and floor over a period of some forty-five years have weathered badly. The floor surface is cracked and broken and its grade does not permit easy cleaning or drainage. The drain from the pool joins that from the pit housing the black bears before flowing to the Assiniboine River and both drainage lines are cracked or broken in a number of places," W.A. Mildren reported. When workers attempted to repair the floor and wall cracks in 1953, the male grizzly bear took umbrage, "clawing out the newly bonded cement from cracks and crevices."

A report by zoo Curator R.W. Sutton was even more critical. Sutton attributed the confined quarters as leading to restlessness among its denizens and the trampling death of a valuable grizzly cub. Furthermore, he said the pits were an "affront to the eyes as well as the nose." And if that wasn't convincing enough, there was also the danger to public safety. He said it was lucky no child had fallen into the pit, tumbling amongst the bears. "I feel that the only reason the male grizzly bear has not climbed out of the pit, is that he has not thought of it – yet."

Fearing the loss of its popular grizzly bear exhibit, city council actually agreed to fund the construction of new enclosures. On June 15, 1955, the Parks Board viewed a model of the proposed new structures to accommodate black, grizzly and polar bears in a manner that would emulate their natural habitat. No bars would obstruct the view and the public would be protected by a seven-foot- (over two metre) wide moat. The $80,000 enclosures opened to the public with much fanfare in June 1957. Designed by Winnipeg architects Smith, Carter & Katelnikoff, the enclosures incorporated the recommendations made by the Zoo Advisory Committee based on information from the Brookfield Zoo in Chicago and the Seattle Zoo. The open moat type enclosures encompassed an area of 12,100 square feet

Bear Enclosures as Refurbished, 2018
PHOTO BY AUTHOR

(1,124 square metres), making them one of the largest of their type in the world. To ensure proper rearing of young cubs, the design boasted isolation quarters behind the individual enclosures for male bears "who have no patience with the cubs." The ursine occupants in their new quarters attracted Winnipeggers and visitors for over half a century.

For almost fifty years, the Assiniboine Park Zoo amazingly lacked proper food refrigeration facilities. Each year, significant numbers of animals died of food poisoning. In 1952, tainted rations took the lives of a fisher and a cougar. Finally, Parks Superintendent T.R. Hodgson decided to act. In June 1952, city council gave approval for a forty by twenty-five-foot (twelve by eight metre) enlargement of the lion house. The addition would function as a food storehouse and winter quarters for parrots, beavers, ducks, and monkeys. The architects included a small staff office in the design. It was assumed that the lions would not escape and devour the food, monkeys or humans.

The Parks Board installed a proper food refrigeration system in the extension. The improvements reduced animal deaths. The lions did not escape. And the press recorded no deaths of monkeys or humans.

Since 1951, the Parks Board and Zoo Advisory Committee had shared the goal of constructing a children's zoo in Assiniboine Park. Higher priorities such as new bear enclosures had shunted the project to the wayside. However, funds became available in the late 1950s. In September 1957, the Parks Board approved plans for the children's zoo, which would display selected varieties of North American farm animals and some birds. Named Aunt Sally's Farm to honour the pioneer work of Sally Warnock in protecting animals in Winnipeg, the attraction would be located north of the new bear enclosure and east of the lions' house but in view of neither. Within its perimeter, plans called for construction of a pony corral, a miller's wheel, a miniature railway with station and platform, a playground and a small picnic area. Construction of this children's zoo commenced in 1958.

Aunt Sally's Farm –
Waterwheel, 1959
MANITOBA ARCHIVES
PHOTO

Entrance to Aunt
Sally's Farm, 1959
MANITOBA ARCHIVES
PHOTO

Aunt Sally's Farm opened to the public on August 7, 1959. In his typical eccentric style, Mayor Stephen Juba led a white goat to a ribbon on which a succulent carrot had been attached. After a few tentative sniffs and an encouraging pat on the head from the mayor, the goat ripped at the carrot and the ribbon was broken.

Aunt Sally's Farm enjoyed widespread press and public support. On its inaugural day, the *Free Press* commented that "in this zoo there are no fences around the animals. Children may wander freely among the animals, feeding them at certain times, petting them and generally getting much closer than they ever have before the zoo." In Aunt Sally's Farm, children mingled with alpacas, yak calves, rabbits, Shetland ponies, ducks, Sicilian dwarf donkeys, and Australian horned sheep. They enjoyed their first guided pony ride, travelled on a miniature railway and revelled in the delight of a water wheel in motion. For a span of thirty years, Aunt Sally's Farm would entertain children and parents alike.

Aunt Sally's Farm, 1959 MANITOBA
ARCHIVES PHOTO

Throughout Assiniboine Park's first half century, no consideration had been given to protecting the public against the escape of dangerous zoo animals. That proved to be an unfortunate omission on February 19, 1958. That is when a bull buffalo bolted to freedom. The RCMP were summoned and shot the animal dead.

The Parks Board took immediate steps to reinforce the buffalo compound with quarter-inch cables. The board considered the consequences of other animals escaping from the zoo. Monkeys could be enticed back with plentiful supplies of bananas. If lions, tigers or cougars leaped to freedom, human lives would be imperilled. The only response lay in shooting them. This was something the president of the Manitoba Zoological Society, Richard Glover, wished to avoid. In March 1958, he recommended also fencing the perimeter of the zoo. Escaped animals, he reasoned, would be confined until captured. The Parks Board endorsed his proposal, authorizing fence construction "at the earliest possible date." Despite financial constraints, money was allocated for this purpose.

In spring 1958, the Parks Board attempted to address the shortfall in zoo funding by evaluating proposals best described as "unparklike." One such proposal by Winnipeggers Theodore Buzunis and sons lay in constructing a circus midway known as Kiddieland within zoo boundaries. The lessees would operate miniature airplane and racing boat rides, a Ferris wheel, merry-go-round and roller coaster. Under the proposal, in return for this commercial concession, the Parks Board would receive about $20,000 per year based on gross percentage of revenue for a term of five years. Other business operators entered the fray with competing proposals. The scheme sparked public outrage. The Chamber of Commerce, Zoological Society of Manitoba, Winnipeg Council of Women, and the Humane Society all passed resolutions opposing the

scheme. Letters from angry citizens arrived at the Parks Board office. The *Free Press* asserted that "the park exists to bring nature to city dwellers; there are other places for other attractions." As Dominion Day 1958 drew near, the Parks Board abandoned the ill-considered scheme. The zoo would continue to rely on public funding – sparse though it was – for its operation.

Original Mill Stones for Ogilvie Flour Mills, Aunt Sally's Farm, 1959
MANITOBA ARCHIVES PHOTO

On the eve of the Metro takeover in 1961, little had been done to enhance the zoo. From 1954 to 1960 only $291,292 had been spent – much of it on the new bear enclosures. The *Free Press* lamented that "many of the cages and enclosures are hopelessly inadequate, some are downright offensive and inhumane." It remained to Metro to invest in zoo upgrades.

An Inclusive and Multicultural Park

In the aftermath of World War II, Assiniboine Park embraced a wide range of social activities. The park continued as a favoured venue for church, social club, and labour union picnics and field days. Events including an ethnic festival, a community club jamboree, and a powwow drew huge appreciative crowds intent on sharing Winnipeg's many cultures. One group, the criminal element, received no welcome. In 1947, criminals targeted the pavilion safe but were quickly apprehended. Queen Elizabeth II's visit in 1959 crowned a period in which Assiniboine Park celebrated Winnipeg's social, ethnic and racial diversity.

The former Deer Lodge Hospital (now Deer Lodge Centre) is located on Portage Avenue just three blocks west of the northern pedestrian entrance to Assiniboine Park. Established by the Dominion Government in 1916, the hospital rehabilitated wounded soldiers, enabling them to re-enter civilian life. During and after the Second World War, many wounded veterans benefited from its care. Physical fitness training comprised part of the Deer Lodge rehabilitation program. However, the hospital possessed little outdoor space to undertake this activity. In May 1946, the Department of Veterans Affairs requested permission to use a portion of Assiniboine Park for remedial games and physical training, a continuation of its activities during the war. Wishing to meet the needs of returned veterans, the Parks Board readily agreed. Its only condition stipulated that the area used was to "be kept in good condition." The availability of Assiniboine Park for re-integrating veterans constituted the first of many examples of a park which embraced everyone.

Greater Winnipeg's Community Clubs performed an important function in creating a harmonious society in the war's aftermath. Men, women, and children, including returned veterans, took part in social activities organized by the community clubs. Once a year, all community clubs met for a day of song, dance and sports. In mid-June 1947, members of the Associated Community Clubs of Greater Winnipeg congregated in the verdant and spacious grounds of Assiniboine Park. The program catered to diverse interests. Two large stages were erected in different parts of the park to host comedy juggling acts, Ukrainian dancers, YMCA tumblers, Scottish dancers and pipers, tap dancers, acrobats, and a maypole dance by pupils of General Wolfe School. Nearly 1,000 contestants representing twenty-nine community clubs competed for championship ribbons, prizes and club trophies in community club races. Bringing their own picnic suppers, visitors enjoyed entertainment by the Navy, Army and Air Force Band. In the evening, the program featured dance music by the same band and by

Maurice Libman's orchestra and at a second locale, community singing. Regardless of their background or ethnicity, everyone could enjoy the festivities at Assiniboine Park.

Winnipeggers embraced multi-culturalism at the park. On Thursday, June 9, 1949, a United Citizens Day was held in the commodious green space. In his opening remarks, master of ceremonies, Doug Coats, declared that the event "symbol-ized the contribution to Winnipeg's development by peoples of many races and ethnic groups." A massive crowd, estimated between 30,000 and 40,000 by the *Free Press* and 60,000 by the *Tribune*, enjoyed the festivities. The program represented a kaleidoscope of Winnipeg's many cultures. Choirs, bands and dancers from twelve ethnic groups performed.

An ensemble of 300 choristers and bandsmen from the Ukrainian Canadian Committee led off the evening. A sword dance by four male dancers in traditional Cossack cos-tume "won rounds of applause." Next, forty young kilted dancers performed the Highland Fling. A French-Canadian dance troupe directed by

Georges Forest sang as they "swung through an energetic folk dance." Canadians of African ancestry were represented. According to the *Free Press*, "Mrs. Beatrice Browne led the coloured choir in the beauti-ful harmonies of some of the best

loved spirituals including 'The Year of Jubilee' and 'Let us Break Bread Together.'" The Winnipeg Council of the Canadian Jewish Congress sponsored one of the largest groups at the event. Participants included a mixed choir, orchestra, dancers and young gymnasts. The Chinese com-munity took part in the festivities. Its

dance group staged the Lion Dance accompanied by Chinese gongs and symbols. Lithuanian and Polish Canadians and Italians all contrib-uted with songs and folk dances. The *Free Press* complimented the Lithuanian girls in their embroidered,

long full skirts and aprons and the Italian choir for its "haunting songs." An incredible evening of entertain-ment ended with colourful Russian dancing and music. Virtually every ethnic group had made its contri-bution. Winnipeg's multicultural composition manifested itself fully in the Assiniboine Park celebration.

The park continued as a favoured venue for church, social club, and labour union picnics and field days.

Assiniboine Park witnessed its first Indigenous powwow in mid-June 1949. Members of the Blackfoot Nation presented Winnipeg Mayor Garnet Coulter with the title of

Assiniboine Park witnessed its first Indigenous powwow in mid-June 1949.

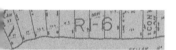

honorary chief. Close to 2,000 spectators according to the *Free Press* and 5,000 based on a *Tribune* account watched as twenty-six Blackfoot dancers performed an anniversary powwow to honour the mayor – the first Canadian mayor to receive this honour.

Events began with an historic Red River ox cart carrying the mayor to the podium as his wife and civic officials walked behind.

According to the *Tribune*, Mayor Coulter "was made chief with the proper rites, ceremonies, dances and prayers which are bestowed upon an Indian when made chief." The mayor danced with the Indigenous participants during the powwow. Honourary songs were sung on his behalf and prayers given for his leadership of the civic administration. Drum performances, dances and chanting accompanied the investiture. At the conclusion of the ceremony, Coulter thanked the Blackfoot. "This is a great honor conferred upon me" he said. "The ceremony was spectacular and interesting. The honor touched me very deeply."

One event which the Parks Board did not sanction was an attempted pavilion safe-cracking. In early morning on June 16, 1947 park night

warden William Hampton heard a noise emanating from the pavilion, "a kind of whisper" and saw a flash of light inside the main floor of the tower room. Immediately, he rushed to the caretaker's residence and phoned the police. Hampton located the safe upside down with its handle knocked eight feet from its moorings. Windows on the north side of the pavilion had been opened and a hole drilled in the frame near the catch. A screen had been forcibly removed.

Detective A.J. Manning arrived at the scene at 2:25 AM. He witnessed a man seventy feet away, running westward from the pavilion. Manning lost sight of him. Another officer, Constable Lawrence Carpick reached the park at 2:55 AM. He saw the thief scampering across the bridge towards Portage Avenue. With police in hot pursuit, the thief jumped off the bridge, ran along the riverbank and hid in the bushes. Using his flashlight, Carpick located, captured, handcuffed and arrested the thief and marched him back to the pavilion.

Arthur Wurch of no fixed address was charged with his part

in the pavilion robbery attempt. A notorious thief, he had once escaped from Stony Mountain Penitentiary. Wurch returned to the penitentiary with a four-year sentence. In January 1948, his accomplices had still not been apprehended.

Queen Elizabeth II's visit to Assiniboine Park on July 24, 1959 marked the highlight of over a half century of social activities in Winnipeg's suburban playground. Over 25,000 well-wishers gathered three hours early for the arrival by motorcade of the Queen and Prince Philip. Elected representatives attended: Premier Duff Roblin, Mayor Steve Juba, all eighteen Winnipeg aldermen and their spouses. Visitors witnessed an historic rent paying ceremony. In front of a Cree and Ojibway encampment reminiscent of the Red River settlement era, the Queen received the traditional tribute from the Hudson's Bay Company of two elk heads and two black beaver skins. Under the Hudson's Bay Company Charter of 1670 such payment was required when the reigning monarch

entered company lands. To the tune of the RCAF Edmonton Band the company fulfilled its responsibility for only the second time in its history. As the royal couple left the dais, the Queen looked around the park and remarked "It's very pretty."

A day after the Queen's departure, officials scheduled a giant barbecue for up to 10,000 visitors from Ontario, Saskatchewan, and the United States. Appropriately held near the buffalo enclosure at the southwest corner of the park, events also featured entertainment by the fifty-piece Royal Canadian Horse Artillery Band capped by a mammoth fireworks display. The barbecue and entertainment provided an appropriate end to a memorable occasion.

As the year 1960 passed into history, an era in Assiniboine Park had ended. Assiniboine Park would come under the control of the Metropolitan

Corporation of Greater Winnipeg. The Parks Board would lose its responsibility for Assiniboine Park and would no longer guide its future. A number of achievements had been realized in fifteen years. The zoo had been placed on a professional footing

with the institution of management planning procedures and the animals cared for using best zoological practices. And the park embraced the cultures of all people regardless of their race, religion or ethnic origin.

Queen Elizabeth's Visit to Assiniboine Park, 1959 CITY OF WINNIPEG ARCHIVES, WINNIPEG BOARD OF PARKS AND RECREATION ANNUAL REPORT, 1959

Chapter Nine:
A Flourishing Park, 1961–1971

Second Conservatory –
Interior, 2018
PHOTO BY AUTHOR

The brand-new Metropolitan Corporation of Greater Winnipeg, commonly known as Metro, transformed Assiniboine Park from a professionally administered recreation area with an ageing infrastructure into one of the finest urban parks in Canada. In the space of Metro's decade-long life, Assiniboine Park developed one of the most modern zoos in North America and a spanking new conservatory. In addition, Assiniboine Park evolved from a warm-weather playground to one enjoyed by citizens in all seasons.

Metro accomplished this feat by orderly and targeted spending without bankrupting city taxpayers or straining city hall finances. With a larger tax base than the old city, Metro achieved this objective without imposing user fees. The much-improved zoo attracted a million visitors per year with free admission. During Metro's tenure, Assiniboine Park attracted all Winnipeggers regardless of their ability to pay.

The Metropolitan Corporation of Greater Winnipeg (Metro)

The Province of Manitoba created the Metropolitan Corporation of Greater Winnipeg (Metro) as an answer to the lack of common services between the City of Winnipeg and the growing suburban municipalities. According to historian Alan Artibise in *Winnipeg: An Illustrated History*, before the advent of regional government in Winnipeg, the Province of Manitoba established independent commissions to administer water supply and services, sewer services, an airport authority, regional planning, and public transit. As the urban area grew, it became evident by 1960 that Greater Winnipeg needed unification of some required services. The final of a series of provincially-funded studies, the Greater Winnipeg Investigating Committee, recommended the creation of a "strong central authority with responsibility of a large number of inter-municipal services."

The Metropolitan Winnipeg Act of 1960 established a second tier of regional government in the City of Winnipeg and its independently incorporated suburbs. Metro assumed responsibility for administering traffic control, zoning, public transit, sewers, water, major streets, bridges, garbage disposal, major parks and public golf courses. Metro council consisted of ten members elected in ten divisions who elected a chairman from amongst themselves. Metro levied a sum against area municipalities to finance its operations. It did not tax individual property owners. Section 173 of the Act stipulated that "the metropolitan council may pass bylaws for acquiring land for and establishing, laying out and improving and maintaining public parks in the metropolitan area or in an adjoining municipality." Section 174 empowered the corporation to assume jurisdiction of any existing public park over fifteen acres within its geographic area. Section 176 authorized Metropolitan council to appoint a superintendent of parks "to operate, manage and supervise the parks of the corporation under the general direction and control of the council."

On April 1, 1961, Metro officially took over Assiniboine Park, including Assiniboine Park Drive (now the western part of Wellington Crescent), the Assiniboine Park Conservatory, and the Assiniboine Park Zoo. Metro assigned the operation and maintenance of the park to the Winnipeg Parks Board on condition that Metro would pay all costs of services rendered, plus fifteen percent for superintendence and overhead.

The agreement was supposed to be renewed annually. But just one year in, on December 31, 1961, Metro terminated its agreement with the Parks Board and assumed direct operation and maintenance of its parks and golf courses. Employees of Assiniboine and the other included parks were transferred to Metro. Metro asked the Parks Board to reassign qualified personnel to fill the positions of assistant superintendent, administrative officer and supervisor of maintenance and construction. Ultimately, the number of full-time employees transferred in Assiniboine Park were small: nine in the park, seven in the conservatory, fourteen in the zoo. Those employees would report to Metro council's Committee on Parks and Protection via the Metro parks superintendent.

Park Planning

Upon its creation, Metro immediately took over the park planning process from the Parks Board. In a letter to Zoo Director Gunter Voss dated June 16, 1961, Parks Board General Superintendent T.R. Hodgson wrote that the Parks Board merely acted as Metro's agent in respect to normal zoo operations and maintenance. "All procedures concerning the planning and capital improvements have been specifically excluded and these matters will

be perused by the Metro Council and its administrators by direct negotiation with the Zoo Director in consultation with the General Superintendent as may be required."

In the spring of 1961, Metro proposed spending $377,960 for a one-year upgrade to the Assiniboine Park Zoo as part of a larger borrowing bylaw. Angered by what they saw as Metro's usurpation of their responsibilities, Winnipeg's mayor and city council appealed Metro's plan to the province's Municipal Board. The Board declared the work non-essential. Its ruling stipulated that borrowing for park development could be fitted into Metro's yearly programs for essential services. A year later, Metro prepared a five-year zoo development plan and appropriated $566,430 from the member participants for this purpose. Upgrades included a refreshment stand and restaurant, more benches,

Second Conservatory – Exterior, 2018
PHOTO BY AUTHOR

Fish Pond in Second
Conservatory, 2018
PHOTO BY AUTHOR

sidewalks, fences, animal enclosures, road paving, parking, and landscaping. This time, the Municipal Board limited Metro's plans and approved spending of just $170,930. Each succeeding year, Metro would be forced to seek Municipal Board consent for zoo expansion. According to the *Free Press* of June 22, 1962, Metro councillors "feel, however, the municipal board have given its approval in principle of the five-year plan." Year after year, with the blessing of the Municipal Board, Metro transformed its zoo management plan into a brick, concrete, and steel reality.

In mid-May 1968, Professor Martin Searle of Metro's Zoological Advisory Committee submitted a five-year, $2,265,000 plan for further zoo development. The proposal contained four priorities: The first would create in the zoo's northwest corner an "Asiatic and Foothills Range" where yak, wisent, Formosan sika, wild horses and tigers would roam. A second priority entailed the construction of a "Fauna Subtropics" enclosure at the southwest corner populated with twenty-five species of subtropical animals and birds

including ostriches and antelopes. A third component, "Mountain Dwellers" would house bighorn sheep, mountain goats, marmots and pika. An "African Hills" segment completed the plan. To be placed a short distance north of the proposed Corydon Avenue parking lot, it would exhibit African animals and birds.

Zoo Director Gunter Voss saw the proposal as a revised version of his own unexecuted 1960 management plan. Lack of funds had derailed his proposal. In much the same way, lack of funds derailed Metro's plans. Metro had to shelve its proposal until 1970 when it revisited the idea. However, except for beginning work on the tropical house, Metro had no opportunity to realize its grand dreams. Within a year, Metro itself had been dissolved.

Infrastructure Improvements under Metro

In its decade-long jurisdiction, Metro substantially upgraded Assiniboine Park's infrastructure. Underground utility installations, road paving, landscaping, and tree planting were

Second Conservatory –
Interil, 2018 PHOTO
BY AUTHOR

undertaken. Picnic shelters and a new conservatory parking lot were constructed. The opening of a new conservatory highlighted Metro's tenure.

Sanitary services and road paving constituted a Metro priority. In 1964, Metro spent almost $50,000 for storm sewers in the park, followed by the installation of sanitary sewers to the picnic shelter, pavilion and conservatory a year later. Road paving stood high on Metro's agenda. In 1964, Tallman Paving asphalted the park's entire driveway system. By 1965, years of City of Winnipeg neglect on utilities and infrastructure or roads had been largely reversed.

Metro upgraded Assiniboine Park's picnic shelters. During 1963,

the corporation awarded a $32,000 contract for a new picnic shelter on the park's Crescent Drive. Two years later, a second picnic shelter was constructed for over $21,000. Assiniboine Park's capacity for protecting picnickers in inclement weather had been enhanced.

Prior to the construction of the new conservatory, the original structure was improved, and new outbuildings added. In 1962, Metro contracted fibreglass building repairs to Canadian Pittsburgh Industries for $5,763. To enhance visitor experience, in 1964 a coffee shop was erected at the eastern end of the conservatory. Costing about $55,000, it opened to the public on July 31, 1964. Built under the Winter Work Incentive Program, the federal government contributed $5,000 towards its costs. Metro constructed new greenhouses at the conservatory in 1967. Engineers Crosier & Greenberg and Partners prepared plans and specifications for the glass structures. For a tender of $16,275 Ickes-Brown Glasshouses of Canada Ltd. received the construction contract.

Yet despite its upgrades and the addition of new outbuildings, the conservatory continued to deteriorate. In 1964, the *Free Press* reported that the conservatory "may need replacing." Four years later, the paper declared the building "structurally unsound. The old structure is iron, and rust accumulates because of the abundance of moisture. A lot of time and money are spent in scraping rust. The heating plant is outdated." Clearly a new facility was needed.

Metro delivered. The crowning achievement of Metro's tenure over Assiniboine Park was surely the construction of a new conservatory. In May 1969, Metro secured tenders for the construction of a new conservatory structure. For the sum of $577,584, contractors Wallace & Aikins successfully won the contract. In addition, Metro spent $25,000 on landscaping and new walkways and $31,900 for professional fees.

Better lighting conditions promoted improved plant growth.

Almost a decade before the advent of the heritage movement in Winnipeg, architects Lundgren, Snider, Tomcej and Associates of Winnipeg with Crosier Greenberg and Partners as consulting engineers prepared plans that preserved the mature plants in the palm house – many of which dated back to 1914. A rectangular canopy was placed over the palm house and the new conservatory built around the old structure. Once the building was complete, workers demolished the old buildings. The completed edifice was substantial.

It measured two-and-a-half times the size of its antecedent. Constructed of glass and brick, it featured a central dome forty-two feet high (nearly seventy-three metres) at the centre – ten feet (three metres) higher than the earlier building. Better lighting conditions promoted improved plant growth. The foyer featured a sunken meeting area for horticultural groups. The building constituted a modern version of Burnham & Company's original glass house, managing to retain the historic banana tree, Japanese orange tree and fig trees.

New Park Attractions

Under Metro's jurisdiction, two new park attractions opened to the public. The placement of Canadian National Railways steam locomotive Number 6043 was the more minor addition. Moved to the southeast corner of

the park in 1962, it was hoisted onto a solid platform costing $3,000. The platform design received the CN Railways chief engineer's approval. To prevent children from injuring themselves while playing on it, the City of Winnipeg authorized the erection of a chain link fence to encircle the locomotive.

The miniature steam train concession proved more popular. In April 1964, local businessman Peter Buzunis received permission to install and operate a scale model steam railway south of the zoo parking lot. Costing $42,000, the railway boasted 3,000 feet (914.4 metres) of twenty-four-inch (.61 metre) track complete with plank platform, tunnel, coal dock, water tank, ticket seller's cabin and crossing signs. A Pennsylvania-built train travelled on the tracks at six mph, accommodating ninety-six riders in three passenger cars. Metro Council set the initial fare at twenty-five cents for both adults and children. At an official opening ceremony, Metro Chairman Dick Bonnycastle drove the last spike into the miniature track. The miniature train made its inaugural run on July 30, 1964. Today, the railway continues to delight adults and children alike.

An All-Season Playground

In the 1960s, Metro transformed Assiniboine Park from a summer playground into a hive of year-round activity. In 1962, Metro formulated plans to construct toboggan slides, "nursery ski slopes," and winter animal quarters "so sightseers can go for walks in the park during the winter and stop to see the exhibits." Four years elapsed before Metro was able, for the first time in history, to open the zoo in winter. A year later, parks staff converted the duck pond into a skating rink and erected a heated shelter for changing. They

Miniature Steam Train & Station, July 29, 1964 UNIVERSITY
OF MANITOBA ARCHIVES, WINNIPEG TRIBUNE PHOTO 18-399-012

Animals including two humped camels, vicunas, alpacas, guanacos, llamas, Arctic fox, polar bears, Chinese leopards, Siberian tigers, pronghorn antelope, moose, white-tailed deer, bison, wisent, Tibetan yaks, sika deer, Pere David deer, cougars, and lynx embraced Winnipeg's brisk winter weather.

1954 LANDS

1904

also constructed a toboggan slide and cleared walkways and paths for snowshoeing, cross-country skiing and walking. To enable visitors to warm up after vigorous outdoor activities, the coffee shop and conservatory opened daily.

Winnipeggers embraced winter activities in Assiniboine Park. In late February 1965, before completion of all of the winter infrastructure, the *Free Press* reported extensive public usage. "Countless families were tumbling down hills and riverbanks on sleds, toboggans, flying saucers, skis and anything that would hold them, snowshoers were struggling to stay upright, a group of 25 boys were playing football in a field of knee-deep snow." One boy attempted "to mush in a homemade sled harnessed to a cocker spaniel, spring-minded people were hopefully visiting the conservatory and even dignified parents could be seen belting the occasional snowball." The zoo posed an attraction to those willing to undertake a vigorous stroll. Animals including two humped camels, vicunas, alpacas, guanacos, llamas, Arctic fox, polar bears, Chinese leopards, Siberian tigers, pronghorn antelope, moose, white-tailed deer, bison, wisent, Tibetan yaks, sika deer, Pere David deer, cougars, and lynx embraced Winnipeg's brisk winter weather.

The numbers of Winnipeggers enjoying outdoor winter activities in Assiniboine Park were substantial. In February 1968, 9,578 people visited the zoo, with 3,645 coming on one day – February 25, 1968. The duck pond lured 10,000 skaters from December 1967 to February 1968, while 2,800 people used the toboggan slides. Metro had truly converted Assiniboine Park into a year-round visitor destination.

Zoo Modernization

In ten short years, Metro council and Zoo Director Gunter Voss transformed the Assiniboine Park Zoo from a small collection of mainly Western Canadian animals into a mid-sized zoological garden dominated by exotics. By 1970, Assiniboine Park housed one of the top zoological collections in North America.

Throughout the 1960s, by both purchase and donation, Assiniboine Park undertook a sizeable animal

Free Zoo Animals

Periodically, the Assiniboine Park Zoo has supplemented its collection with animals captured in the wild or animals which have intruded into the city. On Saturday morning July 22, 1972, a young bull moose, likely from Sandilands Forest Reserve, led police and wildlife officials on a moose chase through the inner city, Fort Garry, St. Boniface and St. Vital before being captured on the banks of the Seine River. Requiring a virile male for its female specimens, the Assiniboine Park Zoo welcomed the beast into its fold. According to the *Tribune*, the moose appeared to be fourteen to sixteen months old and weighed 600 to 700 pounds. One police officer remarked that "it's saved the taxpayer a few dollars."

acquisition program. In 1961, the zoo purchased an eight-month-old Siberian tiger from Germany at a cost of $3,500. Five years later, the program reached its apex. From funds provided by the Royal Trust Company, the zoo imported a rare lesser panda from India. In a swap with East Germany, Assiniboine Park received two North Chinese leopards in exchange for two cougars. To end the year, the zoo obtained by donation a four-year-old female zebra and a two-year-old male zebra born in New York's Catskill Game Farm.

Successful breeding further increased the zoo's population. In 1962 four wallabies and two camels were born. In 1968, the zoo welcomed a litter of three Siberian tigers and raised them to full size. According to Director Voss, "no other zoo in Canada can make such a claim." Voss boasted that in terms of reproduction, the Winnipeg Zoo was one of the most successful on earth. "I would like people to realize it is seldom animals held in captivity will reproduce." By 1970, the Assiniboine Park Zoo exhibited 900 birds and animals representing 100 species.

At the outset of Metro's tenure, many animal enclosures stood in a decrepit state. Within a decade, by selective and judicious spending and the deployment of specialists in enclosure design and planning, Metro transformed a zoo dominated by ancient cages into a modern zoological park.

The combined lion enclosure, winter animal quarters and small office illustrate the state of zoo accommodation. On January 27, 1962, the *Free Press* dispatched a reporter and photographer to interview Gunter Voss. The *Free Press* reported that Voss shared an office "with some 40 screeching, quacking and chattering animals." "Every animal requiring heated accommodation is jammed into the rear of the zoo's lion house. No more than a yard from the dozing lions is a row of monkey cages." Next to the office "is a mynah bird that responds to the ring of the telephone with piercing screeches and wolf whistles. The room's star boarder is Angie a Japanese Macaque monkey who's not yet ready to join the Chinese monkeys in the adjoining room. Unfortunately, Angie

has rheumatism." The interview with Voss resulted in bedlam. Voss released Angie to pose for the photographer. Angie "wrenched herself from the arms of Dr. Voss and proceeded to make a shamble of the room. She tipped over cages, setting a pair of chinchillas free, knocked over water pans, frightened the geese out of their wits and attacked Puli, the curator's amiable Hungarian sheep dog. In her effort to avoid recapture, Angie took refuge on the head of a reporter, scampered over the office desk and made her stand behind a stack of cages. After 10 minutes, she wearied of the chase and allowed herself to be seized. Asked if Angie would bite, Dr. Voss said merely, no so far." At the end of Metro's tenure similar situations did not recur. Proper heated enclosures had been built for less hardy specimens.

To develop the zoo into a world-class facility, Metro installed state of the art underground utilities – water mains, storm sewers and electrical services. Sewer lines comprised a priority. According to Metro council minutes, beginning in 1963, Metro spent $10,750 for sewer, pump and water lines. Two years later, the figure rose to $103,837 for a water main and sanitary sewer extension. In Metro's later years, water main and sanitary sewer figures declined but still remained significant – $26,168 in 1966 and three sections of water main and sewer extensions totalling $12,900, $7917 and $8017 in 1967. By 1970, the Assiniboine Park Zoo boasted modern water mains and storm sewers within its confines.

Underground electrical services complemented water utilities. Metro's director of Parks and Protection vowed to eliminate overhead wires within the zoo's boundaries. For several years the superintendent of Electrical Distribution in the Streets and Transit Division acted as Consultant Supervisor in converting the zoo from overhead lines to buried cables in addition to installing much needed communication devices. As the zoo was modernized, Metro excavated trenches for underground cables on a project by project basis. By the end of Metro's tenure,

Successful breeding further increased the zoo's population. In 1962 four wallabies and two camels were born. In 1968, the zoo welcomed a litter of three Siberian tigers and raised them to full size.

The Incarceration of Gunter Voss

Zoo Director Gunter Voss led an imperfect career after leaving Winnipeg. In late April 1970, he resigned as director of the Assiniboine Park Zoo to occupy a similar position in Toronto. There he guided the early development of the new $20,000,000 Toronto Zoo, which was located in the Rouge River Valley on the eastern edge of that city. Development costs ballooned. Within four years, Voss was removed for "grave managerial inadequacies" but was retained as a part-time consultant for another year. In 1979, the City of Detroit offered Voss an opportunity to redeem himself. Appointed as director of that city's zoo, Voss survived only two years in the position. In 1981, Detroit Mayor Coleman Young dismissed him for taking an unauthorized vacation.

But Voss soon landed on his feet. Relocating to Victoria, BC in 1982, he worked for the BC Environment Ministry as staff development co-ordinator in the personnel services office. This was the last responsible position he would occupy.

While in the employment of the BC Government, activities of a criminal nature back in the United States came to light. On November 24, 1982, the *Free Press* reported that the FBI sought Voss's extradition from Canada for receiving a kickback on the purchase price for seven African antelope and three guanacos which he acquired for the Detroit zoo. Voss contested the extradition order to the United States. On June 23, 1983, it was overturned by the BC Supreme Court because "the charges had not been properly documented and certified under the Canada Extradition Act."

Two years later, Voss was back in the USA. Pleading guilty to the Detroit charges, on June 21, 1985 he was sentenced to six months in jail, fined $5000 and ordered to repay the bribe he had received.

the zoo stood free of overhead electrical wires.

Landscaping and the construction of paved walkways constituted a priority. In the mid-1960s, Metro expended tens of thousands on landscaping the zoo. In 1965 alone, it allocated $9,715 on an area between the Children's Zoo and the zoo office and $3,448 for a space east of the zoo entrance. Asphalt walks were laid to all exhibits. In 1965, Metro awarded a $25,000 contract to Maple Leaf Construction to pave the zoo walks. Metro emphasized the co-ordination of landscaping with zoo enclosure upgrades. Metro council declared that all new animal accommodations must be tied into landscape and walkway design. For one year at least, Metro assigned a consulting firm, Underwood, McLellan & Associates Ltd., this task. Comprehensive planning had triumphed at the zoo.

During Metro's tenure, the zoo underwent the greatest upgrade to animal enclosures in its history. Existing accommodations were improved. In the decade following their construction, the bear pits had deteriorated. Metro appointed Consulting Engineer T.A. Crosier to prepare plans for renovating the bear accommodations. Contracted without tender, Louis Ducharme and Associates repaired the structures for a flat fee of $8,500 plus $80,000 for building materials.

Most animals in the zoo received spacious and substantial new quarters. From 1962 to 1971, Metro constructed individual enclosures for a variety of mammals – monkeys, leopards, zebras, caribou, bison– and specialized housing for beaver and muskrat. Expenditures were substantial. The mammal house cost $94,000, a small enclosure for raccoons, hyenas, and prairie dogs $36,000, the leopard quarters almost $23,700 and the zebra enclosure (which also housed kangaroos and emus) about $33,400. The hoofed stock compound necessitated a significant outlay of $210,000. One of Metro's major achievements, the tropical house (now Toucan Ridge) cost taxpayers $585,000. By 1971, animals in the Assiniboine Park Zoo enjoyed accommodations comparable to the continent's finest zoological parks.

New quarters attempted to duplicate life in the wild for some species. Opened on June 8, 1971, the beaver and muskrat house typified the new design philosophy. As its centennial project, Investors Group donated funds for the enclosure. Divided in half, the house separated beavers from muskrats, and featured an indoor pool and an outdoor pond. According to the *Free Press* the beaver pond discharged via a trickling outflow stream. Water sounds stimulated dam building by its rodent denizens. Tree branches were placed in the water and around the pool enabling the public to view beavers at work. For the first time in Winnipeg, conditions encouraged beavers to breed. Four decades in abeyance, Grey Owl's dreams finally bore fruit.

To defray zoo capital costs for the purchase of animals and the construction of new enclosures, Metro both solicited and welcomed donations from citizens and businesses. All donations were acknowledged. To avoid blatant commercialization, Metro granted only subtle

recognition. In July 1964, the director of Parks and Protection advised Metro council that the new zoo entrance offered a focal point for visitor information. Here a plaque could be mounted honouring individuals and corporations who donated funds for animals. Metro council agreed. The names of donors over $100 would be acknowledged in an "Honour Roll" for a period of five years. Metro also dealt with contributions for animal quarters. Donations would be acknowledged with an appropriately worded metal plate affixed to the structure. In this manner the Assiniboine Park Zoo under Metro remained a public space. Individuals and corporations wishing garish naming rights would be disappointed.

In June 1967, heavy fighting during the Arab-Israeli Six Day War damaged the Jerusalem Biblical Zoological Gardens. The Jerusalem institution suffered significant losses to its collection. Assiniboine Park Zoo Director Gunter Voss recommended that Metro assist that zoo in replenishing its stock. Metro

Parks Committee agreed to the request. The Committee of Parks and Protection wrote to the Jerusalem authorities identifying surplus animals. In response, Jerusalem selected one female palm civet, one pair deodorized skunks, three squirrel monkeys and one pair of mottled ducks. Private donations covered air freight transportation. The Assiniboine Park Zoo had emerged as an important player on the international scene. It would contribute its part in assisting other zoological gardens.

From 1965 to 1970, the Assiniboine Park Zoo reached its zenith as an internationally recognized and highly praised institution. Outside experts complimented the zoo's achievements. In June 1965, the American Society of Mammologists assembled in Winnipeg for their annual convention. Delegates took a particular interest in the herd of Pere David's deer and a white female camel soon to give birth. Some delegates recognized Metro's zoo as Canada's finest while others noted that the exhibits required better explanatory signage.

Four years later, two American zoo specialists, Les Fisher, director of Chicago's Lincoln Park Zoo, and Marvin Miles, an Oakland, California zoological authority, visited Winnipeg. The zoo's master plan impressed them. "The fact that the zoo is in a healthy growing stage is most encouraging" noted Fisher. The experts appreciated the safety features in animal areas such as sliding doors in the bear enclosures. They admired the natural and semi-natural habitats of the animals. "This is not really common in America" said Miles. "The natural settings promote breeding and the animals appear more relaxed." Fisher and Miles rated the zoo among the world's best in terms of attendance.

In April 1970, Gunter Voss resigned as director of the Assiniboine Park Zoo to take up a similar position in Toronto. With Voss at the helm, Metro spent $1.5 million in developing the zoo from 1961 to 1969. In the words of the *Free Press*, "Dr. Voss changed a run-down zoo to an institution which has been recognized as a model of animal care, conservation,

sanitation and viewing facilities." *New Leisure Magazine* described the zoo "as one of the foremost zoological gardens in North America."

Organized Public Activities

During the 1960s, Assiniboine Park embraced, or at the least tolerated, all aspects of outdoor recreation. From Pan American Games field hockey in 1967 to hippie love-ins, Assiniboine Park remained the chosen destination for Winnipeggers to relax and play. As with other Metro-operated recreational areas, Assiniboine Park hosted band concerts of a wide variety, including country and western, polka, jazz and rock and roll in order to appeal to all citizens.

Metro's bucolic park fostered artistic endeavors. In the summer, the Women's Committee of the Winnipeg Art Gallery sponsored a Painting in the Park program. Started in 1958 with thirty-four students and two teachers, the numbers rose to two hundred students aged six to seventeen and nine teachers in 1963. Also organized were adult classes with about thirteen students in the latter year. For two hours Monday to

Friday, students attended three weeks of classes in Assiniboine Park and one week in Kildonan Park. Students presented two exhibitions of their work – one in Assiniboine Park, the other in an art gallery.

In the late 1960s, Canada and the western world experienced the hippie phenomenon. A youthful rebellion against authority, it manifested itself in distinctive attire, long hair, music, drugs, and an idealistic quest for world peace. Every summer across North America and Western Europe hippies attended "love-ins."

Hippies in Winnipeg organized love-ins and selected Assiniboine Park as their venue. Winnipeg's first love-in took place on June 25, 1967. The organizer requested attendees bring balloons, kites, pets, toys, and incense. He asked them to wear colourful clothing. A total of 2,500 attended and enjoyed music from

The Safe and Sound, The Gentry, and The Electric Jug and Blues Band. Youth in psychedelic attire and bell-bottomed pants roamed the crowds carrying multi-coloured crepe flowers. During the afternoon's events, a petition for peace was circulated for submission to the United Nations. In an editorial, the *Free Press* praised the orderliness of the proceeding. It "went beautifully...

it did not turn out to be an orgy of drug taking, sin and loose behaviour. Hippies and police co-operated to ensure there were no incidents." The *Tribune* expressed similar views. According to its account, not much happened except a rock and roll concert. "There was no marijuana or LSD in evidence at the park."

Despite its success, Metro councillors remained wary of a repeat

Hippie Love-In, June 25, 1967 UNIVERSITY OF MANITOBA ARCHIVES – WINNIPEG TRIBUNE PHOTO PC 18/3512/18-2470-037

performance. On March 26, 1970, Councillor Bernie Wolfe expressed concern about a proposed love-in to be held under the direction of "Rick the Freak." He asserted that the event "would have to be under the direction of qualified and responsible personnel." Better yet, the hippie organizer should be informed that "Assiniboine Park is at the present time functioning to its full capacity."

Throughout the 1960s, Metro continued the longstanding practice of sponsoring public concerts in Assiniboine Park. At first the Winnipeg Musicians' Association and later the Musicians' Performance Trust Fund helped defray the cost. In the early 1960s, general concerts appealed to a wide audience while later in the decade performances concentrated on specific music genres. One notable general concert took place on June 21, 1964. Five thousand people assembled to hear some of Winnipeg's top musicians perform. Jimmy King's Band started the event by playing big band era tunes, including selections from Glenn Gould, Bennie Goodman and Count Basie. Guest artist Wally Keep followed with Hollywood film theme songs, including "Hello Dolly", "San Francisco" and "Get Away from it All." To interest younger people in the audience, Chad Allen and the Reflections played Beatles tunes – "I Want to Hold Your Hand" and "She Loves You." The background band for the performances consisted of four trumpets, four trombones, five saxophones, brass, drum, piano and vibes.

Towards the end of the decade, Metro focussed on specifically themed concerts. To capitalize on the interest in Latin American music after the successful Pan American Games, Jose Poneira and his Pan Americans performed "a Musical Fest Latin American Style." Two weeks later the Vic Davies Combo entertained audiences with "Jazz in a Pastoral Scene." The succeeding year witnessed an even wider variety

Jose Poneira and his Pan Americans Concert October 8, 1967 UNIVERSITY OF MANITOBA ARCHIVES

of music. On June 29, 1969, the Bavarian Polka Band introduced that genre of music to Winnipeggers. An old favourite, Country and Western, obtained Metro sponsorship. In July 1969, Melodie and her Country Western Review staged a "Musical Round Up." Regardless of one's musical preferences, the public could enjoy a free concert in Assiniboine Park.

In summer 1967, Winnipeg hosted the largest sporting event in its history – the Pan American Games. The secretary of the organizing committee was granted permission to stage field hockey events on Assiniboine Park's cricket field and utilize its modern pavilion changing rooms. Pan Am officials divided the cricket pitch into two fields and scheduled games during mornings and evenings. Canada, the USA, Jamaica, Argentina, Mexico, the Netherlands Antilles, Bermuda and Trinidad Tobago participated in the field hockey competition. On one day, more than 1,000 fans witnessed four games. The *Free Press* commented "a week ago if any Winnipegger had seen a field hockey player practicing for his sport he could easily have been excused for thinking him a poor weekend golfer. But with the Pan Am Games the scene has changed."

The Demise of Metro

The Metropolitan Corporation of Greater Winnipeg met its end in 1972. According to historian Alan Artibise, almost from its inception, Metro faced uniform resistance from both municipal politicians and the public. Mayor Stephen Juba and city council took deep offence to the reduction of their responsibilities. They envisaged a single-tier Winnipeg which would absorb the suburbs and provide governance to all in the Greater Winnipeg area. The suburbs also objected to their loss of power and the imposition of a new taxation regime. The fragmented authority had segmented Winnipeg's financial capacity. And the lack of citizen involvement confused and troubled citizens of Winnipeg and the suburbs alike.

In 1969, the New Democratic Party under Ed Schreyer was elected to provincial office. The Schreyer government replaced the City of Winnipeg, the suburban governments and Metro with a one-tier structure – Unicity. Initially, the fifty elected members of city council received assistance from thirteen community committees through which the public could exercise its voice.

Assiniboine Park had flourished under Metro's administration. With only a few parks to oversee, Metro allocated the required financial resources and transformed an antiquated and failing zoo into one of the finest in North America. It had constructed a fine new conservatory while preserving the historic subtropical gardens. Under Unicity's tenure, Assiniboine Park would fare less favourably as the new governmental structure balanced multiple funding demands.

Chapter Ten:
The Path to Privatization, 1972–2007

From 1972 to 2007, Assiniboine Park travelled a winding path to privatization – first to provincial government control and abandonment, then benign neglect by Unicity, and finally to a non-profit corporation made up of park "friends" who loved the park and contributed financially to its upkeep. Along the journey, park officials, city councillors and the public dreamt grandiose new visions for the park and zoo – none sustained by government or private funding. Towards the end of Unicity's tenure, the zoo, duck pond and conservatory all required multi-million-dollar upgrades.

English Garden, 2013
PHOTO BY AUTHOR

To supplement shortfalls in its operational budget, officials even took to counting coins in the conservatory fish pond and to soliciting donations for zoo animal upkeep. Several bright spots emerged: voluntary organizations called "friends" took steps to restoring the pavilion, establishing the Leo Mol Sculpture Garden, erecting and maintaining the Lyric Theatre and programing conservatory activities. In a period where The Forks superseded Assiniboine Park as Winnipeg's prime public meeting place and free entertainment venue, city council evaluated its options for reversing the decline of the suburban playground. It chose privatization.

Metro's Legacy

Metro bequeathed Unicity, the new governmental organization representing Winnipeg and its suburbs, a state-of-the-art park with a world-class zoo and conservatory. Focussing on exotic animals, the zoo was expensive to maintain and operate. It placed prohibitive financial demands on a city council tasked with multiple priorities. For the first three years

of its administration, Unicity did manage to complete or expand on legacy projects and activities initiated by the former regional government.

One major objective entailed the acquisition of lands for a buffer zone west of the zoo. The properties in question stretched from Roblin Boulevard to the Assiniboine River and added more river frontage for visitor enjoyment. The purchases took place in two stages. In 1974, the city acquired just over fourteen acres (more than five and a half hectares) fronting Roblin Boulevard and a former convent school at 2799 Roblin Boulevard with almost ten acres (nearly four hectares) including 330 feet (100.58 metres) along the Assiniboine. A year later, Winnipeg expropriated three additional parcels totalling 17.20 acres (6.96 hectares). A buffer zone for Assiniboine Park now stood complete and bordered in part on adjoining residential areas.

Unicity completed Metro's plans for a native animal section at the zoo. In June 1972, city council approved a $300,000 expenditure for preliminary work on a twenty-acre

site in the zoo's undeveloped south half. City council authorized the installation of underground gas, water mains, sewers and electrical conduits. A large musk ox paddock and major native waterfowl lake awaited development. Over the long term, the new section was designed to accommodate twenty species of animals, including skunks, badgers, wolverines, martens, mink, and white-tailed deer.

Open areas would house the existing collection of elk, cougars, lynx, mule deer as well as flight aviaries for the zoo's bald and golden eagles. Winding through the new section, paths would guide visitors to the displays. Deep ditching and concealed fencing eliminated the need for enclosures. In November 1973, the city transformed the preliminary work into reality.

Councillors voted $850,000 for the project, subject to a $23,500 contribution under the Province of Manitoba's Special Municipal Loan and General Emergency Fund. Metro's plans continued to guide Assiniboine Park development, though provincial funding was required.

Metro's last major initiative, the zoo's Tropical House, became a reality under Unicity jurisdiction. Designed by Architects' Consortium of Winnipeg and Consulting Engineers Reid Crowther and Partners, it was erected by contractors Wallace and Akins Ltd. of Winnipeg.

The building was sizeable. Oval in shape, it measured 136 feet long and 100 feet wide. It ascended to a glass and steel dome almost fifty feet overhead. At the time of its construction, the edifice was divided into two areas – a large open space with winding paths, slopes of jungle foliage and a waterfall, plus a tunnel section for exhibits behind glass. Under the auspices of Zoo Director Clive Roots, over 1,400 plants, tree shrubs

and evergreens were planted – all "carefully selected for their resistance to inquisitive birds" and sustained by daily watering from a concealed sprinkler system. Two types of birds moved freely – "brilliantly colored flyers which sail through the air and perch in high dead trees and ground skulkers which strut among the low foliage." Exhibits selected included two-toed sloths and Aldabra tortoises from the Indian Ocean, grey

tree kangaroos and iguanas. Visitors entered the tunnel section through bamboo curtains impenetrable by free-flying birds. Behind glass they viewed De Brazzus monkeys from Central Africa, giant pythons, several varieties of baby crocodiles and oriental otters. Still in use today for a Central and South American exhibit, the tropical house marked the apex of Metro's legacy to the Assiniboine Park Zoo.

Tropical House – Now Toucan Ridge, 2018
PHOTO BY AUTHOR

Mayor Stephen Juba, 1957 MANITOBA ARCHIVES PHOTO

During its administration of Assiniboine Park, Metro had sponsored free public concerts featuring various genres of music – rock & roll, big band, South American, jazz, polka. After Unicity's takeover, the process towards diversification continued. In 1974, *New Leisure Magazine*, through its regular schedule of events, advertised a third annual series of concerts presented by the Winnipeg Symphony Orchestra. Conducted by Maestro Piero Gamba, the orchestra performed selections from Dvorak, Rossini, Tchaikovsky, and Handel. To appeal to a popular audience of non-symphony attendees, an artillery and fireworks show followed. The Royal Winnipeg Ballet introduced park goers to its offerings. As part of Festival Manitoba's Dancing in the Park celebrations, the internationally renowned dance troupe performed a series of free ballets over a five-day period. Park visitors could enjoy ballets such as The Variations on Strike, Up the Meadow Lark, The Still Point and Le Corsair Pas de Deux. With its diversity of free public entertainment to suit all tastes, the modern Assiniboine Park had arrived.

Under Provincial Control

The NDP government of Ed Schreyer recognized Assiniboine Park as a destination for all Manitobans, one that should be placed under provincial control and financed by all taxpayers. In April 1973, the province offered to assume responsibility for the park. Premier Schreyer declared that "it is really a provincial zoo rather than a city park." Winnipeg Mayor Stephen Juba expressed skepticism of provincial intentions and perceived it as a power grab. A year elapsed before the province outlined terms of its proposed takeover. In a letter to city council, the premier proposed leasing the park for twenty-five years and paying the full costs of developing and maintaining it. Under a five-year management agreement, the city would operate the park and zoo as a provincial park and recreational facility available to all Manitobans.

During the life of the twenty-five-year lease the province would determine both the operating and capital budgets for the park and pay all costs as approved. Yet another year passed before city council acted. Retroactive to January 1, 1974, the lease prohibited admission charges being imposed without mutual city and provincial consent. To allay municipal concerns, the city or province could cancel the agreement on one year's notice. The park retained its existing name – Assiniboine Park and Zoo.

For a few years, Assiniboine Park prospered under provincial control. In 1975, the province allocated $717,500 for park improvements. The southeast zoo area reached completion. Enclosures for puma, lynx and wolverines were constructed, as well as washrooms, concession buildings, roadways, walkways and

sewer, water and electrical installations. The park received funding for a quarantine building for rare and costly animals and isolation quarters for sick beasts. Two years later, the park continued to be funded adequately. On March 18, 1977, the *Free Press* reported that Assiniboine Park and Zoo obtained the "lion's share" of the province's $5.1 million grant with 100 percent of its costs covered to a maximum of $2.6 million. For a short time at least, park officials did not have to scramble for funding.

In 1977, voters replaced the NDP provincial government with the Progressive Conservatives led by Sterling Lyon. Ushering in a period of austerity, the new provincial government cut funding to

In July 1978, Zoo Director Clive Roots complained that the zoo "is falling behind other Canadian cities because of continued budget restraints."

Assiniboine Park. In July 1978, Zoo Director Clive Roots complained that the zoo "is falling behind other Canadian cities because of continued budget restraints." Roots asserted that the zoo required an adequate yearly operating budget to maintain its "reputation and attractiveness." Two months later, he indicated that cash cuts to the zoo's operating budget would force a reduction in the size of its animal collection and a

we're barely getting enough to maintain the zoo."

On January 12, 1979, the province announced changes to its funding policy. In a letter to Acting Mayor William Norrie, cabinet minister

funding priorities without reference to the Province… All provincial responsibilities for these nine grant programs will terminate on or before March 31, 1979." The province had effectively cancelled its lease to Assiniboine Park. The park reverted from provincial park back to municipal status. In the future the city would solely fund Assiniboine Park requirements.

The province had effectively cancelled its lease to Assiniboine Park. The park reverted from provincial park back to municipal status.

downgrading of its status as a major Canadian facility. At a meeting of the city's Civic Parks and Recreation Committee, he concluded that "we are not a progressive zoo…We haven't got enough money to expand;

Gerald Mercier wrote that "the province will be making one unconditional Block Grant to the City of Winnipeg in lieu of nine conditional grants…The City is entitled to allocate these monies with its own

The Park Under Unicity

Once again, under Unicity, Assiniboine Park experienced benign neglect. Limited public funding had placed the park and zoo in a holding pattern for over a quarter of a century. Unicity changed little, undertaking few upgrades to the park. Private citizens involved themselves in park activities and raised funds to complement whatever financial resources the city was willing to disburse. Examples of privately- or partial-privately-funded projects included the Children's Zoo – Kinsmen Discovery Centre, a restored and modernized pavilion, the Lyric Theatre, the Leo Mol Sculpture Garden and upgrades to the conservatory.

Non-profit co-operating organizations became involved in the administration of the park. By 2000, the park was operated by a patchwork of organizations and city departments with no central direction. That same year, the city created Assiniboine Park Enterprise to co-ordinate park activities and formulate a governance model for the future. City council opted to privatize the park by transferring administration to an amalgamation of "friends" groups including Partners in the Park, Friends of the Conservatory, and the Zoological Society of Manitoba.

The Zoo

Upon reassuming control over Assiniboine Park, the city set about finalizing the most ambitious zoo master plan in the park's history. Initiated in 1976 with provincial government funding, the plan was prepared by Reid, Crowther and Partners, Consulting Engineers and Hilderman, Fein, Witty, Landscape Architects and Planners. City council struck a steering committee of several municipal officials and Zoo Director Clive Roots to oversee the planning process. Confined to the undeveloped western area of the zoo, the review was completed in February 1980. In its introduction, the report noted that the existing collection remained incomplete and devoid of large mammals, great apes, reptiles and aquatic animals. Moreover, the zoo offered no heated winter viewing for visitors. The master plan proposed "a rather unique concept." Accessible from the south gate, a series of major animal buildings would be linked by heated passageways providing year-round viewing for "delicate" animals indoors and hardy varieties outdoors in winter. During the summer months, most animals would be exhibited outdoors. Specimens to be acquired included elephants, rhinoceroses, giraffes, hippopotamuses and the great apes – gorillas, orangutans and chimpanzees. The zoo would also develop an aquatic collection – penguins, seals and beluga whales. The plan envisaged the construction of "natural-appearing exhibits" with moats and ditches restraining the inmates from devouring one another and the public. To improve public access, the document proposed construction of a second footbridge across the Assiniboine River with a direct zoo entrance. Costly in the extreme, the master plan scheduled the expansion in five phases from 1980 to 1994. The end result, the authors predicted, "will undoubtedly be one of the world's finest zoological gardens." The expected increase in attendance, the increased year-round use, and the improved tourist potential would obviously produce definite advantages for the city's business community."

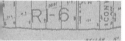

On February 20, 1980, city council adopted the master plan in principle with development to be phased in over a fifteen-year period. Council appointed a task force comprised of several city councillors and Director Roots to investigate additional means of funding the development. Yet city councillors expressed little enthusiasm for the project even though they just adopted it! Finance Committee Chairman Abe Yanofsky said that zoo expansion, estimated at $29.6 million, lay at the "lower end of Winnipeg's spending priorities." The report of the city's Committee of Finance declared that "the financial implications of the proposal are of such a magnitude that it should only be considered in conjunction with all of the city's capital requirements." The 1980 zoo master plan never received public or private funding. It remained a pie-in-the-sky dream of zoo enthusiasts.

Constructed in the mid-1950s and repaired during the Metro era, polar, grizzly, and black bear enclosures required renovations. Work on these enclosures constituted one of the few zoo improvement projects initiated solely at city expense. In 1980, city council allocated $201,300 for repairs to polar bear quarters. Unforeseen problems during construction resulted in a cost overrun of over $42,000 which the city happily approved. Two years later, polar, grizzly, and black bear pits needed further upgrades. As in 1980, M.M. Dillon Ltd. received a commission to provide engineering services. The work was spread over three years – in 1982, further polar bear accommodation improvements, in 1983, black bear renovations, and in 1984, similar repairs to grizzly bear quarters. The cost outlays were sizeable – $135,271 for polar bears, $132,420 for black bears and a hefty $240,281 for grizzly bears. All three bear enclosures featured simulated rock work completed by Titan Construction at a cost of $222,805.

Funding shortages for zoo improvements plagued city council in the mid-1980s. In November 1986, the city partnered with the Zoological Society of Manitoba to share costs and responsibilities for zoo development. In an agreement with the society, the city officially recognized the organization as the sole citizens' advisory group pertaining to zoo matters. The city encouraged the society to promote community and government support for the zoo. Most importantly, that group could solicit and accept donations for city-approved zoo projects. To have a say in its operations, the city secured representation on the organization's board and steering committees.

Kinsmen Discovery Centre, 2018 PHOTO BY AUTHOR

Construction of the Kinsmen Discovery Centre, successor to Aunt Sally's Farm, constituted the first major achievement of the partnership between the City of Winnipeg and the Zoological Society of Manitoba. Taking the lead for the $1.75 million project, the Zoological Society obtained a $400,000 Federal/Provincial Tourism Grant and a $300,000 donation from the Kinsmen Club of Winnipeg. It raised a further $125,000 on its own. The Winnipeg Foundation and numerous small private donors contributed to the project. The city disbursed the lion's share of funding – $1,025,000.

Designed by Smith Carter Architects and Engineers following an architectural competition, the Kinsmen Discovery Centre opened to the public in 1990. It consisted of two buildings. In the main structure, wildlife was displayed in six habitat galleries. The water gallery exhibited fish and underwater plants and featured rock formations and a two-metre high waterfall. The grasslands gallery contained two domed sand dunes into which children could crawl and come face to face with a meerkat. An air gallery, underground gallery and two forest galleries awaited children's exploration. A petting zoo and an outdoor amphitheatre completed the arrangement. The city operated the facility at a cost of $40,000 to $50,000 per year. The Discovery Centre constituted the first of a number of projects in Assiniboine Park which the city undertook in conjunction with co-operating organizations.

After eight decades, free zoo admittance had ended.

Throughout the 1980s, the zoo continued to experience funding shortfalls. City council attempted to address the problem by brainstorming on revenue generation possibilities. In July 1983, city staff advised the Council Committee on Recreation and Social Services of potential revenue sources – donation boxes, stroller/wheelchair rentals, animal feeding dispensers, animal adoption programs and zoo admission charges. Councillors selected animal adoption and the placement of feeding dispensers to raise much needed funds. They also established a zoo reserve fund with an unspecified amount of capital intended solely for animal purchases. City council rejected an admission fee as it would reduce zoo visitation.

The "Adopt an Animal" program achieved a very modest success. Instituted in 1984, the zoo placed 1,200 animals up for "adoption." The animal's size and appetite determined the donor's yearly cost. Smaller animals commanded $15, while Siberian tigers and grizzly bears cost $1,000. In 1984, the zoo received funds for 165 of its 1,200 beasts, the most expensive "adoption" being by St. James Legion No 4.,

which contributed contributed $1,000 a year to feed a grizzly bear. In 1989, the zoo raised its rates of "adoption." While tiny prairie dogs brought in $25, grizzly bears set donors back $2,000 – all tax deductible. The *Free Press* demonstrated its support for the Assiniboine Park Zoo by donating $2,000 to feed a Siberian tiger. But donors did not acquire special rights to the animals. According to Zoo Director Clive Roots "the only contact with animals is whatever communication [the sponsor] can establish outside the cage. You wouldn't want to take them out of their cages. None of them are tame."

Adopt an Animal campaigns and feeding dispensers generated only token revenue. In 1993, the city finally initiated an admission fee – $3 for adults, $1.50 for youths, $1 for children and $7.50 for families. Later in the year, the city introduced annual individual and family zoo passes. After eight decades, free zoo admittance had ended.

Despite funding shortfalls, Assiniboine Park Zoo and its partner, the Zoological Society of

Manitoba, mounted a number of special exhibits. Best known was the giant panda exhibit. In September 1987, the Chinese government offered to loan two giant pandas for display at the Assiniboine Park Zoo. The City's Protection, Parks and Culture Committee immediately approved travel to China for four representatives to negotiate an agreement with the Chinese government. The city solicited donations and sponsorships to offset expenses incurred. In July 1988, an agreement between the Chinese and the City of Winnipeg was finalized.

Capitalizing on Winnipeggers' love for cute and cuddly critters, Communist China proved to be an astute business operator and struck a hard bargain. Winnipeg would donate $350,000 US to the Chinese Association of Zoological Gardens for giant panda conservation, breeding and research. The city would also purchase $500,000 US insurance from the Peoples Insurance Company of China at a cost of $12,500 US. In addition, the Chinese received other benefits – one third of all gate receipts over $587,000 and all proceeds from panda souvenir sales.

To top matters off, Winnipeggers would pay expenses for a Chinese party of two to inspect the exhibition facilities, food and medical conditions, and the residence of a Chinese animal specialist, veterinarian and interpreter for the duration of the exhibit. The city would cover costs of transportation, housing and feeding the animals and a delegation of seven Chinese officials to attend opening and two for closing ceremonies. In return, the Chinese agreed to send two healthy pandas of non-breeding age to Winnipeg – sleepy middle-aged or senior denizens of the panda world requiring more veterinary attention than more playful youngsters. The Chinese had clearly struck a beneficial deal.

The panda exhibit took place in Assiniboine Park from May to September 1989. On May 11, 1989, the $330,000 enclosure opened to visitors. While awake, the elderly pandas ate 350 pounds of bamboo per week – imported from Georgia at a cost of $4 per pound plus shipping costs.

The *Free Press* expected up to 600,000 people to witness the display at admission fees of $3 per adult and

$1.50 for children. However, that figure proved optimistic as only 500,000 visitors passed through the turnstiles. Revenues generated did cover construction costs for the animal enclosure and the financial commitments made to the Chinese government.

The exhibition elicited controversy. The Manitoba Animal Rights Coalition demonstrated in front of the zoo entrance. Ignorant of the pandas' age, their spokesman Todd Lawton mistakenly claimed that the exhibit "exploits the panda and makes a mockery of their status as an endangered species." Furthermore, he said, panda visits interrupt breeding activities and lead to "more specimens being taken out of the wild to augment Chinese population."

The relative success of the giant panda exhibit enticed Assiniboine Park and its partners to launch further programs. In July 1992, the Zoological Society of Manitoba proposed a display of Australian animals for the zoo. City council approved an expenditure of $380,000 subject to receipt of an acceptable marketing plan and a detailed budget and confirmation of federal and provincial government funding commitments. Two months later, the city authorized the Zoological Society to demolish what was left of Aunt Sally's Farm and in its place tender contracts for construction of enclosures for the Australian exhibit. The scope of the project was significant. It would cost $2.6 million to mount. Animals from the Australian outback including kangaroos, wallabies, Tasmanian devils, red pandas, and exotic birds such as lorikeets and cockatoos would entice visitation to the zoo. To highlight the show, the San Diego Zoo would loan two koalas. After its termination, the city would adopt several red kangaroos and wallabies for its permanent collection. In summer 1993, the Winnipeg Down Under exhibit proceeded with an interesting variety of animals. Visitors paid a special fee of $4 for adults and $2.50 for children to see the exotic species from Australia.

Assiniboine Park Zoo staged seasonal activities designed to generate much needed funds. In the first week of October in the mid-1990s, the Zoological Society organized a Hallowe'en children's exhibit called Boo at the Zoo. For a full week of evenings, zoo displays offered children an alternative to the usual one evening of door-to-door trick or treating. From the zoo entrance a one and a half kilometre-long pumpkin-lined path led children to a building where treats were handed out. The route passed structures decorated as the Ultimate Haunted House, Dracula's residence, Gingerbread House, Lost Curator's Cabin and a Discovery Castle. At seventeen locations, sound and light effects including talking trees and howling wolves were designed to frighten passersby. En route, children and their parents encountered scary ghosts, ghouls and goblins. The Hallowe'en show proved highly profitable. In 1996, 42,000 tickets were made available while a year later the first three days alone drew 37,000 paying customers.

A Christmas light show met similar success. In 1995, the Lights of the World exhibit featured illuminated sculptures, including a cherry red lion, several tall giraffes ascending five metres high in "glowing yellow," a lime green rhinoceros, "radiating" pink swans and other animals. A year later, the show treated visitors with thirty-five new sculptures including Zoorasic Park's illuminated dinosaurs. Costing only $50,000 to launch in 1995, the three-week long display attracted 70,000 paying customers. At last Assiniboine Park had found a means of supplementing zoo revenue.

In late April 1991, the acclaimed great ape conservationist Jane Goodall visited Winnipeg to mark Earth Day activities. In a tour of the Assiniboine Park Zoo, she noted that "it's sort of in the middle of the old-fashioned zoos that haven't done anything to improve, and the new zoos that have somehow managed to raise a lot of money." Goodall was pleased that the Winnipeg facility exhibited no chimpanzees, gorillas or orangutans as the severe Winnipeg winter would force these large primates to spend too many months indoors. Goodall's comments indicate that the zoo had failed to keep pace with international developments. It had remained fixed in time since Metro's dissolution. The absence of great apes reflected a lack of funding to achieve Unicity's management plan – not a decision to spare primates from unsuitable weather.

The English Garden and Conservatory

Eighteen years into Unicity's tenure the English Garden began showing signs of decline. In the past, its reputation had rested on the annual flower display. Since the Unicity takeover, budgetary restraint

English Garden, 2013
PHOTO BY AUTHOR

diminished the variety of annuals in the garden. In 1991 the city prepared a master plan. It proposed phasing in over a three to five-year period a range of perennials to supplement and complement the annual flower display. Altogether a total of 325 species of annuals and perennials would replace the existing 100 annuals. The management plan called for the replacement of concrete walkways with more rustic cobblestone pathways, the restoration of greenery around the garden, a new pathway to the Leo Mol Sculpture Garden, new gates, lighting and benches.

The project received city council approval. The city struck an advisory committee of citizens to assist in the plan's fulfilment and to identify outside funding sources. From the outset, the project required ongoing funding. On September 20, 2000, the *Free Press* reported on the eighth annual English Garden clean-up event. Participants purchased a bag for $5, strolled through the garden and picked up seeds and cuttings from a variety of plants. With an average seventy-five donors, the fundraiser generated $375 – small

change for the purchase of new plants for the English Garden display.

During the first twenty years of Unicity's tenure, the conservatory experienced only routine maintenance and a few upgrades. One of the last and the most significant of Metro's major projects, the conservatory could expect structural soundness for several decades.

In May 1989, a new group called Friends of the Assiniboine Park Conservatory was formed. Composed of about sixty volunteers interested in botany, plants and horticulture, the organization worked with the city on educational and recreational programs and suggested ideas for the facility's long-term development. By 1995, Friends of the Assiniboine Park Conservatory had grown to over 327 individual and seven institutional and organizational members. At that point, the city appointed them as formal "partners in planning for development of the Conservatory and in the implementation of the Conservatory's mission." Continuously short of funding for conservatory activities and upgrades, the city welcomed

Friends' contributions for service unachievable through tax-based funding. Friends' contributions led to several conservatory upgrades – $40,000 of a $60,000 sliding wall system to shield an area required for programing purposes and a gift shop operated by that organization. Coins thrown into the conservatory's fish-pond raised $1,000 to $2,000 annually for Friends' programs and building improvements.

The Pavilion, Leo Mol Sculpture Garden & Lyric Theatre

The withdrawal of Unicity from adequately funding Assiniboine Park encouraged private citizens to fill the gap. A group led by businessman Hartley T. Richardson spearheaded the drive to establish the Leo Mol Sculpture Garden. Pavilion Gallery Trust Inc. (later re-named Partners in the Park) raised capital and with government assistance restored the pavilion and transformed it into an art gallery, restaurant, and administrative offices. Private funding enabled arts groups to realize their long-sought dream of a permanent

Restored Pavilion,
2013 PHOTO
BY AUTHOR

bandstand, the Lyric Theatre, where they staged performances for appreciative audiences. By their actions, private citizen groups established a stake in park administration equal to that of the city.

The pavilion presented Unicity with a particular challenge. In the 1960s,

Metro had opened Assiniboine Park to year-round recreation. Yet the pavilion remained closed because it was poorly insulated and unheated. Upgrades would cost in the millions – funds unavailable to the city. The city sought private partners to fund its goals.

In early 1982, the Curling Hall of Fame and Museum of Canada Inc. proposed converting the pavilion into a year-round facility. Initially, the city's Committee on Recreation and Social Services expressed concern that the reuse would be inappropriate in terms of "ideology and practicality." The Curling Hall of Fame modified its submission. Under a twenty-five-year lease approved by city council, the curling group would winterize and heat the pavilion. The main floor would house a public concession, washrooms, and a number of administrative offices while the curling hall of fame would occupy the second floor. The lessee would spend $1,000,000 to upgrade the building. Several years elapsed and no renovations took place. Failing to raise the required capital, the curlers abandoned the project in March 1985.

Leo Mol Sculpture Garden and Garden House, 2018 PHOTO BY AUTHOR

In October 1996, a non-profit group, Pavilion Trust Inc. chaired by Richardson, presented city council with a plan to renovate and operate the pavilion. Under a management agreement, the trust would undertake at no cost to the city the restoration of the pavilion, including the pergola, lily pool, and front courtyard. The Trust would convert the interior, including the tower, to art gallery, restaurant and banquet purposes, and install proper insulation and a heating system. The gallery would exhibit collections of three local artists – Walter J. Phillips, Ivan Eyre and Clarence Tellenius. Inside the pergola, the group proposed constructing a glassed-in restaurant. Moreover, Pavilion Gallery Trust Inc. promised to cover annual maintenance costs of $27,000 per year and $4,000 in utility bills. City council approved the privately funded $4-million pavilion makeover. The project proceeded with private funding and a $2.25 million infusion from the Canada-Manitoba Infrastructure Works Program. The restoration proved a resounding success.

A non-profit organization developed the Leo Mol Sculpture Garden with combined public and private funding. In 1989, Leo Mol offered to donate his lifelong collection of sculptures to Assiniboine Park for placement adjacent to the English Garden. On May 9, 1989, a meeting took place to discuss the proposal. H.T. Richardson representing Mol, the mayor, and members of the Committee of Parks and Protection attended. The group selected a site encompassing the former gardener's house, private yard and remnant of the original plant nursery. Within the confines of the land parcel, a garden containing fifty to seventy-five bronze statutes with a Victorian-style garden house to accommodate smaller indoor sculptures would be erected. In February 1990, the city approved the project and instructed the city solicitor to prepare an agreement with Mol for the donation of the sculptures. Five months later, the Parks and Recreation Department presented a financial plan for the development of the project. Relying partially on city funding, the Friends of Leo Mol Sculpture Garden set up a trust fund for the endeavour. The city provided start-up capital of $100,000. The sod turning ceremony for the Sculpture Garden took place on September 28, 1990.

Leo Mol Sculpture Garden, 2018
PHOTO BY AUTHOR

The Lyric Theatre comprised the third project completed by friends of the park utilizing private finances. From the demolition of the original carousel bandstand in the 1930s

until the late 1990s, concerts were performed on a series of temporary stages. In 1959, park officials erected such a structure to accommodate Queen Elizabeth's visit. Over successive decades, musicians, dancers and thespians deployed the city's "bandmobile" to stage plays, dances and concerts in the meadow backing the pavilion. By the early 1990s an informal stage was constructed. It backed onto the pavilion's pergola. The Royal Winnipeg Ballet paid for this temporary platform. Yet performing arts groups craved a permanent band shell. In 1997 Pavilion Gallery Trust Inc. proposed constructing the structure. Private funds would be utilized, and a $500,000 endowment fund would be established. Performers of the Winnipeg Symphony Orchestra, Royal Winnipeg Ballet, Manitoba Theatre Centre and jazz and folk festivals would benefit greatly from the new facility. Pavilion Gallery Trust Inc. offered to manage band shell activities. In return, the Trust obtained the right to cordon off selected areas fronting the stage where admission could be charged.

City council approved the proposal in principle and the city solicitor prepared a management agreement between the city and Pavilion Gallery. Since 1998, the Lyric Theatre has been a summer destination for concert, ballet and theatergoers.

Decline of Assiniboine Park

By the mid-1990s, The Forks superseded Assiniboine Park as Winnipeg's most popular attraction. Previously a Canadian National Railways marshalling yard, its focal point, the Forks Market, had functioned as two stables for horses and carts. Officially opened for business in 1989, The Forks soon attracted multitudes of people. By 1998, visits to The Forks topped seven million annually with 120 public events being staged. In the early 1990s, the city selected The Forks as its site for Canada Day celebrations. Assiniboine Park reverted to a secondary location for public events and essentially an overflow site for Canada Day festivities.

Bird's Hill Provincial Park also drew potential visitors away from

Lyric Theatre, 2018
PHOTO BY AUTHOR

Assiniboine Park as a result of its close proximity to Winnipeg. Created as a project to honour Canada's 1967 centennial, the park boasted hiking and cycling trails as well as a man-made lake and bathing beach. The site's vast expanse enabled it to stage the ever-popular Winnipeg Folk Festival and various sports competitions including marathon and bicycle races. To enjoy nature in suburban surroundings, Winnipeggers possessed a choice of destinations – a short drive to Assiniboine Park or a somewhat longer journey to Bird's Hill.

Beginning in the 1980s, the construction of trails throughout the city and its suburbs further reduced visits to Assiniboine Park. Winnipeggers could enjoy picturesque walking and cycling close to home. Paved paths were laid adjacent to the Red and Assiniboine Rivers downtown. Along stretches of the Seine River, Bunn's Creek and Sturgeon Creek pedestrians could enjoy pretty views from the new walkways. New subdivisions such as River Park South, Waverley West and Sage Creek

incorporated public paths alongside water retention ponds. Even close to Assiniboine Park, new paths enticed residents to exercise. Walkways through the Assiniboine Forest and the Harte Trail in Charleswood offered opportunities for healthful recreation. Winnipeggers residing a considerable distance no longer travelled to Assiniboine Park to walk or cycle the riverine paths. Visiting for exercise purposes attracted mainly local residents.

The Assiniboine Park Zoo and Conservatory fell into decline. According to the *Free Press* in 1998, the zoo had not undergone a facelift in twenty-five years "and it's beginning to look old, tired and a little frayed around the edges." The Winnipeg Foundation, which had donated $1 million for park improvements from 1995 to 2000, reported that vandalism, messy washrooms and an ageing playground plagued the park. The conservatory stood in dire need of repair. The city admitted that the roof and crumbling brickwork required replacement and the heating, electrical and plumbing

systems needed upgrades. Friends of the Conservatory estimated the cost of conservatory repairs at $4,000,000. On September 19, 2005, the *Free Press* editorialized that the zoo was "crumbling and out of date…years behind the model zoos in other North American cities. Same said for conservatory." The park "needs imaginative play spots, fountains and programs to draw families and individuals every day, year-round." Yet no funds were forthcoming. On September 6, 2000, Mayor Glen Murray indicated "that spending more money maintaining Assiniboine Park is not a high priority." He even refused a $150,000 expenditure for permanent washrooms for the Lyric Theatre.

At the dawn of the twenty-first century, the city amalgamated its various departments which operated in Assiniboine Park. In April 2000, several city departments administered Assiniboine Park. Community Services/Cultural Amenities took responsibility for the zoo subject to Zoological Society control of the Carousel Restaurant, Zootique Gift

Condos in the Park?

In the early 2000s, the need to secure new sources of funding for the redevelopment of Assiniboine Park had grown urgent. Addressing this issue, Mayor Sam Katz proposed constructing condominiums on two unused parking lots facing Corydon Avenue that functioned as the city's yard waste and Christmas tree depots. On September 18, 2005 the *Free Press* reported that up to 280 units could be built on the parcel. The lease fees and property taxes would generate more than $1 million per year. The money would be deposited into an endowment fund to help finance Assiniboine Park's makeover.

The response from some city councillors was swift. On September 18, 2005, River Heights Councillor Donald Benham stated, "I am disgusted that the person who is entrusted with our public legacies like Assiniboine Park would try to sell them off for the private benefit of developers and rich people." Four days later, Benham suggested that the city apply profits from the sale of surplus lands to Assiniboine Park's redevelopment. Councillor Justin Swandel offered another solution. The city could give the park all taxes from the future development of Kapyong Barracks – lands owned by the federal government with an uncertain future.

Reporter after *Free Press* reporter directed an unrelenting and furious barrage of criticism at Mayor Katz's proposal. On September 20, Gordon Sinclair Jr. wrote that "a million bucks is a pittance compared to the parcelling off of a priceless park in the surrendering of our children's legacy... Now Sam Katz wants to create an enclave for the privileged there in what amounts after hours to a gated community." Two days later, Val Werier called the condos "a regressive step" and the unsightly parking lot "a minor matter." He questioned how it could be called "visionary to promote a private, privileged complex within our finest park sustained by the public purse for a century." A third columnist, Shawna Mackinnon, declared that "the only winner would be the developers and those fortunate enough to be able to afford the cost of purchasing the upscale condos. These folks would have Assiniboine Park, Winnipeg's crown jewel as their personal playground." Clearly the press perspective was single-minded.

Through letters to the editor and a public opinion poll, citizens expressed more balanced views. By September 20, the *Free Press* had received ninety-four letters and e-mails on the subject. Half the writers supported condos while the other half opposed them. The paper also commissioned a Probe Research poll. Released on September 29, 2005, its findings revealed fifty percent opposition and forty-three percent support. Seven percent of respondents took no stance. Indeed, the proposal for condos in Assiniboine Park divided Winnipeggers.

Mayor Katz's proposal died a slow death. In a year-end review of city council's deliberations, *Free Press* reporter Mary Agnes Welch and Patti Edgar concluded that Katz's trial balloon had initiated a public discourse on Assiniboine Park's future. In raising the issue of alternate funding for Assiniboine Park and ultimately the creation and revitalization of Winnipeg's iconic green space under the Assiniboine Park Conservancy, Sam Katz deserves credit.

Shop and educational programs. Community Services/Cultural Amenities also managed the conservatory subject to Friends of the Conservatory responsibility for the gift shop and educational programs. The two city departments of Public Works, and Parks and Open Spaces

Services division of the Community Services Department as Assiniboine Park Enterprise. The new division would manage the zoo, conservatory, park maintenance and event support function. Above all it was tasked with physical and financial planning for the park as a whole. Assiniboine Park Enterprise would develop plans for the park's redevelopment and governance structure.

Under the auspices of Assiniboine Park Enterprise, the city formulated a ten-year zoo redevelopment plan. Prepared by landscape and zoo architect Azeo Torre, the plan became public on July 12, 2002. The document envisaged displays simulating a tour of Canada and featured animals of the boreal forest, Canadian Shield, Arctic tundra and ocean. According to the *Free Press*, visitors would access the zoo from Corydon Avenue. The entrance would open to a prairie meadow populated with deer, elk, and bison. The path would lead

Under the auspices of Assiniboine Park Enterprise, the city formulated a ten-year zoo redevelopment plan.

shared park maintenance and event management responsibilities. By necessity, the city excluded the Pavilion, Leo Mol Sculpture Garden and the Lyric Theatre – all operated under lease by Partners in the Park, the successor to Park Pavilion Trust Inc. To administer the park, the City renamed the Cultural Amenities and visitors northward. There moose, timber wolves, and wolverine would be displayed. The trek culminated in the Arctic. A domed polar bear enclosure with an underground viewing area would enable visitors to view both polar bears and walruses. A second phase of the project foresaw a transformation of the existing aviary units into a children's discovery centre complete with classrooms for interpretation and animal demonstrations. A third phase focussed on northern Asia and proposed exhibits of Siberian tigers and Amur leopards. To attract visitors, the plan transformed Assiniboine Park Zoo into an educational and cultural experience. To fund redevelopment, the city required public and private partnerships.

Two years after the zoo proposal, the city released the Assiniboine Park Framework Plan. It incorporated views of Assiniboine Park Enterprise,

Friends of the Assiniboine Park Conservatory, Partners in the Park and the Zoological Society of Manitoba. The scope proved far-reaching. The proposal embraced the Torre development plan. Among other recommendations, it called for construction of a new conservatory at the southeast entrance on Corydon Avenue as a focal point for the Formal Gardens and the redevelopment of the existing conservatory area into a public information and park visitor centre. The duck pond would be rehabilitated, enlarged and connected to the English Garden via a wide pedestrian walkway. The Assiniboine River shoreline and riparian forest would be restored to its original condition. The zoo would be integrated into the park and offer views and vistas of its activities from outside zoo boundaries. The Park Framework Plan recommended changes in administration. The

English Garden, Leo Mol Sculpture Garden and duck pond would be managed as one unit.

City council concurred in the recommendations of Executive Policy Committee and adopted the plan. In combination with the zoo master plan, the Park Framework constituted Assiniboine Enterprise's only real achievement. Both plans formed the base for future park development.

Privatization

In 2006 to 2007, city council took steps to establish a new governance model for Assiniboine Park. Either unable or unwilling to raise sufficient funds to operate the park and fulfil terms of the zoo management and park framework plans to upgrade it, city council laid the ground for privatization. In 2005, the *Free Press* cited New York City's Central Park governance structure as a model. In an editorial dated September 19, 2005,

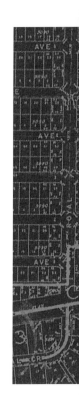

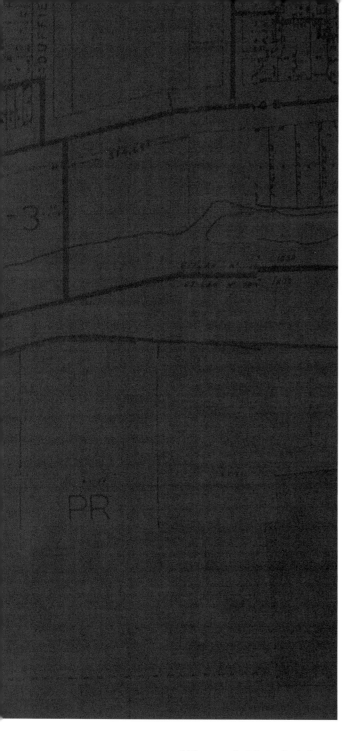

it concluded that Central Park "was saved in the 1980s from deterioration by a not-for-profit partnership that harboured ambitious plans to be bankrolled by entrepreneurial zeal. This can happen here. Partners in the Park might be a template." Evidently city council agreed. On July 10, 2006, Bartley Kives of the *Free Press* reported that the city would create a new agency, the Assiniboine Park Conservancy to operate the park. Its board would include representatives from the city, province, Friends of the Conservatory, the Manitoba Zoological Society and Partners in the Park. The decision to privatize the park had been taken.

Park privatization elicited a spirited debate. The non-profit groups operating parts of the park expressed doubts. According to *Free Press* reporter Mary Agnes Welch, they feared that existing volunteers "will be shunted aside if a new board is set up to run the park. And they worry a plan to govern the park has come without any guarantee of increased city funding leaving the door open for more corporate involvement and reduced public access." City councillors and the mayor expressed a range of views. Councillor Russ Wyatt of Transcona opposed "private sector control of the park." He said that "just because the city has underfunded the park for 20 to 25 years, it doesn't mean we have to get rid of it." Councillor Dan Vandal of St. Boniface commented that privatization "is a surrendering of city council's responsibilities" and "councillors were elected to look after the park and zoo, not to give it to an outside group." Mayor Sam Katz retorted "that the general public doesn't care who runs the park, as long as its facilities are improved and maintained."

On June 20, 2007, city council voted by a ten to six margin to lease Assiniboine Park to the newly-created, non-profit Assiniboine Park Conservancy. The Standing Policy Committee on Protection and Community Services set out terms of the handover. The committee report stipulated that the not-for-profit corporation "would operate independently from the City of Winnipeg with a mandate to lead, manage, fundraise, restore and redevelop the overall park and its amenities." The Conservancy would assume responsibility for the park in a phased-in approach. The initial Board of Directors would be selected by the mayor and include representatives from the City of Winnipeg, Province of Manitoba, Zoological Society of Manitoba, Friends of the Assiniboine Park Conservatory, Partners in the Park, Charleswood Rotary Club, and the community at large. A city council community advisory committee would advise the Conservancy on matters of public interest. Within six months of incorporation, the Conservancy would negotiate a park management agreement with the city. The city allocated $100,000 in start up capital to ensure that the Conservancy met its strategic plan deadline.

In 2008, 103 years of municipal administration and control of Assiniboine Park ended. Privatization had probably been inevitable. From 1980 to 2007, Assiniboine Park had been one initiative in competition with other initiatives – and probably a low priority in terms of public need. From its inception, the

In 2008, 103 years of municipal administration and control of Assiniboine Park ended.

zoo had evolved from an inexpensively maintained menagerie to a multi-million-dollar operation – unaffordable by a city with multiple demands. Friends had partnered with the city and successfully raised funds for creation of the Leo Mol Sculpture Garden, Lyric Theatre, Pavilion rehabilitation, and some conservatory and zoo improvements. In 2007, friends administered

considerable elements of the park. Facing a major park makeover, a small majority of city councillors believed that the friends could duplicate their limited successes on a park-wide scale – and save taxpayers the need for increased expenditures.

Chapter Eleven: A New Vision, 2008–2019

Qualico Family Centre, 2018
PHOTO BY AUTHOR

On the eve of its takeover, the new Assiniboine Park Conservancy (APC) acquired a park in a mixed state of repair. The pavilion had been restored by Pavilion Trust Inc., predecessor to Partners in the Park. The Leo Mol Sculpture Garden and Lyric Theatre consisted of relatively new structures initiated by park friends. The English Garden had recently been transformed by Unicity into a colourful and mixed annual-perennial garden and stood in fine shape.

But major elements of the park were crumbling. Having witnessed few upgrades or maintenance since 1980, the zoo required extensive rehabilitation. The conservatory was obsolete and needed extensive repairs or replacement. The duck pond required rehabilitation and the children's playground no longer met modern standards. City council expected and demanded the APC to address these issues.

The APC took control of Assiniboine Park in March 2008. At that time the city was eager to rid itself of its Assiniboine Park responsibilities. Consequently, the APC operated for almost three years without a management agreement or development plan. These agreements awaited negotiation. The Lease and Funding Agreement between the City of Winnipeg and the Assiniboine Park Conservancy was finally signed on October 1, 2010. The Development Plan was finalized three months later. Based on a preliminary plan submitted in March 2009, the latter's concepts echoed those of the Assiniboine Park Zoo Management Plan of 2001 and the Assiniboine Park Framework Plan of 2004. The APC also filed an undated refurbishment plan for existing park structures. On October 1, 2010, the Assiniboine Park Conservancy Inc. and the City of Winnipeg finalized the management agreement. The document is far-reaching. Except for funding, the city seems to absolve itself of responsibility for Assiniboine Park. The agreement is long term: a fifty-year lease to the APC with two twenty-five-year renewals for control, occupation and park usage. The APC acquires the right to develop new facilities and pursue commercial activities within the park, subject to city council approval for major projects. The city commits itself to long term funding of APC activities while the APC accepts responsibility for fundraising from private and senior government sources to match the city's capital cost contributions.

Public accountability is incorporated into the agreement. At the beginning of each decade, the APC presents a new ten-year development plan to city council for approval. Each year, the APC provides city

Duck Pond, 2013
PHOTO BY AUTHOR

Picnic Shelter, 2018
PHOTO BY AUTHOR

New Children's Playground,
2018 PHOTO BY AUTHOR

council through the Executive Policy Committee with an audited financial statement, progress report on park development and rehabilitation, intended building and restoration plans and an annual report on APC activities. To ensure that the APC is achieving its goals, it opens all its records to city inspection. Under terms of the agreement, the public retains free access to park green areas while the APC can charge for all attractions and parking should it wish to do so. Above all, the agreement stresses the retention of Assiniboine Park's character as an early twentieth century "English landscape" – a vision which would be subsequently challenged. Should the city terminate its agreement with the APC, eighteen months notice is required plus a mutually satisfactory agreement between the parties on the development of the park and the expenditure of funds.

The Development Plan of January 12, 2011 is the blueprint for the refurbishment of Assiniboine Park. To secure city funding as specified in the lease, the APC must renew the park within ten years. By the time of this book's publication in 2019, the APC was fulfilling its obligations on time or ahead of schedule. The Development Plan presents the city and the public with a comprehensive vision of Assiniboine Park and its new attractions.

The preamble to the document elucidates the APC's vision for park renewal. It commences with the usual platitudes – a vibrant park for all, guided by the collective views of the community and a space with various attractions, amenities, services and programs. Then the plan strikes a new chord. The APC envisages a "signature park," world-class in design. "Natural attractions such as gardens and green spaces will be further enhanced to reinforce the park as Canada's most spectacular representation of the Olmsted model." The park will be "a unique and engaging dynamic laboratory for life-long learning." To finance the improvements, revenue generation is integrated into all activities.

The APC vision differs markedly from Assiniboine Park's original concept – a place laid out with a limited budget, a few attractions, a sanctuary with wide open spaces amenable to rest and rejuvenation by Winnipeg citizens, a park devoid of revenue-generating user fees and amusement park attractions. The very antithesis of the 1903 vision, the APC's plan strikes a new chord.

The crux of the development plan is "The Transformation of Assiniboine Park – Restore, Enhance, Preserve." The revitalization of Assiniboine Park is divided into three phases of change and renewal. The first is "The Heart of the Park." It encompasses creation of a Children's Nature and Adventure Playground, an expanded duck pond, and a family centre with restaurant. The second phase, "The Transformation of Assiniboine Park Zoo" entails the zoo's rehabilitation, the construction of the Journey to Churchill exhibit and the Polar Bear Conservation Centre. Phases 1 and 2 have been successfully completed. The final

The crux of the development plan is "The Transformation of Assiniboine Park – Restore, Enhance, Preserve."

phase, "The Iconic Conservatory and Conference Centre" entail the construction of a new conservatory and garden in the eastern part of the park. One of the three gardens will feature a native forest complete with rock climbing wall, and an aerial park with a zip line and rope ladders. It will engage youth "in confidence-building activities and promote physical activity." At this time of writing, Phase 3 is well underway.

The undated Refurbishment Plan for Assiniboine Park is the second document to which the 2010 lease is subject. It calls for renewal of many structures in the park. The City of Winnipeg has committed $3.1 million annually for a ten-year period beginning in 2010 for the restoration and improvement of park structures. Included in the plan are virtually all animal enclosures except new builds. Outside the zoo perimeter, the Lyric Theatre, Cricket Building, Leo Mol Gallery and Cottage among others are being restored or improved. In spring 2019, renovations were ongoing.

Why did city council issue such a long-term lease to the APC, approve its grandiose development plan, and abrogate its responsibility to maintain the park? One obvious reason was the city's inability to fund the desired $200-million park makeover. In a June 23, 2012 interview with APC Chief Executive officer Margaret Redmond, *Free Press* columnist Gordon Sinclair Jr. proffered an additional explanation. In a column he paraphrases Redmond as stating that the city undertook a series of studies, "one of which canvassed Winnipeg's Big Money on how much they would donate for the redevelopment of the park. The No. 1 message was that as long as the city was at the helm of this, I won't give."

The *Free Press* welcomed the APC takeover. In an editorial dated March 17, 2008, it declared that "after years of decline and neglect Assiniboine Park appears to finally be on the path to recovery." The *Free Press* based its confidence on the leadership role in park renewal taken by some of the city's most influential citizens. Most importantly, the new APC board agreed "on a broad vision of the park and zoo that is based on environmental principles, as opposed to the razzle-dazzle of Coney Island." The *Free Press* applauded the goal of raising $50 million privately to leverage another $150 million from three levels of government.

How does today's governance of Assiniboine Park compare with large parks in other major cities? Como Park in St. Paul and Stanley Park

Riverine Forest, 2018
PHOTO BY AUTHOR

in Vancouver remain among the only large parks operated by municipal government – Como Park by the St. Paul Parks Department and Stanley Park by the publicly-elected Vancouver Parks Board. Como Park operates a zoo and conservatory and charges no zoo admission. However, its original park landscape has been severely compromised. To provide park funding, Como Park encompasses a golf course, an amusement park, mini golf and "a historic carousel." On the other hand, Stanley Park no longer operates a zoo. Opened in 1905, its zoo closed its gates ninety-one years later. In 1994, voters rejected a proposal to expand the zoo and instead did away with it altogether. The disposal of its collection, partly to the privately-owned Greater Vancouver Zoo in Aldergrove, BC likely enabled Stanley Park to be operated more economically and ensured public control.

In terms of governance, New York's Central Park Conservancy (CPC) is often cited as the model for the Assiniboine Park Conservancy. On close scrutiny, however, the Central Park Conservancy and APC share little in common. Started as a "friends" group in 1980, the CPC initially assisted the New York City Parks Department in routine park maintenance and refurbishment. The most recent agreement in 2013, a ten-year pact, assigns the Central Park Conservancy responsibility for day-to-day park management in return for grants based on its ability to raise private funds. The City of New York retains overall control and policy responsibility for Central Park. In essence, the Central Park Conservancy performs a caretaker function.

The creation of the APC constitutes a made-in-Winnipeg solution to

Sculpture on North Side of Assiniboine River, 2018 PHOTO BY AUTHOR

Giant Insect Display at Zoo, 2018 PHOTO BY AUTHOR

the problems confronting Assiniboine Park. As an arms-length, not-for-profit corporation, it plans, develops and operates the park with minimal city input. Its creation represents a desire to redress a decline in Winnipeg's most distinctive green space.

Duck Pond, 2013
PHOTO BY AUTHOR

A Park Makeover

In its first decade, the APC has undertaken a flurry of improvements. Assiniboine Park's makeover has proceeded according to the 2011 development plan. Construction of the first phase, the $10 million "The Heart of the Park," was started in 2009, two years before the plan's finalization. The centrepiece of the project, the duck pond, was reconstructed and tripled in size. Facing the east side of the pond, a heated, glassed-in picnic shelter, complete with modern washrooms, was erected. To the west of the pavilion, the APC laid out a new children's playground. Entering through a pint-sized, blue door with a circular portal, the facility utilizes natural building materials and features a river-like water play area, wooden tree houses, "saucer-like" swings and green bouncing rubber hills. It opened to the public on May 19, 2011. Outside the playground, a toboggan run delights children of all ages. Overlooking the duck pond, a new family centre provides much-needed restaurant facilities, meeting rooms and a children's play area. Welcoming its first customers on November 24, 2011, the structure encompasses 10,000 square feet of interior space and boasts exterior glass walls, a wood-slat ceiling assembled from reclaimed diseased elm trees and a roof covered in vegetation. To help finance the structure Qualico Developments donated $3 million for naming rights while the RBC Foundation contributed $400,000. By late 2011, "the Heart of the Park" was complete. Today, thousands of Winnipeggers, young and old, visit the new facilities to play, observe waterfowl, dine in the family centre and in winter, skate and toboggan.

The second phase of the development plan, "The Transformation of Assiniboine Park Zoo" is complete and extensive zoo renovations and upgrades have been undertaken. The zoo now has a new layout with the relocation of its main entrance from inside the park to a new entry point complete with large parking lot off Roblin Boulevard. The revitalized zoo boasts four major components – a prairie exhibit featuring a herd of buffalo, an Arctic exhibit concentrating on polar bears, an Asian exhibit with Siberian tigers, and a seasonal Australian display of kangaroos. Within the zoo's rearranged configuration, improvements consist of a new zoo entrance and visitor centre, transformation of the tropical house into an environment for Central and South American animals, construction of the Journey to Churchill exhibit and the opening of a heavy horse centre.

The first project completed at the zoo was Toucan Ridge in April 2011. Expending $3.1 million, the APC transformed the former tropical house into a Central and northern South American microclimate. Housed within its walls are capybaras (the world's largest rodent), toucans, ibises, small toucanets, pink flamingoes, squirrel monkeys, and Goeldi monkeys. To enhance the display, the exhibit acquired crocodiles, bats and ocelots. Visitors can imagine themselves in the South American jungle without leaving Winnipeg's boundaries.

In 2013, work started and was completed a year later on a new zoo entrance costing $5.5 million. Located east of the earlier

entrance, it features 11,410 square feet (1,060 square meters) of interior space including a gift shop, a welcoming place and guest services centre. The new edifice provides a fitting entry to a revitalized zoo.

The Journey to Churchill exhibit constitutes the most awaited and publicized zoo project undertaken by the APC. It was partly funded by private capital with the Richardson Foundation contributing $5 million, Opened on July 3, 2014, it provides a simulated natural habitat for polar bears, Arctic fox, grey wolves, musk ox, caribou, seals and snowy owls. The display enables visitors to view polar bears and seals at eye level

Journey to Churchill
Visitor Centre –
Exterior, 2018
PHOTO BY AUTHOR

Journey to Churchill
Visitor Centre –
Interior, 2018
PHOTO BY AUTHOR

swimming in simulated sub-Arctic waters. An adjacent restaurant with reinforced glass walls permits visitors to view polar bears at play on simulated sub-Arctic barrens. Prince Charles and his wife, the Duchess of Cornwall visited the exhibit three weeks before its official opening.

Comprising part of the complex, the International Polar Bear Conservation Centre rehabilitates orphaned polar bears and conducts research pertinent to polar bear survival. An interpretive centre is connected to the research facility and according to Melissa Martin of the *Free Press* "is replete with interactive games, displays and videos explaining the impact of climate change on polar bear icy habitats." Utilizing the refurbished and updated mid-1950s bear enclosures to house orphaned animals, the Polar Bear Conservation Centre opened in January 2012, two years before completion of the primary exhibit. The Journey to Churchill forms the focal point of the refurbished, reconstructed and upgraded zoo.

Announced in September 2014, the APC constructed a heavy horse centre on a 1.9-hectare site at the north end of the zoo. It features a barn, pasture, paddock, a carriage shed and walking paths. Barn tours and wagon rides in summer and sleigh rides in winter are offered. Included in the development plan, the facility provides entertainment for children. A former president of Great West Life, Ray McFeetors, donated $2 million for the facility.

The final piece of the development plan, "Canada's Diversity Gardens," is now under construction and is expected to be completed in 2020. It occupies the southeast corner of the park and consists of a new conservatory and gardens. It replaces the Formal Garden, which has drawn visitors since the park's 1909 opening. The cost is being largely shared between the levels of government; the federal government is financing the lion's share at $35 million, while

McFeetors Heavy
Horse Centre, 2018
PHOTO BY AUTHOR

Construction of the Diversity Gardens, 2018
PHOTO BY AUTHOR

the Province of Manitoba is contributing $15 million and the City of Winnipeg, $10 million. Among private pledges totalling over $10 million, the Asper Family is donating $2 million.

Indigenous perspectives, cultural practises and contributions, through First Nations knowledge, appreciation and understanding of plants. A second garden, the Cultural Mosaic, will celebrate immigrants from

according to the APC, "visitors will encounter an abundance of plant life in the spring, a cool retreat in the summer, breathtaking views of fall foliage and refuge from the cold winter along beautiful snow-covered woodland paths."

The Grove is where Canada's Diversity Gardens is supposed to change its focus to the majesty of trees. According to its advance publicity, the Grove "will wrap visitors in a tranquil arboretum setting that reminds us of the simple beauty and calming nature of trees." It could be said to be a bit redundant. Just a few steps to the north, park visitors now enjoy a revitalized riparian forest along the Assiniboine River completed through APC efforts. And within easy walking distance south of the park, the public can stroll along the Assiniboine Forest's well-maintained paths in a natural setting.

The old conservatory closed its doors on April 2, 2018. For almost 105 years, citizens had escaped Winnipeg's often brutal climate with a visit to this subtropical paradise.

Plans call for the creation of several new gardens. The Indigenous Peoples' Garden will be a gathering place for the public to learn about

climates similar to Canada's through their garden styles and horticultural experiences. A third garden, the Grove, will feature a forest where,

The centrepiece of Canada's Diversity Gardens will be the new conservatory, to be called the Leaf.

Designed by Architecture 49 and the KPMB Group, this building will offer over 6,000 square metres of display space. Several galleries will transport visitors through different climates and environments. A tropical biome will immerse the visitor in a garden of tropical leafy plants, some growing over six storeys high. A Mediterranean biome will surround visitors with plants grown in Greece, Italy, South Africa, Southwest Australia, Central Chile and California. Here the plants will reach their peak textures and greenery during the cold prairie winter. A third space, the Babs Asper Display House, will program rotating floral exhibitions. It is designed to entice the public to visit the facility frequently. And above all the luscious plant growth, an elevator will lift visitors to the Shirley Richardson Butterfly Garden. Here the public will experience the beauty of tropical and exotic butterflies year-round. Supporting facilities, including a restaurant, classrooms and meeting rooms, will make a visit to the new conservatory a memorable experience.

The old conservatory closed its doors on April 2, 2018. For almost 105 years, citizens had escaped Winnipeg's often brutal climate with a visit to this subtropical paradise. Few of the existing plants are being transplanted in the new facility. But the Norfolk pine will be grafted and stored. On January 31, 2018, Gerald Dieleman, project director for the Diversity Gardens indicated that "we don't know what the success rate will be, but it is worth trying." As a result of "structural and mechanical deficiencies" the old conservatory has met the wrecker's ball. In its place greenhouses for Canada's Diversity Gardens will rise. Eventually the old site will revert to green space.

Vacant Plot looking West after demolition of Second Conservatory, October 2018
PHOTO BY AUTHOR

APC Educational Programing and Entertainment

Since its takeover of Assiniboine Park in 2008, the APC has focussed on educating both schoolchildren and adults in the need for conservation. The APC philosophy connects people with nature without destroying it. APC educational programs offer summer zoo day camps where children aged four to twelve learn about nature and animals. Other programs, including the popular keeper talks, delve into the lives of animals. Adults are not ignored and can enroll in short presentations including those on spring birding, yoga, and zoo photography. The APC provides a range of guided tours for both school and adult groups. For adults, guided tours of

the zoo, English Garden, Leo Mol Sculpture Garden and Pavilion Art Gallery raise revenue for the APC. Conspicuously absent are courses on the 110-year history of Assiniboine Park – a past which the APC has ignored and at times destroyed.

The APC limits its participation in arts and entertainment to a basic minimum. At present, arts groups and businesses are financing these activities. In 2017 and 2018 the Casinos of Winnipeg, the Johnston Group, Royal Winnipeg Ballet and Steinbach Credit Union have sponsored a line-up of free musical acts, ballet and movies. The Lyric Theatre is home to these activities. Concerts by the Winnipeg Symphony Orchestra, big band, rock and roll groups, barbershop quartets, and great musical hits groups attract visitors with free presentations. The Royal Winnipeg Ballet's park performances draw huge crowds. Free children's movies encourage families with young children to spend evenings together outdoors. Canada Day celebrations and the Folklorama kick-off highlight the summer season.

Other Assiniboine Park venues prove popular with visitors. With the support of the Richardson Foundation in 2018, the Leo Mol Sculpture Garden hosted the annual series of Sunday jazz concerts in July and August. The Winnipeg Art Gallery presents exhibitions in the pavilion. In 2018, the APC attracted visitors to the Pooh Gallery with its presentation on the real Winnie. Under APC direction and private funding, Assiniboine Park has resumed its traditional role as a place where Winnipeggers gather amidst beautiful surroundings for free summer entertainment.

A New Vision

The Assiniboine Park Conservancy has transformed Assiniboine Park with a new vision of its own. No longer a vast expanse of playing fields and floral gardens with a small zoo and conservatory, the 1904 design of Frederick G. Todd as enhanced by park superintendents D.D. England and George Champion lies defunct. Gone is part of the green space in front of the pavilion, now occupied by an extended duck pond and a new family centre. The plants and

trees in the old conservatory have been uprooted. The Formal Garden and surrounding open areas are giving way to Canada's Diversity Gardens. The APC's new vision of a three-section, pay-per-use educational and environmental theme park has been established. Given the decline of Assiniboine Park before the APC takeover, the changes were probably inevitable in order to restore the park as a destination for all Winnipeggers.

Led by Henry Sandison and a supportive city council and mayor in the early 1900s, the Public Parks Board envisaged and developed a suburban park with vast open spaces creating an Arcadian view of nature. Here, Winnipeggers could relax and rejuvenate away from the city's hustle and bustle. The park would be free and welcoming to residents from all walks of life and devoid of all signs of commercialism. For the first two decades of its existence, the park fell short of this ideal. It first attracted a crowd of middle-class Sabbatarians who picnicked, engaged in sports and on Sundays enjoyed liturgical music. By the 1920s, the park had changed when it began welcoming all

Under the Assiniboine Park Conservancy, the future of Assiniboine Park looks promising.

citizens regardless of their religion or ethnicity. During the two world wars, the public congregated in the park to support patriotic activities. The original concept of Assiniboine Park reached its zenith during Metro's administration of 1961 to 1971. In that decade, Assiniboine Park boasted one of North America's leading zoos and conservatories and attracted record crowds to enjoy picnics and concerts. At its height, more than one million people per year visited its free zoo.

In the 1980s, Assiniboine Park fell into a slow decline. With multiple civic priorities, Unicity could no longer afford the maintenance and development of a world-class zoo nor upgrade Assiniboine Park's ageing infrastructure. The creation of green areas into new suburban design and the construction of walking paths along Winnipeg's riverbanks reduced the need for travel to Assiniboine Park to enjoy these amenities. The emergence of The Forks as a more accessible site for concerts and public functions reduced park visitation. By 2000, the state of Assiniboine Park had reached crisis proportions. Unable and unwilling to raise funds for a park makeover, the city convinced participating "friends" groups into undertaking this task. The Assiniboine Park Conservancy was born.

Under the Assiniboine Park Conservancy, the future of Assiniboine Park looks promising. An upgraded zoo, enlarged duck pond, and family centre have encouraged Winnipeggers and out-of-town visitors to return to the park. In the future, a new conservatory and gardens will once again create public interest. If the Assiniboine Park Conservancy refrains from park overdevelopment, demonstrates transparency in its dealings with the public, and keeps user fees to a minimum, Assiniboine Park will thrive.

However, the APC does have a responsibility to honour those pioneers who envisaged, planned and developed the park as a series of vast open spaces for relaxation, rejuvenation and education for all citizens regardless of race, religion or ability to pay or to be enticed by "catch penny" attractions. Interpretive panels at appropriate locations should commemorate the visions and accomplishments of John Arbuthnot, Thomas Sharpe, Henry Sandison, and George Champion. Educational programs should integrate into their presentations the achievements of the park visionaries who preceded the APC. At a minimum, it is hoped that this book will restore their legacy.

Selected Bibliography

I   CITY OF WINNIPEG ARCHIVES RECORDS

City of Winnipeg. Public Parks Board Minutes, 1903–1961

City of Winnipeg. Public Parks Board Letter Books – Outgoing Correspondence, 1905–1921

City of Winnipeg. Public Parks Board Correspondence – Incoming, 1931

City of Winnipeg. Public Parks Board Annual Reports, 1892–1964

City of Winnipeg (Unicity). Minutes, 1972–2008

Metropolitan Council of Winnipeg (Metro). Minutes, 1961–1971

Rural Municipality of Assiniboia. Minutes, 1905–1922

Municipality of St. James. Minutes, 1923–1931

Town of Tuxedo. Minutes, 1954

Winnipeg Suburban Municipal Board. Minutes, 1925

II   CONTEMPORARY NEWSPAPERS & PERIODICALS

Manitoba Free Press, Winnipeg, Manitoba 1903–1931; *Winnipeg Free Press*, 1931–2016

Manitoba Sun, Winnipeg, Manitoba, Selected Issues

Northwest Review, Winnipeg, Manitoba, Selected Issues

Park and Cemetery, Chicago, Illinois, 1908–1916

Town Topics, Winnipeg, Manitoba, 1903–1913

The Voice, Winnipeg, Manitoba, 1898–1914 – Selected Issues

Western Labor News, Winnipeg, Manitoba, 1919

Winnipeg Daily Times, Winnipeg, Manitoba, 1880s – Selected Issues

Winnipeg Telegram, Winnipeg, Manitoba, 1901–1913 – Selected Issues

Winnipeg Tribune, Winnipeg, Manitoba, 1891–1978 – Selected Issues

III   UNPUBLISHED ESSAYS & THESES

Rostecki, R.R., "The Growth of Winnipeg, 1870–1886," Unpublished MA Thesis, University of Manitoba, 1986

Rostecki, R.R., "The Pre-Parks System of Winnipeg, 1880–1893," Unpublished essay in possession of author, ca. 1983

IV   STATUTES

Statutes of Canada, Chapter 53, An Act respecting the Lord's Day, RSC, 1906

Statutes of Canada, Chapter 140, An Act respecting the Protection of Navigable Waters, RSC, 1927

Statutes of Manitoba, 50 Victoria, Chapter 10, An Act to amend the Manitoba Municipal Act, 1886. Assented to June 10, 1887

Statutes of Manitoba, 55 Victoria, Chapter 31, Ac Act to Provide for the Establishment and Maintenance of Public Parks in Cities and Towns, Assented to April 20, 1892

Statutes of Manitoba, 61 Victoria, Chapter 27, An Act to provide for the Better Observance of the Lord's Day, Assented to April 27, 1898

Statutes of Manitoba, 1–2 Edward VII, Chapter 77, Ac Act to provide for a Charter for the City of Winnipeg and to repeal all Acts and parts of Acts in Conflict Therewith, Assented to March 1, 1902

Statutes of Manitoba, 4–5 Edward VII, Chapter 53, An Act to further amend The Winnipeg Charter, Assented to January 31, 1905

Statutes of Manitoba, 19 George V, Chapter 99, An Act to Legalize By-Law 13123 of the City of Winnipeg, Assented to April 19, 1929

Statutes of Manitoba, 19 George V, Chapter 102, An Act to Legalize By-Law No. 30 of The Public Parks Board of the City of Winnipeg, Assented to May 7, 1929

Statutes of Manitoba, Chapter 93, An Act Relating to the Tuxedo Planning Scheme, 1954, Assented to March 31, 1955

Statutes of Manitoba, Chapter 40, An Act to establish The Metropolitan Corporation of Greater Winnipeg and to provide for the Exercise by The Corporation of Certain Powers and Authority (The Metropolitan Winnipeg Act), Assented to March 20, 1960

Statutes of Ontario, 46 Victoria, Chapter 20, An Act to provide for the establishment and maintenance of Public Parks in Cities and Towns, Assented to February 1, 1883

V BOOKS AND ARTICLES

Artibise, Alan, *Winnipeg – An Illustrated History*, James Lorimer & Company, Toronto, 1977

Barbour, Dale. *Winnipeg Beach – Leisure and Courtship in a Resort Town, 1900–1967*, University of Manitoba Press, Winnipeg, 2001

Bellan, Ruben, *Winnipeg First Century – An Economic History*, Queenston House Publishing Company Ltd., Winnipeg, 1978

Beveridge, Charles & Hoffman, Carolyn ed., *The Papers of Frederick Law Olmsted Supplementary Series 1 – Writings on Public Parks, Parkways and Park Systems*, Johns Hopkins University Press, Baltimore, 1997

Bowman, William D., "Hakoah Vienna and the International Nature of Interwar Austrian Sports," *Central European History*, 44 (2011), pp. 642–653

Boy Scouts of Canada, *Moments and Memories – A Glimpse at Manitoba Scouting, 1908–1982*, Boy Scouts of Canada Manitoba Council, Winnipeg, 1983

Braz, Albert, *Apostate Englishman – Grey Owl, The Writer and the Myths*, University of Manitoba Press, Winnipeg, 2015

City of Winnipeg Parks and Recreation Department, *The History and Development of Assiniboine Park and Zoo*, Winnipeg, December, 1972

Creighton, Donald, *Canada's First Century, 1867–1967*, Macmillan, Toronto 1970

Jacobs, Peter, "Frederick G. Todd and the Creation of Canada's Urban Landscape," *Association for Preservation Technology Bulletin*, 15, No. 4, 1983, pp. 27–34

Kitz, Janet & Castle, Gary, *Point Pleasant Park: An Illustrated History*, Pleasant Point Publishing, Halifax, 1999

Kheraj, Sean, *Inventing Stanley Park: An Environmental History*, UBC Press, Vancouver, 2013

Laverdure, Paul, *Sunday in Canada*, Gravelbooks, Yorkton, Saskatchewan, 2004

Macdonald, Catherine, *A City at Leisure: An Illustrated History of Parks and Recreation Services in Winnipeg, 1893–1993*, City of Winnipeg Parks and Recreation Department, Winnipeg, 1995

McCormack, A. Ross, *Reformers, Rebels and Revolutionaries: The Western Canada Radical Movement, 1899–1919*, University of Toronto Press, Toronto, 1977

Masters, Donald C, *The Winnipeg General Strike*, University of Toronto Press, Toronto 1950

Morgan, Henry James, *The Canadian Men and Women of The Time*, William Briggs, Toronto, 1912

Pioneers and Prominent People of Manitoba, Canadian Publicity Co., Winnipeg, 1925

Rosenzweig, Roy & Blackmar, Elizabeth, *The Park and the People – A History of Central Park*, Cornell University Press, Ithaca, NY 1992

Rostecki, R.R., "Donaldson Park" in R. Thain ed., *Brookside Cemetery – A Celebration of Life*, E.R. Publishing & Communications Ltd., Winnipeg, 2004

Russenholt, E.S., *The Heart of the Continent*, McFarlane Communications Services, Winnipeg, 1968

Schmidt, Andrew J., "Pleasure and Recreation for the People: Planning St. Paul's Como Park," *Minnesota History*, Vol. 58, No. 1, Spring, 2002, pp. 44–50

Schofield, F.H., *The Story of Manitoba*, Vol. 3, S.J. Clarke Publishing Company, Winnipeg, 1913

Smith, Donald B., *From the Lord of Shadows – The Making of Grey Owl*, Western Producer Books, Saskatoon, 1990

Spector, David, *Monuments to Finance, Vol. 11 – Early Bank Architecture in Winnipeg*, City of Winnipeg Historical Buildings Committee, Winnipeg, August, 1982

Waite, P.B., "Sir Oliver Mowat's Canada: Reflections on an Un-Victorian Society," in Swainson, Donald ed., *Oliver Mowat's Ontario*, Macmillan, Toronto, 1972

Wallace, W. Stewart & McKay, W.H. ed., *The Macmillan Dictionary of Canadian Biography*, Macmillan, Toronto, 1978

Winnipeg Public Parks Board, "Summer Outings Round Winnipeg," Winnipeg, ca. 1905

Wencer, David, "Historicist: John Howard's Enduring Monument," *Torontoist*, 2013/2

Wilson, William H., *The City Beautiful Movement*, Johns Hopkins University Press, Baltimore, 1989

VI ONLINE SOURCES

www.centralparknyc.org – Central Park Conservancy, January, 2017

wwwcityparksblog.org. – Angela Howe, "Lessons from the Masters – The City of New York and Central Park Conservancy Partnership," City Park Blog, January 14, 2013.

www.comozooconservatory.org – "History Como Park Zoo and Conservatory," January, 2017

www.lemontroyal.qc.ca. – Les amis de la montagne, Short History of Mont Royal, 12/03/2013

Index